D1017326

INVENTING ENGLISH

A Portable History of the Language

Seth Lerer

COLUMBIA UNIVERSITY PRESS : NEW YORK

Columbia University Press : *Publishers Since 1893* : New York   Chichester, West Sussex

Library of Congress Cataloging-in-Publication Data

Lerer, Seth, 1955–
    Inventing English : a portable history of the language / Seth Lerer.
      p. cm.
    Includes bibliographical references and index.
    ISBN-10 0–231–13794–X (cloth : alk. paper)
    ISBN-13 978–0–231–13794–2 (cloth : alk. paper) —

    ISBN-10 0–231–51076–4 (e-book)
    ISBN-13 978–0–231–51076–9 (e-book)
    1. English language—History. 2. English language—Etymology. 3. English
language—Old English, ca. 450–1100. 4. English language—Middle English,
1100–1500. 5. Linguistics. I. Title.

PE1075.L47   2007
420.9—dc22   2006030652

Printed in the United States of America
c 10 9 8 7 6 5 4

CONTENTS

All texts from different periods of English appear here in original spellings. Texts from Old and Middle English use some letters not found elsewhere. These are

Þ, þ	"thorn," indicating a -th- sound
Ð, ð	"edth," indicating a -th- sound
æ, Æ	"aesch," indicating the vowel sound as in Modern American English, "cat"
3	"yogh," indicating a sound like a "y" at the beginnings of words, and a sound like a "gh" in the middle of words
7	the abbreviation for "and"

In addition to these letters, I will occasionally represent sounds by using the International Phonetic Alphabet. Each vowel and consonant sound in a language has a special symbol in this alphabet. The appendix to this book lists these symbols, the sounds they represent, and the ways in which speech sounds are described by linguists.

Words that are discussed as words, or words from other languages, appear in *italics*. Words that explain, translate, or define other words appear in "quotations." Words that are transcribed into the International Phonetic Alphabet to record their pronunciation appear between /slæʃ marks/.

At the end of this book are chapter-by-chapter lists of references and suggestions for further reading. In addition to the specific sources and editions I use, there are often many different editions available—in books and on line.

Throughout this book, I use the following abbreviations:

CHEL *The Cambridge History of the English Language,* general editor
      Richard M. Hogg, 6 vols. (Cambridge: Cambridge University
      Press, 1992–2002).

OED   *The Oxford English Dictionary,* originally edited by James A. H.
      Murray (Oxford: Oxford University Press, 1889–1928); Supple-
      ment, 1933; second edition, 1989. Online at http://dictionary.
      oed.com.

Finally, unless otherwise noted, all translations from Old English, Middle English, and early Modern English, and from other languages, are my
own.

Inventing English

Finding English, Finding Us

I GREW UP ON A STREET FULL OF LANGUAGES. I heard Yiddish every day from my parents and grandparents and from the families of my friends. There was Italian around the corner, Cuban Spanish down the block, Russian in the recesses of the subway station. Some of my earliest memories are of their sounds. But there were also words of what seemed to be my own family's making and that I have found in no dictionaries: *konditterei*, a strange blend of Yiddish and Italian calibrated to describe the self-important café set; *vachmalyavatet*, a tongue-twister used to signify complete exhaustion; *lachlat*, a cross between a poncho and a peacoat that my father pointed out one afternoon.

Still, there was always English, always the desire, in my father's father's idiom, to be a "Yenkee." My mother was a speech therapist in the New York City schools; my father, a history and English teacher. For the first decade of my life, we lived a dream of bettering ourselves through English. We tried to lose the accent of the immigrant. We memorized poetry. Days I would spend with Walt Whitman (de facto poet laureate of Brooklyn) until I was called in, *O Captain*-ing together with him straight to supper. I read *Beowulf* in junior high, and in the arc of Anglo-Saxon or the lilt of Chaucer's Middle English I found words that shared the Germanic roots of Yiddish. There was that prefix for the participle, *ge-*, in all those languages. If Grendel's mother was *gemyndig*, mindful, remembering, harboring a grudge, then so too was my mother. Everything in my family was *gehacktet*—ground up, hacked to bits, whether it was the chicken livers that we spread on toast or the troubles that beset us all (the Yiddish phrase *"gehacktet tsuris,"* hacked up troubles, has always stayed with me. I think of Grendel's leavings—the dismembered bodies of the Danes—with no more apt phrase).

At Oxford, I studied for a degree in medieval English languages and linguistics. J. R. R. Tolkien and W. H. Auden had died only a couple of years before I arrived, and Oxford in the 1970s had an elegiac quality about it. Tolkien and Auden were the two poles of its English studies: the first philological, medieval, and fantastic; the second, emotive, modern, and all too real. My tutors were their students and their self-appointed heirs. I learned the minutiae of philology, details whose descriptions had an almost incantatory magic: Frisian fronting, *aesh* one and *aesh* two, lengthening in open syllables. I went to bed dreaming about the *Ormulum* and the orthoepists. And then, one evening in the spring of 1977, in some grotty dining hall, I heard the poets Ted Hughes and Seamus Heaney read. Heaney got up, all red-faced and smiling, brilliant in his breath. He read poems about bog men—ancient Germanic people who had been preserved in peat for fifteen hundred years. Twenty-five years later, I found in Heaney's *Beowulf* translation what I had felt on that evening: the sense that the study of the word revealed not just a history of culture but a history of the self. "I had undergone," Heaney writes of his study of Old English in the introduction to his *Beowulf*, "something like illumination by philology."

Philology means "love of language," but for scholars it connotes the discipline of historical linguistic study. For Seamus Heaney, or for you or me, philology illuminates the history of words and those who speak them. My goal in this book is to illuminate: to bring light into language and to life. Whether you grew up in New York or New Mexico, whether your first words were in this or any other tongue, you are reading this book in the language of an early-twenty-first-century American. Writing at the beginning of the nineteenth century, Washington Irving called America a "logocracy"—a country of words. We all still live in a logocracy—invented then and reinvented everyday by citizens of language like ourselves.

This is a book about inventing English (*invent*, from the Latin *invenire*, to come upon or find). Each of its chapters illustrates how people found new ways to speak and write; how they dealt with the resources of language of their time and place; and how, through individual imagination, they transformed those resources into something uniquely personal. These chapters may be read in sequence, as you read a textbook or a novel; or they may be read as individual essays, each one suitable for bed or as a pause in the day's tasks. My book, therefore, is less a history of English in the traditional sense than it is an episodic epic: a portable assembly of encounters with the language. Each episode recalls a moment when a person or a group finds something new or preserves something old; when someone writes down something that exemplifies a change; when the experience of language, personally or professionally, stands as a defining moment in the arc of speech.

All of us find or invent our language. We may come up with new sentences never heard before. We may use words in a unique way. But we are always finding our voice, locating old patterns or long-heard expressions, reaching into our thesaurus for the right term. And in inventing English, we are always inventing ourselves—finding our place among the welter of the words or in the swell of sounds that is the ocean of our tongue.

And this, it seems to me, is what is new about this book—its course between the individual experience and literary culture, between the details of the past and the drama of the present, between the story of my life I tell here and the stories you may make out of your own. Histories of the English language abound, and different readers find themselves in each. Scholars research and write out of the great six-volume *Cambridge History of the English Language*. Teachers work from textbooks such as Albert C. Baugh and Thomas M. Cable's *History of the English Language*. The interested public has had, for the past half century, books ranging from Mario Pei's *The Story of the English Language*, to Anthony Burgess's *A Mouthful of Air*, Bill Bryson's *The Mother Tongue*, and the illustrated companion to the PBS series *The Story of English*. A university professor such as David Crystal has sought wider audiences for his arguments in *The Stories of English*. And I have spent the last decade addressing listeners and viewers of my lecture series prepared for the Teaching Company, *The History of the English Language*. I have spoken to college students, adult education classes, social clubs, and professional organizations. The fact remains that people of all vocations or politics are fascinated by the history of English, and my book invites the reader to invest in his or her (and my own) fascination with the word.

I think that we are fascinated by English not only because of how it has changed over time but because of how it changes now. Within a single person's lifetime, words shift their meaning; pronunciations differentiate themselves; idioms from other tongues, from popular culture, and from commerce inflect our public life. English is in flux. E-mail and the Internet have altered the arc of our sentences. Much has been made of all these changes: by the linguist Geoffrey Nunberg in his provocative radio and newspaper essays (collected in his book, *The Way We Talk Now*), or by the journalist William Safire in his weekly *New York Times Magazine* column. For all the nuance of their observations, however, neither of these commentators (nor really anyone else) locates our current changes in the larger history of English. The shifts we see today have historical precedents. Our debates about standards and dialects, politics and pronunciation recall arguments by pedagogues and poets, lexicographers and literati, from the Anglo-Saxon era of the tenth century, through the periods of medieval, Renaissance, and eighteenth- and nineteenth-century society. This book therefore grows out of my conviction that to understand a language it is necessary to appreciate its history. We speak and spell for reasons that are often lost to us. But we can rediscover these reasons.

This book recovers answers to our current questions, and it illustrates how language is a form of social behavior central to our past and present lives. Throughout its historical survey, this book sets out to raise some basic questions for the study of our language—questions that have been asked at all times in its history.

Is there, or should there be, a "standard English"? Should it be defined as the idiom of the educated, the sound of the city-dweller, the style of the business letter? As early as the tenth century, teachers in the monastic schools of Anglo-Saxon England asked this question. Some claimed there should be rules for spelling, speech, and usage. Such rules were grounded in a particular dialect of Old English—the one that was geographically central to the region of the king's court and the church's administration. Similar attentions to dialect and standards were the subject of debates throughout the Middle Ages and the Renaissance. Was there, asked teachers and students alike, a particular regional form of English that should form a national standard? Should we write the way we speak? Should speech display one's education (and thus something that could be learned) or should it reveal one's class and region (and thus something that reflected birth)?

In asking questions such as these, teachers and scholars throughout history have raised another major question. Should the study of language be prescriptive or descriptive? Dictionaries, for example, record spelling, pronunciation, meaning, and usage. Are they simply recording habits of language or are they also codifying them? Isn't any description also a prescription? When we present the features of a language—and when we do so through authoritative venues such as dictionaries, school texts, or public journalism—are we simply saying *how* we speak and write or are we also saying how we *should* speak and write?

Few debates about standards and prescription have been so fraught, especially in English, as those on spelling. Why do we spell the way we do? Why is there such a difference between spelling and pronunciation? As this book illustrates, English spelling is historical. It preserves older forms of the language by using conservative spellings. English spelling is also ety-mological: that is, it preserves the earlier forms of words even when those forms no longer correspond to current speech. We spell words such as *knight* or *through* in these ways because we maintain an old convention of spelling these words in their earliest forms (in Chaucer's time, they would have been pronounced "k-nicht" and "throoch"). In Britain, the disparity between spelling and pronunciation can be even more extreme: a name such as *Featherstonehugh* is now pronounced "Fanshaw." A city such as *Worcester* (pronounced "Wooster") preserves the remnants of an Old Eng-lish form: originally, *Wigoraceaster* (*ceaster*, originally from Latin, *castrum*, meaning a fort or a town; *Wigora* referring to a clan or tribe in ancient England: hence, the town of the Wigors). These habits are the legacy of me-dieval scribes, Renaissance schoolmasters, and eighteenth-century diction-ary makers who fixed spelling and pronunciation according to particular ideals of language history, educational attainment, or social class. There was a time when English and American men and women spelled much as they spoke. By the end of the eighteenth century, however, English spelling and pronunciation had divorced themselves from one another. Spelling had become a system all its own.

The history of English pronunciation is a history of sound changes. The periods we call Old English, Middle English, and Modern English were distinguished not just by vocabulary, grammar, or idiom but also by pro-nunciation. Scholars of our language have codified sets of sound changes that, in particular historical periods, created systematic shifts in the Eng-lish speech. For example, words that had a long *a* sound in Old English changed their pronunciation over time, so that by the time of Chaucer they had a long *o* sound. Thus Old English *ban* became *bone*; *ham* became *home*; *twa* become *two* (now pronounced like "too"). Old English had consonant clusters at the beginnings of words (*hl-*, *hw-*, *hr-*) that were simplified by the Middle English period. Thus *hlud* became *loud*, *hwæt* became *what*, *hring* became *ring*. Sometimes, sounds were twisted around (this phenom-enon is known as metathesis—the same thing that makes children mis-pronounce *spaghetti* as "psghetti," or that generates dialect pronunciations of *ask* into "aks"). The Old English word for *bird* was *brid*; the word for *third* was *thrid*. Contact with languages, especially with French after the Norman Conquest, provoked changes in pronunciation. Contacts among different regional dialects also provoked changes. The famous Great Vowel Shift—the change in the pronunciation of English long vowels—that oc-curred in the fifteenth century may have been due, in part, to new contacts among different dialect groups of late Middle English. Different dialects pronounced, say, the long *u* sound in Middle English differently; eventually a new form settled out as a double sound (or diphthong), usually written *ou*. Thus, *mus* became *mous*; *hus* became *house*; *lus* became *louse*. In addition to these historical changes, regional dialects survived in England, and American English descends from several of them. We need to understand how American English developed from these particular regions, and how these dialects were separated and later came into contact, after the periods of colonial settlement.

Finally, there are questions about grammar. Anyone who has studied another language, especially another European language, will know that English grammar seems "simple." We have no grammatical gender of nouns, as French, German, Spanish, and other languages do. We do not have case endings: that is, we do not use different endings to show that nouns are subjects, direct objects, or indirect objects in sentences. Our verbs end in a relatively limited set of forms. Why did this happen? Old English was, like its contemporary European languages, a highly inflected language. Meaning was determined by word endings that signaled the number and gender of nouns; whether they were the subject, direct object, or indirect object in sentences; and whether relationships of agency or action operated among nouns and verbs (we now use prepositions for this function). Verbs were classed in complex groups, each with different kinds of forms or endings. Sometimes, tense could be indicated by the ending of a verb (talk, talked); sometimes, it was indicated by a change in the root vowel of the verb (run, ran). Some of these features do survive in Modern English, but the history of the language as a whole is, generally speaking, a story of a shift from an inflected to an uninflected language. Meaning in a sentence is now determined by word order. "The man loves the woman" is a very different statement from "The woman loves the man." But in Old English the statements "Se monn lufiað ðone wif" and "ðone wif lufiað se monn" say the same thing. What matters are the grammatical cases (here, the nominative, or the subject case, signaled by the article *se*, and the accusative, or direct object case, signaled by the article *ðone*), not the order of the words.

But English has not completely lost these features. In fact, it preserves, in what might be called "fossilized" forms, certain very old patterns, endings, and inflections. Some regional British and American dialects preserve old forms, often because their speakers have been geographically or socially isolated for a long time. Some great works of literature—the

King James Bible of 1611, the plays of Shakespeare from the sixteenth and early seventeenth centuries, the novels of Charles Dickens from the mid-nineteenth century—deliberately preserve forms of the language that were deemed old-fashioned in their own time. Biblical English, for example, is full of old verb forms like *hath* and *doth* (even though we know from the evidence of letters, schoolbooks, and works of literature that people were saying "has" and "does" by the early seventeenth century). Shakespeare is using double negatives and comparatives (e.g., "the most unkindest cut of all") even as they are passing out of common speech. And Dickens's characters spout forms and phrases that echo a linguistic past preserved in little pockets of class or region (witness, for example, Joe Gargery in *Great Expectations*: "I hope Uncle Pumblechook's mare mayn't have set a forefoot on a piece o' ice, and gone down").

The experience of English and American literature is, therefore, a linguistic as well as an aesthetic one. To illustrate the history of the English language, I will often draw on examples from poetry, prose fiction, drama, and personal narrative. To understand that history is to give us greater access to the imaginative scope of poets, playwrights, novelists, and philosophers of the past. If we are worried about language, we are also worried about literature: about the so-called canon of writers, about what we all should read and teach, about where our literature, not just the English or American language, is going. To deal with questions such as these, we need to understand how literature engages with the history of language. Often, word origins or etymologies can be a source of stimulus or humor for a writer. Often, too, literary works play with dialect. In many ways, the history of American literature—from Washington Irving, through Mark Twain, to Norman Mailer, to Toni Morrison—is a history of recording and reflecting on the differences in American language. Those differences are not always simply regional; they embrace race, class, gender, and social standing.

We always hear the history of English, whether we know it or not. For speakers and writers, for readers of literature, Web surfers and e-mailers, this book sets out to provide a portable history of the language and in the process to provoke us to consider histories of ourselves.

Some Preliminaries and Prehistory

A language's words may come from many sources. Sometimes, words may stay in a language for thousands of years. They may change in pronunciation or spelling, or even in meaning, but their root will be the same. These kinds of words make up a language's core vocabulary. In English, that core vocabulary consists of short words often of one syllable for basic natural concepts (e.g., sky, sun, moon, God, man, woman), parts of the body (e.g., head, nose, ear, tongue, knee, foot, leg, heart), and basic foods, plants, or animals (e.g., cow, horse, sheep, oak, beech, water).

A language's words may also come from other languages. They may be borrowed to express a new concept. Or they may be imposed upon speakers of a language by conquerors or colonizers. Throughout the history of English, many periods of contact and conquest, scientific study and exploration left us with such loan words from different languages.

Sometimes groups of language speakers may separate. Over time, new languages may emerge from the old ones. The languages of Europe and those of Northern India, Iran, and part of Western Asia belong to a group known as the Indo-European Languages. They probably originated from a common language-speaking group about 4000 BC and then split up as various subgroups migrated. English shares many words with these Indo-European languages, though some of the similarities may be masked by sound changes. The word *moon*, for example, appears in recognizable forms in languages as different as German (*Mond*), Latin (*mensis*, meaning "month"), Lithuanian (*menuo*), and Greek (*meis*, meaning "month"). The word *yoke* is recognizable in German (*Joch*), Latin (*iugum*), Russian (*igo*), and Sanskrit (*yugam*). The word *wind* appears in Latin as *ventus*, in Russian as *veter*, in Irish Gaelic as *gwent*, and in Sanskrit as *vatas*. Words that share a common origin are known as cognates.

As the Indo-European language groups split off, however, certain language families developed words of their own. Words common to those language families are also said to be cognate, but only in that family. Latin, for example, gave rise to many different yet related languages known as the Romance languages: French, Spanish, Portuguese, Italian, Romanian. Because these languages are historically related, they share words in common; but those words may be pronounced very differently in each language. Thus the word for "wolf" would have been *lupus* in Latin. In Spanish it is *lobo*; in Italian it is *lupo*; in French it is *loup*; in Romanian it is *lupu*.

English is a branch of the Germanic languages. Thus there are many words in English which are cognate with words in German, Dutch, and the Scandinavian languages. In fact, one of the features that distinguishes the Germanic languages as a group is their shared, cognate vocabulary. Numbers, for example, are cognate.

English: one, two, three, four, five, six, seven, eight, nine, ten, hundred

German: eins, zwei, drei, vier, fünf, sechs, sieben, acht, neun, zehn, hundert

Dutch: een, twee, drie, vier, vijf, zes, zeven, acht, negen, tien, honderd

Danish: en, to, tre, fire, fem, seks, syv, otte, ni, ti, hundrede

The Germanic languages also share words, for example, for "bear" and "sea." Compare the Germanic with the non-Germanic forms here to notice the differences.

English, *bear*; German, *Bär*, Danish, *bjorn*; but Latin *ursus*.

English, *sea*; German, *See*; Dutch, *zee*; Danish *sö*; but Latin *mare* and Greek *thalassa*

The reconstruction of the Indo-European language families and, in particular, the ancient forms of the Germanic languages was one of the great achievements of nineteenth-century linguistics. As this is a book about the history of the English language, I will not be reviewing it. But many standard textbooks of this history detail this fascinating and complex subject. Readers interested in learning more about Indo-European and the techniques of linguistic reconstruction should look at Calvert Watkins, *The American Heritage Dictionary of Indo-European Roots*.

We have no written record of the language of the original inhabitants of the British Isles. By the time the Romans came to Britain and made it part of their Empire (in the middle of the first century BC), the land had long been settled by Celtic speakers. The Romans brought Latin to their colony. By the middle of the fifth century AD, the Roman Empire was disintegrating, and the Romans were leaving Britain. Groups of Germanic-speaking peoples came to Britain from the Continent, some to raid and pillage, some to settle. By the late sixth century, these Germanic-speaking peoples—most of whom were of the tribes known as the Angles and the Saxons—were speaking a language that came to be known as Anglo-Saxon, or what we call Old English. The Celtic-speaking inhabitants were pushed to the peripheries of the islands. Thus, the modern Celtic languages have survived on the edges of Britain: Gaelic in Ireland, Welsh in Wales, Cornish in Cornwall, Erse in Scotland, and Manx on the Isle of Man. Some of these Celtic languages are flourishing (Welsh and Gaelic); some are dead (Manx, Cornish, Erse). But many place names and some particular Celtic words were adopted by the Romans, kept by the Anglo-Saxons, and passed down to modern English speakers. The word *afon*, for example, was the Celtic word for river. There are several rivers in Britain called Avon (most famously, the one with Stratford on it) because that was, quite simply, the old name for river. The Thames is also a Celtic name. A few other Celtic words survive in English: *dun* ("gray"), *tor* ("peak"), *crag*, and the word for a lake, *luh* (which survives in Ireland as *lough* and in Scotland as *loch*).

Latin words came into the Germanic languages during the time of the Empire. On the Continent, as well as in England to some extent, Germanic tribespeople came in contact with the Romans, and certain words entered their language. Such words survive, in various forms, in all the modern Germanic languages. Thus the English word "street" goes back to the Latin expression, *via strata*, meaning "a paved road." The word has cognate forms in all the Germanic languages, for the Romans built the roads and streets that ran through villages and farms (the word also has cognate forms in many other Indo-European languages, a larger legacy of Roman engineering). In the course of history, words came into English from later church Latin, from Scandinavian languages, and (with the Norman Conquest) from French. Part of the story of this book is the story of these loan words.

The earliest records of any Germanic language are in runes. Runic writing was a system that the early Germanic peoples developed for inscribing names and short texts on wood, bone, or stone. It was originally an epigraphic script: that is, a way of writing on objects, not on parchment or paper. No one is quite sure how runes originated, but it is clear that by the fourth century AD, Germanic peoples throughout Europe were writing their names as signs of ownership on objects. One of the earliest, and perhaps the most famous, of such inscriptions went around the lip of a golden drinking horn found in Denmark in the eighteenth century. The inscription is from about the year 400 AD and is written in a form of Old Norse (the horn has since been lost or destroyed). It reads, in a modern transcription: "*ek hlewagastir holtijar horna tawiðo.*" *Ek* is cognate with Modern German *ich* (Old English *ic*), meaning "I." *Hlwewegastir* is a way of writing the name Hlegest (the Old Scandinavian languages put an -*r* ending on nouns in the nominative case). *Holtijar* means "of Holt." *Horna* is the word "horn." *Tawiðo* means "I made." It is cognate with the modern German verb *tun*, meaning to do or make.

In Britain, runes were used to write the language of the Anglo-Saxons. We have no sustained runic documents, however; what we do have are inscriptions on crosses, art objects, headstones, and weapons. There is a beautiful little ivory box in the British Museum with runic writing on it, probably from the early eighth century, telling part of a story about the smith god of Northern mythology, Waeland. There is also a massive cross, also probably from the eighth century, in Northern England on which is inscribed, in runes, part of a poem about Christ's original cross. These runic lines are also incorporated, in an updated version, into a tenth-century Old English poem known as *The Dream of the Rood* (*rood* is the Old English word for "cross," and it still survives in some modern English contexts).

The earliest texts in Old English were written by scribes who learned the Roman alphabet in the Catholic monasteries of Britain and the Continent. They adapted the ways of writing Latin letters and Latin words to their own language. They had to modify the writing somewhat, as there were some sounds in Old English that did not occur in Latin. Sometimes they borrowed the old runic letters to represent these sounds. Sometimes, they made up new spellings from the Roman alphabet. Some of these very early texts are comments or glosses on Latin manuscripts: an English scribe sometimes wrote in his own words above a line of Latin, or along the margins of the text. On rare occasions, some of these scribes would write down scraps of verse that had been circulating orally. Old English poetry, like all early Germanic poetry, was probably composed by singers who might accompany themselves on a harp. Some of this poetry may have been around for centuries before it came to be written down. Some of it may have been written down soon after its composition. And some of it may have been composed by literate poets themselves, perhaps in imitation of the oral performance techniques of their predecessors.

Our first examples of Old English thus come from this transitional moment in British literary history: when singers sang accompanied by harps and scribes were just beginning to write their lines in Roman alphabets in manuscripts. It is with such a moment that I open my history of English.

CHAPTER I

Caedmon Learns to Sing

Old English and the Origins of Poetry

SOME TIME IN THE SEVENTH CENTURY, probably between the years 657 and 680, a Yorkshire cowherd learned to sing. Social gatherings among the peasantry were clearly common at the time. Often, laborers and herders would gather in the evenings to eat and drink, and a harp would be passed among them. But when the harp came to Caedmon, he could not sing. Shamed by his inability, he avoided the gatherings, until one evening an angel came to him in a vision. "Caedmon," the angel called to him by name. "Sing me something." "I cannot," replied the cowherd, "for I do not know how to sing, and for that reason I left the gathering." But the angel replied, "Still, you can sing." "Well, what shall I sing about?" replied Caedmon. "Sing to me about the Creation of the world." And so, miraculously, Caedmon raised his voice and offered this song in the language of his time and place.

Nu scylun hergan	hefaenricaes Uard,
Metudæs maecti	end his modgidanc,
uerc Uuldurfadur,	sue he uundra gihuaes,
eci Dryctin,	or anstelidæ.
He ærist scop	aelda barnum
heben til hrofe,	haleg Scepen;
tha middungeard	moncynnæs Uard
eci Dryctin,	æfter tiadæ,
firum foldu,	Frea allmectig.

[Now we shall praise heaven-kingdom's Guardian,
the Creator's might, and his mind-thought,
the words of the Glory-father: how he, each of his wonders,

the eternal Lord, established at the beginning.
He first shaped for earth's children
heaven as a roof, the holy Creator.
Then a middle-yard, mankind's Guardian,
the eternal Lord, established afterwards,
the earth for the people, the Lord almighty]

These nine lines, weird and wondrous though they may seem to us, make up the earliest surviving poem in any form of the English language. It is known today as *Caedmon's Hymn*. All that we know of this poet comes from a passage in a work by Bede, an English monk and historian who wrote his *History of the English Church and People* in the first third of the eighth century. Bede wrote in Latin, and *Caedmon's Hymn* survives, in Old English, as marginal annotations to the manuscripts of Bede's work.

To understand what Caedmon did, and why his poem and his story were so important throughout Anglo-Saxon England and beyond, we need to understand the central features of Old English, its relationship to the older Germanic languages, and the world in which this tongue emerged as a vehicle for imaginative literature.

Old English was the vernacular spoken and written in England from the period of the Anglo-Saxon settlements in the sixth century until the Norman Conquest in 1066. It emerged as a branch of the Germanic languages, a group of tongues spoken by the tribes of Northern Europe who had developed their linguistic and cultural identity by the time of the Roman Empire. These languages included Old Norse (the ancestor of the Scandinavian languages), Old High German (the ancestor of Modern German), Old Frisian (related to modern Dutch), and Gothic (a form that had died out completely by the end of the Middle Ages). The Germanic languages were very different from the Latin of the Roman Empire. True, like Latin, they had a highly developed inflectional system. Nouns were classed according to declensions (where suffixes signaled case, number, and grammatical gender); verbs were classed according to sets of conjugations (where suffixes signaled person, number, and tense). But the Germanic languages shared distinctive ways of creating new words and a grammatical system unique among other European tongues. And each individual Germanic language had its own system of pronunciation.

Old English shared with its Germanic compeers a system of word formation that built up compounds out of preexisting elements. Nouns could be joined with other nouns, adjectives, or prefixes to form new words. Verbs could be compounded with prefixes or nouns to denote shades of meaning. Thus a word like *timber* could receive the prefix *be-* to become *betimber* ("to build"). Or an ordinary creature such as a spider could be called by the compound *gangelwæfre*, "the walking weaver." Old English poetry is rife with such noun compounds, known as "kennings." Poets called the sea the *hron-rad* (the road of the whale), or the *swan-rad* (the road of the swan). The body was the *ban-loca* (the bone locker). When Anglo-Saxon writers needed to translate a word from classical or church Latin, say, they would build up new compounds based on the elements of that Latin word. Thus a word such as *grammatica*, the discipline of literacy or the study of grammar itself, would be expressed as *stæf-cræft*: the craft of the staff, that is of the book-staff or the individual marks that make up letters (the Old English word for letter, *boc-stæf*, is very similar to modern German *Buchstab*). A word like the Latin *superbia*, meaning pride, came out in Old English as *ofer-mod*: over-mood, or more precisely, too much of an inner sense of self. A word like *baptiserium* (from a Greek word meaning to plunge into a cold bath) was expressed in Old English by the noun *ful-wiht*: the first element, *ful*, means full or brimming over; the second element, *wiht*, means at all or completely (and is the ancestor of our word "whit"—not a whit, not at all).

Old English also shared with the other Germanic languages a system of grammar. All of the other ancient European languages—Greek, Latin, Celtic—could form verb tenses by adding suffixes to verb roots. In Latin, for example, you could say "I love" in the present tense (*amo*), and "I will love" in the future (*amabo*). In the Germanic languages, as in modern English, you would need a separate or helping verb to form the future tense. In Old English, "I love" would be *Ic lufige*. But for the future tense, you would have to say, *Ic sceal lufian*. This pattern is unique to the Germanic languages. Unique, too, was a classification of verbs called "strong" and "weak." So-called strong verbs formed their past tense by a change in the verb's root vowel. Thus, in modern English, we have "I run" but "I ran"; "I drink" but "I drank"; "I think" but "I thought." But there were also so-called weak verbs that formed their past tense simply by adding a suffix: "I walk" but "I walked"; "I love" but "I loved."

These are among the defining features of the Germanic languages, and Old English had them all. But what Old English had in particular was its own, distinctive sound. Modern scholars have been able to reconstruct the sound of Old English by looking at spelling in manuscripts (scribes spelled as they spoke, not according to a fixed pattern across Anglo-Saxon England). But they have also been able to recover the sound of Old English by looking at early textbooks in Latin. The pronunciation of Church Latin has remained very stable over the past thousand years. By comparing the pronunciation of Latin words with Old English words in early textbooks, scholars can learn how certain Old English sounds came out.

What was the sound of Old English? The first thing that strikes the modern English speaker are the consonants. Old English had a set of consonant clusters, many of which have been lost or simplified in later forms of the language. Thus the initial cluster *fn-*, as in the word *fnastian* ("sneeze"), has become *sn-*. Initial *hw-* (as in *hwæt*) has become *wh-* ("what"). Initial *hl-* (as in *hlud*) has become simply *l-* ("loud"). Initial *hr-* (*hring*) has become *r-* ("ring"). Unlike the other Germanic languages (except Old Norse), Old English had voiced and unvoiced interdental consonants (the sounds represented by the Modern English spelling *th*). These were represented by the letters þ (called "thorn") and ð (called "edth") taken from the older Germanic runic system of writing. Such sounds did not exist in Latin or the Romance languages, and thus Anglo-Saxon scribes had to borrow letter forms from the runic alphabet in order to represent such sounds not available in the Roman alphabet (other sounds that distinguished Old English from Latin were the *æ*, or "æsch," a sound akin to the vowel in the modern American pronunciation of "cat," and the sound of the *w*, often written with a runic letter known as a "wynn").

So what did Caedmon do? He took the traditional Germanic habits of word formation, the grammar, and the sound of his own Old English and used them as the basis for translating Christian concepts into the Anglo-Saxon vernacular. England had only recently been converted to Christianity by the time Caedmon composed his *Hymn* (missionaries had arrived in the sixth century; monasteries were well established by the middle of the seventh). The older Germanic poetic forms of expression—shaped to pagan myth and earthly experience—had to be adapted for the new faith.

Caedmon took the many older Germanic words for lord, ruler, or divinity and applied them to the Christian God. *Uard* (pronounced "ward") means guardian or warden, and it was the word used to describe the temporal lord of a people. *Metud* comes from the Old English *metan*, to mete out. Lordship is an act of gift giving in old Germanic cultures, and the image of God as a kind of gift giver seeks to translate a familiar social figure into a new Christian idiom. *Uuldurfadur* is a compound made up of words meaning glory and father, and thus illustrates the technique of noun compounding in the Old English poetic vocabulary. *Dryctin* is the word used for a political ruler in Old English society. It is cognate with other Germanic words for king or lord (for example, the Scandinavian word *Drott*, or king). *Scepen* literally means shaper; creation here is an act of shaping (compare the Old English word for a poet, *scop*, also a shaper). *Frea* was an old Germanic god (compare the Old Norse figure Freyr), whose name means "excellence," or "bloom." Here, we have an old pagan name appropriated into a new devotional world.

Caedmon's Hymn is full of special compounds illustrating how the techniques of Old English verse were adapted to Christian contexts. We are asked to praise not only God's work but his *modgidanc*, what was going on in his mind. Old English *mod* becomes our word "mood," and really means "temper," or "quality of mind." *Moncynnæs* are the kin of men, a transparent compound; but *middungeard* is deceptive. True, it means simply "the middle yard," but it is the term used in Germanic mythology to denote the place between the realm of the gods and the world of the dead. Compare the Old Norse Midgard (or, for that matter, J. R. R. Tolkien's imagined "Middle Earth") and one sees Caedmon reaching back to shared Germanic mythology to articulate a Christian world for newly converted believers. So, too, the idiom *"heben til hrofe,"* to put a roof on heaven, looks back to the Germanic creation myths, where the gods built halls and roofed their dwellings. The most famous of such stories shows up in Snorri Sturlusson's Old Norse *Edda*, written in the mid-twelfth century, where the gods begin by establishing Midgard and building Valhalla, the hall of those killed in battle.

But the text of *Caedmon's Hymn* I have quoted here reveals something more than mythic roots. Old English was a language full of regional dialects, and like all places full of dialect variation, Anglo-Saxon England had a politics of language choice. Depending on where and when it was written and spoken, the language differed in pronunciation, spelling, and the particulars of noun and verb endings. Caedmon and Bede lived in the north of England, north of the Humber River, and their dialect was thus called Northumbrian. This was the original dialect of the *Hymn*, and the form in which I have quoted it here. This form is preserved in the earliest surviving text of the poem—a copy written into the margins of a manuscript of Bede's *Ecclesiastical History*, datable to 737. But the seats of Anglo-Saxon learning were to move soon afterward. Viking raids in the north stripped many monasteries of books and monks. Regional courts and new churches were being established elsewhere, especially in East Anglia. The Anglian dialect of Old English developed in the eighth and ninth centuries, and many of its distinctive forms survive in the great poems of the Anglo-Saxon age (in particular *Beowulf*), leading modern scholars to surmise that these poems were originally composed in that area. By the last decades of the ninth century, power was moving to the south. King Alfred (who would come to be known as "the Great") consolidated his rule at Winchester, in southwestern England, and the dialect of that region was known as West-Saxon.

The West-Saxon dialect emerged as something of a standard Old English by the early tenth century. It was the dialect of King Alfred, and thus had the imprimatur of one of England's leading rulers. King Alfred brought scholars and linguists to his court at Winchester in order to produce manuscripts of classical literature and philosophy and also translate them into Old English. Thus, many of our major Old English manuscripts appear in the West-Saxon dialect. In fact, when Bede's *Ecclesiastical History* was translated into Old English, Alfred's scholars put it into West-Saxon—and in the process, they transformed *Caedmon's Hymn* from its original Northumbrian into West-Saxon (many manuscripts of the *Hymn* therefore have it in the West-Saxon dialect). This is what the poem looks like in West-Saxon:

Nu sculon herigean	heofonrices Weard,
Meotodes meahte	ond his modgeþanc,
weorc Wuldorfæder,	swa he wundra gehwæs,
ece Drihten,	or onstealde.
He ærest sceop	eorðan bearnum
heofon to hrofe,	halig Scyppend;
þa middangeard	moncynnes Weard,
ece Drihten,	æfter teode,
firum foldan,	Frea ælmihtig.

In this form, the poem's words will clearly be more recognizable to a modern English-speaking reader. Instead of the *u*'s and *uu*'s, there are recognizable *w*'s. The noun form of heaven in line 6 (*heofon*) looks and would sound more familiar than the Northumbrian *heben*. The -*th*- sound signaled by the letter þ in the word *modgeþanc* reminds us that at the heart of this compound is the verb "to think." The phrase *"heofon to hrofe,"* literally, to roof heaven, is more transparent to modern eyes and ears than the Northumbrian *"heben til hrofe"* (the preposition *til* still means "to" in the Scandinavian languages). Finally, the West-Saxon translator has given us a far more familiar word in the phrase *"eorðan bearnum,"* than did Caedmon himself in the Northumbrian version. In West-Saxon, it is the children of earth; in Northumbrian it is the children of men, using a word, *ælde*, that

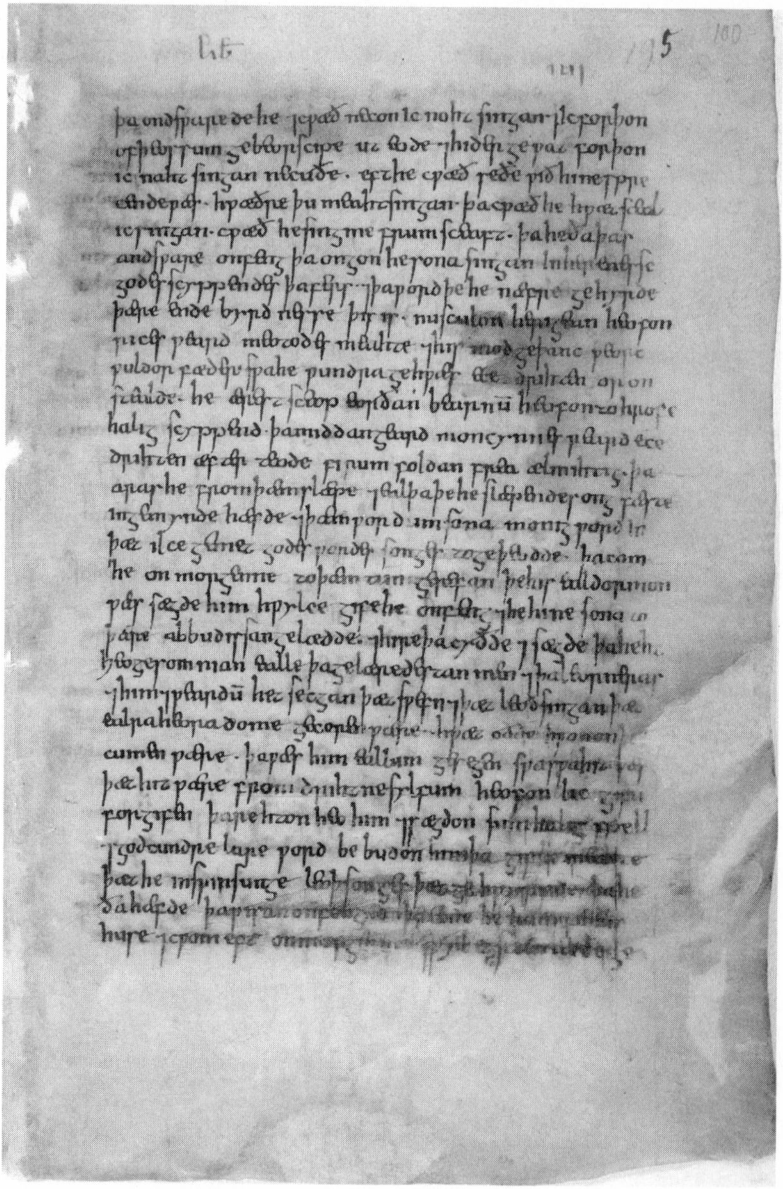

FIGURE I.I

The Old English translation of Bede's *History of the English Church and People*, prepared in the late ninth or early tenth century. Oxford Bodleian Library, MS Tanner 10, fol. 100r. This page contains the story of Caedmon, with *Cademon's Hymn* written into the text as continuous prose.

Reproduced by permission of the Bodleian Library, Oxford.

has passed out of usage (though in both we can see in the word *bearnum* the ancestor of the word *bairn*, still popular in Scotland for "child").

Even this cursory look at West-Saxon shows how indebted our modern English is to this dialect. It emerged as a written form in court and schools; by the eleventh century, it was the mandated standard for many monastic students and scribes—regardless of what region they came from, they had to write in West-Saxon. But it is also important to recognize that other dialects had forms that filtered into what would become modern English. A good example is the sound of certain vowels before the letter -l.

West-Saxon had a phenomenon that linguists call "breaking," where a vowel sound /a/ became a diphthong before l + another consonant. Thus the modern word "old" would have been spelled and pronounced *eald*; "cold" would have been *ceald*. In the Anglian dialect, this breaking did not occur; thus "old," and "cold" are *ald*, and *cald*. These are the forms that, through later sound changes, become our modern English words. Many other such examples illustrate how different dialects contributed to the mix of later Middle and Modern English, but, more significantly, they illustrate how a "standard" form of a language in one period did not necessarily generate the "standard" form of the language in later periods.

Old English dialects were also influenced by contact with other languages. In the north of England, the Scandinavian influence was prominent, in part because of continued raids and settlement patterns by Vikings and later Danish political groups. Northumbrian Old English came to use the Scandinavian sounds of /k/ and /sk/ for the sounds /tʃ/ and /ʃ/ in other dialects. Thus, words like "church" (Old English *cirice*) became *kirk*; *ship* became *skip*. One can chart patterns of settlement and dialect boundaries by place names. The Old English word for a harbor was *wic* (pronounced "wich"). Towns such as Ipswich, Harwich, and Norwich, for example, reflect that pronunciation. But in the North, that word would have been pronounced *wik*: thus, towns such as Berwick, or Wick itself, in modern Scotland.

So, the story of *Caedmon's Hymn* tells us many things: it illustrates how early English poets were adapting the traditional forms of Germanic verbal expression to newer Christian concepts. It tells us about the varieties of dialects in the Anglo-Saxon period. And it tells us, more generally, about the Anglo-Saxon literary imagination and its techniques.

Old English poetry, like all the poetry of the early Germanic peoples, was not written in rhyming lines; it was alliterative. The metrical pattern of each line was determined by the number of strong stresses in the line. Poetry in the Romance languages (French, Italian, and so on) and in Modern English depends on the number of syllables in each line (iambic pentameter, for example, has five feet, each foot made up of a weak and a strong stress, for a total of ten syllables per line). In Old English (and the other old Germanic languages) what mattered was only how many strong stresses each line had (from two to four). And the stressed syllables alliterated with each other: that is, they all had to begin with the same consonant or vowel (for the purposes of poetry, any vowels could alliterate on any other). In *Caedmon's Hymn*, we can see how alliteration governs each line: notice the repeated *h-* words in the first line, the repeated *m*-words in the second, the repeated *w*-words in the third, the repeated opening vowels in the fourth, and so on. The number of syllables varies from line to line, but the strong stresses in each line carry the rhythm through.

These patterns of alliteration also contributed to the formulaic quality of Old English poetry. Each poet drew on a traditional stock of formulas, that is, combinations of words that could be used over and over again to fit into alliterative patterns but that also contributed to the traditional feel of the verse. A good example of formulaic verse comes from the poem *Beowulf.* Early on, the narrator announces how the king, Scyld Scefing, could command his men so that they would obey him from even across the sea: "ofer hron-rade hyran scolde," literally, they should obey him over the whale-road. A little later in the poem, the scene shifts to the court of Hrothgar, which has been attacked by the monster Grendel. Hrothgar sends out over the sea for a hero who can help him: "ofer swan-rade secean wolde," literally, he desired to seek (someone) over the swan-road. There must have been a kind of verbal template for expressing travel across the sea in metaphorical ways: *ofer X-rade.* The X would be filled in by a word that alliterated with the other stressed words in the line. And the sound of both of these lines (separated in the poem by 190 lines) is remarkably similar, as if a larger formulaic expression that covered the whole line was being carefully tailored to each narrative situation.

Together with alliteration and formulaic phrasing, Old English poetry used patterns of repetition, echo, and interlacement to create powerfully resonant blocks of verse. There is an aesthetic quality to this poetry, a quality of intricate word weaving that moves the reader, or the listener, through the narrative or descriptive moment. In fact, one of the expressions used for making poetry in Old English was *wordum wrixlan*—to weave together words. There was a fabric of language for the Anglo-Saxons, a patterning of sounds and sense that matched the intricate patterning of their visual arts:

serpentine designs and complex interlocking geometric forms in manuscript illumination or in metalwork are the visual equivalents of the interlace patterns of the verse.

Caedmon's Hymn seems to come out of nowhere. We have nothing before it, no trials of awkward translators, no half-baked blocks of lines to illustrate the early history of English versification. It is clear that Anglo-Saxons had to have been making poetry long before Caedmon. And, whether or not we believe the miracle that Bede describes, *Caedmon's Hymn* is a miraculous piece of literature.

But so is much of Old English poetry, and the miraculous quality of the *Hymn* is something that many other poems share. Old English verse is constantly calling attention to the remarkably wrought quality of the things of this world. Take, for example, the group of poems known as the Anglo-Saxon Riddles. Over ninety of these short poems survive in a single manuscript, known as the Exeter Book, probably put together around the year 1000. Just about everything in the world is covered by the Exeter Book Riddles, from natural phenomena (wind, sun, moon, fire, water), to earthly animals and plants (fish, oyster, chickens, oxen, trees, onions, leeks), to human artifacts (shield, key, anchor, bread, book, plow, sword, helmet). Taken in tandem, the Riddles constitute a collocation of all creation: an assembly of puzzles whose individual answers contribute to an understanding of the world and the ambiguities of linguistic experience.

The riddles take vernacular literacy as their theme, as they illustrate how a knowledge of the word leads to a knowledge of the world, and in turn, how the world itself remains a book legible to the learned. One of these riddles, for example, is about a book. Told in the first person, it begins by recounting how a thief ripped off flesh and left skin, treated the skin in water, dried it in the sun, and then scraped it with a metal blade. Fingers folded it, the joy of the bird (that is, the feather) was dipped in the woodstain from a horn (that is, the ink in an inkwell), and left tracks on the body. Wooden boards enclose it, laced with gold wire. "Frige hwæt ic hatte," ask what I am called, it concludes. It is a book, but no mere volume. It is made up, sequentially, of all other parts of creation. The natural world and human artifice come together here to reveal the book as a kind of cosmos, and in turn, to demonstrate that the book contains all knowledge. "Gif min bearn wera brucan willað, / hy beoð gesundran and þy sigefæstran . . ." ("If the children of men will use me, they will be the healthier and the more victorious"). That health and victory, however, is not simply bodily or martial, but spiritual. This is a book of creation itself, a great Bible no doubt, bound with glittering ornament: "forþon me gliwedon / wrætlic weorc smiþa" ("on me there glistens the remarkable work of smiths").

That Old English word *wrætlic* appears again and again in the riddles to illustrate how even the most mundane of objects can seem remarkable. In one riddle, a hen and a rooster together appear as a "wrætlic twa," a remarkable twosome. In another, a "wrætlic" thing hangs by a man's thigh. Pierced in the front, it is stiff and hard. It has a good place when the man lifts up his garment to set it in its proper hole. It is . . . a key. But it, of course, is also not a key. Such an object is *wrætlic* in the eye of the poetic beholder, whose double entendre can make this household object seem proudly phallic (much as the riddler elsewhere makes the leek or the sword similarly tumescent; or as the riddle on bread rising in a bowl comes to resemble a pregnant woman's swelling womb).

The Riddles are not just exercises of poetic virtuosity or schoolroom prurience. They lie at the heart of the Old English literary aesthetic. Look at a Riddle on the bookworm.

Moððe word fræt. Me þæt þuhte
wrætlicu wyrd, þa ic þæt wundor gefrægn,
þæt se wyrm forswealg wera gied sumes,
þeof in þystro, þrymfæstne cwide
ond þæs strangan staþol. Stælgiest ne wæes
wihte þy gleawra, þe he þam wordum swealg.

[A moth ate words. It seemed to me
A remarkable occurrence, that I should speak about this wonder,
That the worm (a thief in the night), should swallow
His glorious song, and their strong place. That thieving guest
Was no whit the wiser, when he had swallowed the word.]

The Riddle begins with a deceptively simple statement, and a comment that this action seems a "wrætlicu wyrd," a remarkable event. *Wrætlic* here describes neither a wrought object nor a curiosity of creation but rather a strange juxtaposition of the work of nature and of human hands. The word *wyrd* can mean something as neutral as "event" or "occurrence," but it also means fate, fortune, or destiny (it is the origin of our word "weird," and shows up, in its Old English sense, as late as Shakespeare's *Macbeth*, whose Weird Sisters are not simply odd but prophetic). This, then, is both a strange event and a remarkable fate: strange, that the writings of man should have as their destiny the bowels of an insect. Reading is ingestion—an image central to the monastic tradition of learning, where *ruminatio* connoted the act of chewing over and digesting words as they were read, much as a cow might ruminate its cud. Double meanings are everywhere in this little poem: the "thief in the night" evokes not just a buggy eater but apocalypse itself. The day of the Lord, wrote St. Paul, comes as a thief in the night (1 Thessalonians 5:2; 2 Peter 3:10). The destruction of the page is a terrible thing, especially in a world where writing was a holy project. Not even the great stronghold of binding thread can withstand the mouth of this moth. And yet, for all its eating, this creature is no wiser for the words it swallows.

The bookworm represents a kind of spiritual illiteracy: ingesting the word does little good. How different is the world of *Caedmon's Hymn*. Recall now the setting of his story. It is a gathering of men after a day of work, what the Latin of Bede's *History* calls a *convivio*, a banquet, but what the Old English translator of King Alfred's day renders as a *gebeorscipe*: a beership, a drinking party. This scene of poetic making, like so many similar scenes throughout Western literature, takes place at a site of ritual eating and drinking. Think of the great poetic performances in Homer's *Odyssey*, where the feast is the occasion for a local bard to sing. Think of the opening of Virgil's *Aeneid*, where a harper comes to Dido's palace to sing about creation. Think about *Beowulf*, where Hrothgar commands his poet to entertain his men at their feast:

þær wæs hearpan sweg,
swutol sang scopes. Sægde se þe cuþe
frumsceaft fira   feorran reccan,
cwæð þæt se Ælmihtiga   eorðan worhte... .

[There was the sway of the harp,
Sweetly sang the scop. He, who was able to relate about it, told
About the creation of men from far back in time,
He said that the Almighty wrought the earth... .]

The subject matter of this scop's performance seems the same as that of *Caedmon's Hymn*—and in a way, the same as that of the Riddles. All of creation, whether in its whole or in its many parts, preoccupies the Anglo-Saxon poet. And whether the scene is one of heroic banqueting or barnyard beer drinking or bookworm nibbling, bringing some sustenance into the mouth provokes the performance of words out of the mouth. The little Riddle on the bookmoth offers up, in brilliantly condensed form, a kind of comic commentary on the spiritual and heroic traditions of Caedmon and *Beowulf*. Taken together, these are all lessons in the arts of language: a word that comes ultimately from the Latin *lingua*, meaning "tongue." Old English poetry is always word of mouth—not simply because it was performed orally but also because its controlling metaphors and messages reveal the power of the mouth to shape a sound and give life to letters.

Caedmon's Hymn and Bede's account of its performance hold a larger truth: that all words are miraculous, that we are always translating from one tongue to another, whether it be from the Latin of the scholar to the Old English of the bard, or from the Northumbrian of the cowherd to the West-Saxon of the king. Over three hundred years separate *Caedmon's Hymn* from the Riddles of the Exeter Book. But during those three centuries, a literature flourished in a language most of us can barely parse today. And whether we are looking at the opening of Anglo-Saxon literary culture or its close, the concern always is with the creation of the world, the origins of things, and the first words of poetry. *Frumsceaft*: this is the Old English word for Creation. In the Old English translation of Bede's Latin, this is what the angel commands of Caedmon: "Sing me frumsceaft." See in it now the habits of the old Germanic wordsmiths, who would make up terms rather than borrow them. *Frum* means origin or beginning. *Sceaft* is the shaping. It comes from the same old root as the Old English word for poet, *scop*, the shaper of words. My history of English thus begins with a return to those first shapers, who would move their mouths, as we must do, around strange sounds, to make the voices of creation live again. And to my readers who have started this book, I would advise them: be not like the bookmoth, who ingests the word but does not know. Read well, and ruminate—like cow or cowherd Caedmon—so that you may sing with me.

CHAPTER 2

From *Beowulf* to Wulfstan

The Language of Old English Literature

THE SONG OF THE ANGLO-SAXON *scop* sounded for six centuries. From Caedmon, through *Beowulf*, to the monastic scribes who copied down the legacy of poetry well into the twelfth century, Old English alliterative forms and formulae filled halls and cloisters with their sound. The techniques of that poetry could be applied to any subject matter: Germanic myths, Christian Creation stories, acts of martyrs, Old Testament narratives, current political conditions. Biblical characters, at times, take on the quality of old Germanic heroes. At other times, figures out of the past seem remarkably like contemporary scholars. How does Old English literature refract the inheritance of pagan myth and Christian doctrine; how does it give voice to a unique perspective on the world and the imagination?

These questions can be asked of the whole range of Anglo-Saxon literary life. Not only *Beowulf* worked according to oral-formulaic patterns and alliterative meter. Poems such as *Genesis, Exodus,* and *Daniel* deployed the forms and diction of Old English verse, even when the subject may have seemed far removed from the heroic hall. In *Daniel*, strikingly, the handwriting on the wall that signals the end of the Babylonian kingdom appears, not in Hebrew but in reddened runes—as if the Anglo-Saxon poet needed to imagine an arresting, enigmatic form of writing and turned to the ancient Germanic system of epigraphy. In the *Dream of the Rood*, the figure of Christ on the cross comes off as nothing less than a familiar warrior. *Ongeyrede hine þa geone Hæle—þæt wæs God ælmihtig—strang and stiðmod.* "Then the young hero disrobed himself—that was God almighty—strong and resolute." Christ is *stiðmod*, assured in that *mod* that is so central to the Anglo-Saxon inner life. Even half a century after the Norman Conquest, poets could still conjure up the formulae of heroism, understanding, travel, fear, and worship. The poem known as *Durham*, composed in the first decade of the twelfth century, celebrates the northern English city and the church there, and its words evoke the scope of human and divine creation in distinctively Old English terms.

And ðær gewexen is   wudafæstern micel;
wuniad in ðem wycum   wilda deor monige,
in deope dalum   deora ungerim.

[And there has also grown up [around the city] a fast enclosing woods;
in that place dwell many wild animals,
countless animals in deep dales.]

The great wood stands outside the city much like the forest that encroaches on Hrothgar's hall—and yet, here in the Christian country, woods are filled not with the monsters of the night but with the uncounted animals of God's creation.

The formulae, alliterative patterns, and vocabulary terms concatenate to impress us with a consistency of poetic diction over many centuries. Even in Anglo-Saxon prose, that diction reappears. Translations commissioned by King Alfred in the late ninth century, or sermons written by Bishop Ælfric and Bishop Wulfstan in the early eleventh, strike us not just with words but with rhythm. A good deal of this prose seems to scan, to alliterate, to flow almost like poetry: *Æfter ðan ðe* **Augustinus** *to* **Engla** *lande becom wæs sum* **æðele** *cyning, Oswold gehaten, on* **Norðhymbra** *lande, gelyfed swyþe on* **God** ("After St. Augustine came to England, there was a noble king, named Oswald, in Northumbria, who believed deeply in God"). Some modern scholars have dubbed this a "rhythmical prose," and have argued that the line between the metrical and the prosaic was not as clear as in our time (some modern editions of Ælfric's homilies even lineate it as if it were verse). Whatever the relationship among the forms, one cannot but be struck by resonances between the elegiac oratory of the scop and the exhortations of the bishop.

Old English literary diction lives in nouns and adjectives. The kennings and the synonyms at work in *Caedmon's Hymn* or in the Exeter Book Riddles are the building blocks of literary expression. Relying on specialized knowledge and fitting into metrical and alliterative formulae, the word hoard of Anglo-Saxon poetry challenges the modern reader. Some of the most evocative of terms appear only once in the entire body of the verse. A beautiful example appears when Beowulf returns to Hygelac's court: he presents the king with the rewards he had received, including four horses that are *æppel-fealuwe*, apple-fallow. Other words seem so technical that they must come from a professional experience that few would share. A case in point is the runic inscription at Balthazzar's feast in *Daniel* that appears in *baswe bocstafas*, reddened or purple letters—the word *basu* (the nominative form of *baswe*) shows up in learned glosses to translate the Latin terms for the color derived from the Mediterranean mollusk associated with the dyes of ancient Phoenicia. Some Old English words, too, came from the necessity of translation. Rather than borrowing words from Latin, the Anglo-Saxon translators would often use familiar terms in new ways. Thus, in the translation of Boethius's *Consolation of Philosophy* (a product of King Alfred's circle), the Latin philosophical term *fortuna* becomes the Old English *wyrd*. In the translations of the Latin bible, a word such as *discipulus* ("disciple") finds its rendering in nothing less than a poetic-seeming kenning: *leorningcniht*, a knight of learning.

But the language of Old English literature consists of more than words. Patterns of syntax, rhetorical forms, and structural devices blur the line between grammar and style, between the ways in which you have to speak and the ways in which you want to speak. Because meaning in an Old English sentence was determined largely by the case endings appended to the words, the order of those words could be more flexible than in, say, Modern English. But there were many constraints on that order. In poetry, lines had to alliterate and scan, influencing the sequencing of words. Anglo-Saxon prose, at first glance, seems to pose fewer such constraints. But the fact was that many works of prose were translations from Latin originals, and the word order patterns of the vernacular often mimed those of the Latin. Problems, too, occur for modern readers confronted with a limited number of little words. Many such words did double duty in Old English. The word *þa* (or *ða*), for example, could mean both "when" and "then." *Ðær* (or *ðær*) could mean both "where" and "there." The definite article was used as the relative pronoun (the phrase *se mon se* would need to be translated as "the man who"). Sometimes, especially in poetry, that definite article would just be dropped.

All these conditions make it hard for modern readers to translate Old English texts. But they also made it possible for poets, sermonizers, translators, and teachers to find their distinctive voices in the manipulations of a sentence. Many have found in *Beowulf* such a distinctive voice; many have found it, too, in Archbishop Wulfstan. Indeed, one of the earliest surviving manuscripts of Wulfstan's famous Sermon to the English (the *Sermo Lupi ad Anglos*) may well have been corrected in the bishop's own hand. Amidst the anonymities of scops and scribes, some individuality emerges.

But the most famous individual of all Old English literature is without language at all. The monster Grendel, in *Beowulf*, never speaks. He seems shorn of language itself, capable only of cries. Perhaps this is the reason for his anger at the Danes when, at the poem's opening, he lies in wait to strike at Hrothgar's hall. When he hears the sweet song of the scop, he is, in J. R. R. Tolkien's memorable interpretation, "maddened by the sound of harps." Who is this creature lurking in the shadows? He emerges, at first, only by epithets and adjectives. He is *se ellen-gæst*, the bold spirit (86a), the *feond on helle*, the hellish fiend (101b), *se grimma gæst*, the grim spirit (102b). Only after this string of descriptions is he finally named:

Wæs se grimma gæst Grendel haten,
mære mearc-stapa, se þe moras heold,
fen ond fæsten; fifel-cynnes eard
won-sæli wer weardode hwile,
siþðan him Scyppend forscrifen hæfde
in Caines cynne— þone cwealm gewræc
ece Drihten, þæs þe he Abel slog.

(102–8)

[The grim spirit was called Grendel,
well-known walker in the border lands, he who held to the moors,
the fen and the fastness; the home of the race of monsters
the miserable creature occupied for a while,
ever since the Lord had condemned him
as one of the descendants of Cain—the one whom
the eternal lord condemned to death, because he slew Abel.]

This passage tells us much about the monster, but it also tells us much about the Old English language. We get a mix of Christian and Germanic, of bible and myth. Grendel descends from Cain's kin, from a race of fratricides. He is condemned by God. The biblical names here—Cain and Abel—seem to float like linguistic interlopers on the old familiar diction of belief. From that diction are the words word *Scyppend* and *Drihten*, drawn from the Germanic terms for creator and ruler. There are, too, the brilliant kennings, compounds that distill a set of actions or conditions into single terms. A word like *won-sæli*, for example, brings together two opposing elements into an evocation of despair: *won*, meaning dark, black, or empty (our Modern English word "wan"); *sæli*, blessed, holy (still, in Modern German, *selig*). Grendel is a *won-sæeli wer*, a being empty of blessedness. He inhabits the empty places of the northern European landscape, places called by words that have remained unchanged for a thousand years: *fen*, *moor*, *march*, *fastness*.

But there is also a different kind of word here. The word *forscrifen* is a calque: a bit-by-bit, or morpheme-by-morpheme translation of the Latin word *proscribere*. This Latin term originally meant "to write about": *pro* ("for," or "about") + *scribere* (the verb "to write"). It came to connote the act of making things known, of publicly recording names or actions. Eventually, it meant to outlaw or, as Modern English adopted it, "proscribe," by writing a person's name in a public list. Readers and writers of Old English took this word and translated it in pieces: the prefix *for-* translates the Latin *pro-*; the verb *scrifan* translates *scribere*. Grendel has been outlawed from the book of life.

Calques were a means of adding to the language's vocabulary without bringing in new loan words. As we saw in *Caedmon's Hymn*, the traditional means of building up the old Germanic lexicon was to rely on native words used in new compounds or new ways. More than just a pedantic interest of the linguist, the calque is, for early English, a lens through which we can read the appropriation of a Latin, Christian inheritance into a vernacular idiom. In this way, they share in the larger Anglo-Saxon literary habit of renaming. In *Caedmon's Hymn*, the movement of the poem comes from its string of new names for the divinity. So, too, in *Beowulf*, renaming is the engine that drives poetry. Grendel has many names, as we have seen. Here are some others: *þyrs* (monster), *eoten* (giant), *gastbona* (soul-slayer), *wæl-gæst* (murderous spirit). But more than monsters get their fill of terms. There are myriad words for men: *beorn, guma, hæleð, rinc, wer, man, secg, ceorl*. Do these words have specific registers or connotations, or are they merely terms conveniently slipped into metered patterns in order to alliterate? Is there a difference between this range of simple words and the more complex compounds that seem obviously part of the poetic lexicon: *heaðulac* (battle-play), *gifstol* (throne), *himrceald* (rime-cold), and so on? Or just look, for example, at a glossary of any

Beowulf edition to find an entire lexicography of death: *wæl* (death, slaughter), *wæl-bed* (death bed), *wæl-bend* (deadly bond), *wæl-bleat* (deadly), *wæl-
deað* (deadly death), *wæl-dreor* (the blood of death), *wæl-fæhð* (deadly feud),
wæl-fag (death stained), *wæl-fus* (death ready), *wæl-fyllo* (pile of the dead),
wæl-seax (deadly knife).

What emerges from these lists is the texture of Old English literary
diction. But did the Anglo-Saxon man or woman really talk like this?
What is the relationship between a literary lexicon and the words of
everyday speech? Can we recover something of the idiom of culture
from this heightened diction, or must we turn elsewhere for the talk
of people?

There are some sources for that kind of talk. Early in the eleventh century, Bishop Ælfric of Eynsham (c. 955–1020) composed a *Colloquy* designed to enhance his students' command of Latin syntax and vocabulary.
About a generation after Ælfric composed it, someone (probably one of his
disciples) added an Old English interlinear gloss. This interlinear translation offers valuable evidence for something like the everyday vernacular
at the close of the Anglo-Saxon period. In the *Colloquy* each student plays
a role, taking on the voices of particular professions, crafts, or callings,
and the master asks each in turn just what they do and how they do it.
Much like the Riddles of the Exeter Book, everything is here (the hunter
and his animals, the fisherman and his fish, the fowler and his birds,
and so on), and for the English-speaking student such a text assembles a
vocabulary of experience. "Hwæt wille ȝe sprecan?" What do you want to
talk about? asks the teacher, and he asks again, in phrasing that reveals
both the colloquial idiom of this colloquy and the daily facts of medieval
school life: "Wille beswungen on leornunge?" Do you want to be flogged
into learning? Granted, these lines are translations of a Latin original,
but from them emerge the flavor of speech, not just of vocabulary but of
syntax, too. Take, for example, the episode where one student takes on the
role of hunter.

> Canst þu ænig þing?
> Ænne cræft ic cann.
> Hwylcne?
> Hunta ic eom.
> Hwæs?
> Cincges.
> Hu begæst þu cræft þinne?

Ic brede me max and sette hiʒ on stowe gehæppre, and getihte hundas mine þæt wildeor hiʒ ehton, oþþæt hig becuman to þam net-tan unforsceawodlice and þæt hig swa beon begrynodo, and ic ofslea hig on þam maxum.

[Do you know how to do anything?
I have one occupation (literally, I am able to do one craft).
What?
I am a hunter.
Whose?
The king's.
How do you perform your occupation?
I weave myself a net and set it in a convenient place, and I urge my dogs to pursue the wild animals until they come unsuspectingly into that net and they become ensnared in it and I kill them in the net.]

The first verb of the exchange, *cunnon* means not simply "can," but to have skill of something. Here, it is really, "can you do any thing," or what skill do you have. In the single words of interrogation lie the grammatical markers of gender and case: *Hwyclne*, what kind of thing (masculine, singular, accusative); *hwæs*, whose (masculine, singular, genitive). And when the student answers *cincges*, "the king's," we realize that the answering of a question asked in the genitive case must similarly be in the genitive case.

But there is more than grammar here. Just listen to the student describe the method of hunting. *Plecto mihi retia* he begins in the Latin, I weave a net for myself. But in the Old English, "Ic brede me max," really comes off as, "I weave me a net." You can hear the archaism, or what may be now the regionalism, in that phrase—a realization that the reflexive in what we think of as uneducated modern usage is not uneducated at all; it is but the survival of a past form of English.

Composed as it was for students in a monastery, Ælfric's *Colloquy* did more than teach vocabulary or syntax. It had a doctrinal purpose and an allegorical flavor. How can a Christian student not find spiritual meaning in the story of the hunter who sets out his net for unsuspecting game? Æefric's are lessons in preparedness, in avoiding what may be well foreseen. Elsewhere the Anglo-Saxon monastic student takes on the role of fisherman.

Wylt þu fon sumne hwæl?
Nic.

Forhwi?

Forþam plyhtlic þinc hit ys gefon hwæl. Gebeorlicre ys me faran to ea mid scype mynan, þænne faran mid manegum scypum on huntunge hranes.

> [Would you catch a whale?
> No
> Why?
> Because it is a dangerous thing to catch a whale. It is safer for me to go to the river with my boat than to go with many boats hunting whales.]

It is a dangerous thing to catch a whale. Leviathan may lurk for any foolish Jonah, much as Satan's snares may lurk for the *unforsceawodlice* student. How could a student not see in the word *unforsceawodlice*—literally, "unforseeingly"—the sense of everything that lurks to take us? This word is also a calque, as it translates the *Colloquy*'s Latin word *inprovise*. *In*, or *im*, is the Latin negative prefix; *pro* means concerning or about; *vise* comes from *visus*, seeing. Translate it bit-by-bit and you get *un + for + seeing*.

The unforeseen is everywhere in *Beowulf*, from Grendel's first appearance, to the vengeful visit of his mother, to the final waking of the dragon. The poem operates through a vocabulary of anticipation, vision, light, and darkness. At the heart of the word *unforsceawodlice* is the verb *sceawian*, to look at, see, behold (it is the origin of our modern word "show"). But if there is a great deal that is unseen in the poem, there is much at which its men stare. They look with awe at Grendel's arm, severed and hung from Heorot's roof (*wundor sceawian; hand sceawedon*). They stare at the horrors of the lake that holds his mother (*weras sceawedon*). Hrothgar looks closely at the runically inscribed hilt Beowulf recovers from that lake (*hylt sceawode*). Everyone is looking, so it seems, for a sign.

And so, when Hrothgar's men awaken early in the poem, they behold the horror of Grendel's night visit.

> ða wæs on uhtan   mid ærdæge
> Grendles guðcræft   gumum undyrne
> Þa wæs æfter wiste   wop up ahafen
> micel morgensweg.

> (126–29a)

[Then it was a dawn, early in the day,
Grendel's warcraft revealed to men;
then it was, after the feasting, weeping rose up,
a great morning-sound.]

The gore is *undyrne*, literally "not secret." It is not simply dawn but *uht*, that special time in Anglo-Saxon literature when the mist still clings and the sun has not fully risen. There is no modern English equivalent to this evocative poetic word (even though, when the Anglo-Saxon Catholics sought vernacular terms for the canonical hours, they came up with *uht-sang* for "matins"). On such a frosty morning, the speaker of the poem known as *The Wanderer* must tell his story:

Oft ic sceolde ana   uhtna gehwylce
mine ceare cwiþan.

[Often I have had to speak of my cares,
at each and every dawn.]

But while Grendel's damage may be clear to Hrothgar's men, the order of their actions is unclear to modern readers. Do we have two independent clauses: "Then in the dawn . . . ; then there arose . . ."? Or, do we have a correlative construction: "When in the dawn, then there arose"? In prose, such a distinction could be clearly made with word order. The pattern **þa + subject + verb** indicated a conditional or subordinate clause: when such and such happened. The pattern **þa + verb + subject** indicated a determinative or an independent clause: then such and such happened. This pattern shows up, to great rhetorical effect, in one of the most famous pieces of Old English prose, King Alfred's letter to his bishops on the state of learning in England, appended as the preface to his translation of Gregory the Great's *Pastoral Care*. Written in the last decade of the ninth century, this document has long been studied for its literary power and its testimony to linguistic usage in the West-Saxon world. For the past century, it has remained one of the cornerstones of Old English teaching, often appearing as one of the very first selections in the standard readers, grammars, and anthologies. It is a lament for learning passed, for studies neglected, for scholarship and grammar gone by the wayside (no wonder modern pedagogues have loved to lade their students with its polemics). Alfred works through a pattern of remembrances: "when I recall all this," he often states, "then I think about. . . ." Here are his patterns of recall:

SUBJECT VERB	VERB SUBJECT
ða **ic** ða ðis eall **gemunde**,	ða **gemunde ic** eac hu ic geseah, . . .

When I remembered all of this, then I remembered how I saw, . . .

Such patterns may be harder to adhere to in poetry, though there are clear moments in *Beowulf* when we can see them working.

VERB
Ða **com** of more, under mist-hleoþu
SUBJECT
Grendel gongan, Godes yrre bær.

[Then there came from the moor, under the misty slopes, Grendel walking, bearing God's anger.]

And, with the different word order:

SUBJECT VERB
Snyredon ætsomne, þa **secg wisode**,
under Heorotes hrof;

[They hastened together, when the man directed them,
under Heorot's roof.]

These cases are clear. But many others are not, and scholars have recently debated whether patterns of word order remain looser in the verse or, by contrast, whether most of the *þa*-constructions, especially in the passage I quoted above, are independent then-clauses.

This is the place where arguments about syntax shade into assessments of style. The style of old Germanic verse has long been thought of as moving according to strings of avowals, joined by conjunctions or patterned strings of announcements. This kind of patterning is known as parataxis. Scholars have found the paratactic style, too, in the Bible (with its well-known sequences of sentences beginning with "and" or "then") and in many ancient epics. The great literary critic of the mid-twentieth century, Erich Auerbach, considered parataxis one of the defining devices of early literature. It could be used by St. Augustine to "express the impulsive and dramatic"(Auerbach, *Mimesis*, 71). It could appear in *The Song of Roland* to enable the poet to "explain nothing" and state things "with a paratactic bluntness which says that everything must happen as it does happen, it could not be otherwise, and there is no need for explanatory connectives" (*Mimesis*, 101). Early Germanic poetry, too, writes Auerbach, "exhibits paratactic construction" in which "verbal blocks are . . . loosely juxtaposed"—a stylistic device designed to illustrate not the clear-cut relationships of power and control, but patterns of an enigmatic destiny.

The rhythm of the paratactic, I believe, goes hand-in-hand with the Old English diction of the noun and adjective, of renaming and synonymy. Parallel constructions build to power, and nowhere is this clearer than in one of the great literary performances of the period: Archbishop Wulfstan's *Sermo Lupi ad Anglos* (the Sermon of Wolf—i.e., Wulfstan—to the English), delivered in York in 1014 to a congregation terrified before the invasion of the Danes. There was a Danish king ruling the Anglo-Saxons, and while an English ruler was invited back after that Dane's death, the future of the country seemed unsure. "Leofan men," beloved men, he begins, "gecnawað þæt soð is," know what is true. This world is hastening to its end. Things are growing worse. The devil has led the people astray. Terrible things are happening. Women are being forced to marry against their will; Christians are being sold to heathens as slaves. Nothing has prospered. "Ac worhtan lust us to lage"—but we have made pleasure our law (a phrase, by the way, as powerfully alliterative as anything in poetry).

Wulfstan builds his rhetoric through a series of addresses. Calls to remembrance and exhortations are his mode. He moves through sentences beginning with the word *and*, strings of statements that pile up one after the other:

> And we eac for þam habbað fela byrsta and bysmara gebiden . . .
> And micel is nydþearf manna gewhylcum . . .
> And ne dear man gewanian on hæþenum þeodum . . .
> And we habbað Godes hus inne and ute clæne berypte. . . .
> And Godes þeowas syndan mæþe and munde gewelhwær bedælde . . .
> And gedwolgoda þenan. . . .

Parataxis is his mode. What Erich Auerbach had said about the style of St. Francis of Assisi may well be said of Wulfstan here: that the person who writes these lines "is obviously so inspired by his theme, it fills him so completely, and the desire to communicate himself and to be understood is so overwhelming that parataxis becomes a weapon of eloquence" (*Mimesis*, 166).

Wulfstan's parataxis may owe much to the Latin traditions that St. Francis would later share. But it owes as much to the brilliantly inventive, Anglo-Saxon penchant for word building. Wulfstan's lexicon brims over with compounds, metaphors, and calques. Just look, for example, at how he describes the legal consequences of an escaped slave who, having become a Viking, might encounter his lord once again. What will occur between the thrall and thane is a *wæpngewrixl*: an exchange of weapons. This word comes straight from the Old English poetic vocabulary, with its compound force and its internal alliteration. The word appears in the poem *Christ* (937). In *Genesis*, there is *wælgara wrixl* (the exchange of death spears). But the power of this word comes, too, from the more common contexts of the verb *wrixlan*. For what is more frequently exchanged in Anglo-Saxon literature are words rather than weapons. The scop in *Beowulf* exchanges one word for another, varies his vocabulary when he *wordum wrixlan*. And in the poem known as *Maxims I*, the counseling speaker offers these sage words: *Gleawa men sceolon gieddum wrixlan.* Wise men should exchange speech. Wulfstan's two enemies are, at this moment, hardly wise.

But Wulfstan himself was a master of the art of *wordum wrixlan*. He varies his vocabulary, comes up, it would seem, with more synonyms for crimes, depravities, and sins than almost anyone could conjure. Look at the penultimate section of his sermon.

Her syndan þurh synleawa, swa hit þincan mæg, sare gelewede to manege on earde. Her syndan mannslagan and mægslagan and mæsserbanan and mynsterhatan, and her syndan manswaran and morþorwyrhtan, and her syndan myltestran and bearnmyrðran and fule forlegene horingas manege, and her syndan wiccan and wælcyrian, and her syndan ryperas and reaferas and worolstruderas, and, hrædest is to cweþenne, mana and misdæda ungerim ealra.

[Here are through the injury of sin, as it may seem, too many sorely wounded in the country. Here are man slayers and kinsman slayers and priest slayers and persecutors of monasteries, and here are perjurers and murderers, and here are harlots and child killers and foul lying whorers, and here are witches and valkyries, and here are plunderers and robbers and despoilers, and to speak most quickly, a countless number of all crimes and misdeeds.]

The phrase *her syndan* builds climactically. Each sentence grows longer, the vocabulary more erudite. The alliterations chime in the ear, much as they would in any piece of verse. The nouns denoting all these horrors take on a massive weight, ranging from the learned (*mynsterhatan*, persecutor of churches) to the vulgar (*horingas*, whorers). Wulfstan draws deep into the ancient lexicon: there are witches (*wiccan*) here, and *wælcyrian*, a word that literally means "choosers of the dead" and is the Old English equivalent of the Old Norse *valkyrie*. And at the end of this expostulation, as if exhausting his own dictionary of disaster, Wulfstan wraps it up by saying, shortly, that this place is full of innumerable crimes. His word is *ungerim*, the same word that the poet of *Durham* uses to describe the uncountable wild animals that live in the forest or the uncountable number of relics in the monastery. The poem known as *The Order of the World* used the term (in the form *unrim*) to describe the countless number of blessed who dwell with God in heaven (*eadigra unrim*). What is countless in Wulfstan is not to be found in heaven or on earth, but rather in hell—as if the underworld had ripped through the ground and everyone from harlots to whorers to harpies had come through in a way not to be seen again until the visions of Heironymous Bosch.

Wulfstan was one of the great prose stylists in the history of English, and the sources of his style lie in the literary language of the Anglo-Saxons. At another point in his sermon, his litany of crimes ends with the word *searacræftas* ("magical crafts"). This word has at its root *searo*, or *searwu*, a term of ancient Germanic myth and magic power. Connoting artifice, deception, evil skill, it appears at the heart of many words for marvelous, and freakish, objects in Old English poetry. Grendel's dragon-skin glove is laced up *searobendum fæst* (with cunningly wrought bands). Beowulf's own armor is *searofah* (locked together with magic rings). And Grendel's severed arm, hung up on Heorot, is a *searowunder* for all to see. Summarizing the many uses and registers of this root, the modern scholar Stephen A. Barney evocatively calls it "a word of admirable or dastardly connotation: the reference is to the cunning machinations of the metal-smith or the elaborate artifice of the traitor" (*Word Hoard*, 49). For Wulfstan, the deceits of his fellow men are more than just crimes; they have the flavor of an ancient machination, something as horrible as Grendel's grip.

Canst þu ænig cræft? asked Ælfric's master in the *Colloquy*. It is as if Wulfstan has answered such a question by recording all the crafts of horror, as if the *Sermo Lupi*, as much as the *Colloquy*, or the Exeter Book Riddles, remains an encyclopedia of everything. But the real craft of Anglo-Saxon poets and prose writers was the craft of language: the ability to draw on a vocabulary both old and new, to coin new words, to shape them in alliterative phrases, to use the resources of syntax and of sound for rhetorical effect—to make, in short, weapons of eloquence out of the weaponry of heroes, mythic monsters, and a Christian faith.

CHAPTER 3

In This Year

The Politics of Language and the End of Old English

WILLIAM THE CONQUEROR LANDED IN ENGLAND in October 1066, and though he and his people spoke the dialect of Norman French, Old English was not wiped out overnight. Prose history, poetic lyrics and encomia, and a range of sermons, homilies, and prayers continued to be copied in manuscripts well into the thirteenth century. In the Midlands and the North of England, in particular, linguistic life seemed to go on much as before, with little evidence of French words, syntax, or literary form impinging on the old, alliterative metrics of the Anglo-Saxons. At Peterborough Abbey, about thirty miles northwest of Cambridge, monks continued to compose a chronicle of English history in the style of the Old English annalists. Organized year by year, the so-called *Peterborough Chronicle* limns the political and social life of England from just after the Conquest until 1154. But in addition to its historical record, the *Chronicle* charts the changing English language in the first century of Norman control. Far from the center of that rule, the abbey's monks and scribes preserve an Anglo-Saxon prose almost untouched by Francophone influence. Here, we can see Old English changing, as it were, on its own. Word endings were leveling out. Grammatical gender was disappearing from nouns. The elaborate case system and class system of the nouns was simplifying. The difference between strong and weak adjectives (a feature common to all Germanic languages) was lost, and the old dual form of the verb also disappeared. The spelling of the *Chronicle* text also reveals changes not just in grammar but in pronunciation. The consonant clusters that had characterized the distinctive Old English sound were disappearing. Other changes were affecting consonant sequences, while vowels, too, were altering their length and quality.

It is clear that, whatever the immediate effect the Norman Conquest had on English, the vernacular of Anglo-Saxon England was changing. One theory to explain the loss of endings, and its grammatical consequences, relies on the idea of word stress. Old English, as all Germanic languages, had fixed stress on the root syllable of the word. Regardless of what prefixes or suffixes were added to it, or regardless of the word's grammatical category, the stress remained fixed on the root (other languages, such as those of the Romance family or Greek, have variable word stress). It has been argued that this root stress had a tendency to level out the sounds of unstressed syllables in speech. Some endings may have just been reduced to an unstressed form (say, the short mid-vowel represented in modern phonetic notation as a schwa). In the absence of a fixed and standard system of spelling, late Anglo-Saxon scribes would probably have written what they heard—or, perhaps, written what they thought was correct, even if it was not what they heard.

We can see something of this phenomenon in the *Peterborough Chronicle*. Take, for example, the phrase used to introduce each yearly record—in this year, such and such happened. The entry for 1083 uses the opening formula in precisely grammatical Old English: "On þissum geare" (in this year). The *-um* and *-e* endings signal the dative masculine singular forms of the adjective and noun, following the preposition. As the case endings began to lose their prominence in the spoken language, they became harder to reproduce in the written. The entry for 1117 opens, "On þison geare." Here, the adjectival ending has leveled to an indiscriminate back vowel plus an indiscriminate nasal. Perhaps this spelling represents a scribe's attempt to preserve what he thinks is a grammatical ending. The entry for 1135 opens, "On þis geare." Here, we have a total loss of the adjectival ending, together with what may be thought of as a fossilized dative final *-e* in the noun. Concord in grammatical gender has obviously gone by this time. The last entry for the *Peterborough Chronicle*, 1154, opens, "On þis gaer." Endings have completely dropped away, but the preposition *on* still has its Old English sense of "in" or "at this point," not the more modern sense (emerging in Middle English) of spatial location.

This is a small but revealing illustration of how Old English was changing on its own. These scribal forms, however, may not exactly reproduce the speech forms of the time. Modern scholars, in fact, believe that the entries dated from 1122 to 1131 were all written at the same time and back dated, and that the entries from 1132 to 1154 were similarly written down all at one time (clearly, one scribe wrote out the first section, another scribe wrote out the next). What changes such as these do reveal, though, are the ways in which writers try to represent their language as it changes. We see grammatical confusion, different conventions of spelling and letter formation, changing attitudes towards the relationship of writing to speech. The value of the *Peterborough Chronicle* lies, therefore, not in its transcription of year-by-year spoken English but in its thoughtful evocation of an English prose style passing from the scene.

Even the Peterborough monks could not completely escape Norman influence, and their scribes did not only seek to sustain Old English. They sought, as well, to use new words and forms for distinctive aesthetic, as well as political, ends. Language change is a social phenomenon, and the chronicler's choices of word, syntax, prosody, and diction have implications for the world of lived experience.

And the defining figure of that lived experience during the first decades of Norman rule was William himself. The first king in Britain to build castles on the Continental model, to command a written inventory of the land and holdings of the country (what became known as the Domesday Book), and to close off public lands for private use, William left an indelible mark on the English landscape. For the Peterborough annalist, his death becomes the occasion for a personal review of his rule—an entry (dated 1087) whose emotional pitch echoes the pulpit voice of Wulfstan, with its exhortations and laments and its attention to the transitoriness of worldly goods.

> Eala, hu leas 7 hu unwrest is þysses middaneardes wela! Se þe wæs ærur rice cyng 7 maniges landes hlaford, he næfde þa ealles landes buton seofon fotmæl; 7 se þe wæs hwilon gescrid mid golde 7 mid gimmum, he læg þa oferwrogen mid moldan.

> [Lo, how transitory and insecure is the wealth of this world! He who was once a powerful king and the lord of many lands, received (in death) no other land but seven feet of it; and he who was once clothed in gold and gems lay then covered with earth.]

Such phrasings would have been familiar to an Anglo-Saxon reader not just from the preachers but from the poets. *Beowulf*, for example, is full of such elegiac moments, as when the poet comments on the burial mound of the dead hero.

forleton eorla gestreon   eorðan healdan,
gold on greote,   þær hit nu gen lifað
eldum swa unnyt,   swa hit æror wæs.

(3166–68)

[they let the earth hold the wealth of noblemen,
the gold in the dust, where it now still remains,
as useless to men as it ever had been before.]

The Peterborough annalist's phrasings look back to this linguistic and stylistic Anglo-Saxon inheritance, especially in his alliterative pairings (the phrase "mid golde 7 mid gimmum" here has a formulaic feel and scan to it).

Like several entries in other versions of the Anglo-Saxon Chronicle, the *Peterborough Chronicle* entry for 1087 contains not just prose but poetry (though, as in the case of all Old English poetry, its verse is written out continuously as prose). Especially in entries on the death of kings or the martyrdom of men, the chroniclers would offer verse laments, shaped according to the patterns of alliterative metrics and the formulae of the traditional Germanic idiom. Such poems appear in other versions of the Anglo-Saxon Chronicle on, for example, the death of King Edward (1065), the coronation of King Edgar (973), and, most famously, the Battle of Brunanburgh (937). The poem on the death of William, however, does something different. For one thing, it rhymes. Now while rhyme was not unknown in Old English poetry, it was not used as the governing, organizational principle for verse (the only exception is the so-called "Rhyming Poem" found in the Exeter Book of verse—a tour de force, modeled most likely on the rhyming antiphons of Latin liturgical song). Though rough in meter and in rhyme, the poem on the Conqueror (known to modern scholars as "The Rime of King William") clearly evokes more the short couplets of Continental verse than it does the alliterative metrics of the Anglo-Saxon. Rhyme in the Latin liturgy and in popular, Romance-language song had come to influence vernacular versemaking on the Continent, and it would come by the thirteenth century to control the Middle English lyric. But what we have in "The Rime of King William" may well be the first English attempt at rhymed verse on the Continental model. As such, this poem stands in stark contrast to the surrounding prose annal. It turns formal, metrical and linguistic choice into social criticism. It is a narrative of foreign imposition told through the imported word and meter. Here are the opening lines.

Castelas he let wyrcean,
7 earme men swiðe swencean.
Se cyng wæs swa swiðe stearc,
7 benam of his underþeoddan manig marc
goldes 7 ma hundred punda seolfres.
Ðet he nam be wihte
7 mid mycelan unrihte
of his landleode
for littelre neode.
He wæs on gitsunge befeallan,
7 grædinæsse he lufode mid ealle.
He sætte mycel deorfrið,
7 he lægde laga þærwið
þet swa hwa swa sloge heort oððe hinde,
þet hine man sceolde blendian.

[He had castles built
and poor men terribly oppressed.
The king was very severe,
and he took from his underlings many marks
of gold and hundreds of pounds of silver.
All this he took from the people,
and with great injustice
from his subjects,
to gratify his trivial desire.
He had fallen into avarice,
and he loved greediness above everything else.
He established many deer preserves,
and he set up laws concerning them,
such that whoever killed a hart or a hind
should be blinded.]

"Castelas he let wyrcean," he had castles built: from these first words, the poem signals a new architectural, political, and linguistic order in the land. Castles were foreign to the Anglo-Saxons, who did not build monumentally in dressed stone but rather in timber or flint cobble. The word itself, a loan from Norman French, makes clear the immediate impress of Norman life on English soil. One of the first things William did after the Battle of Hastings was to build a stone castle on the site, and less than three years after the Conquest, castles were marking the main intersections in the old British road system. Norman barons put up castles of their own, and by the close of William's reign, old land divisions were being reformed as feudal castelries. Wulfstan of Worcester, the last Anglo-Saxon bishop who died under Norman rule in 1095 (not the same Wulfstan of the *Sermo Lupi*), lamented these changes: "Our forefathers could not build as we do . . . but their lives were examples to their flocks. We, neglecting men's souls, care only to pile up stones." More than contrasting the monumental Norman stone architecture with the smaller Anglo-Saxon buildings, Wulfstan voices the controlling equation for post-Conquest writing: changes in the built environment represent both cultural displacement and spiritual loss.

William the Conqueror's moral life lives in the landscape. His control of the forest mirrors his control of the people, and his establishment of hunting laws reveals the dissonance between his love for animals and his contempt for the populace:

Swa swiðe he lufode þa headeor
swilce he wære heora fæder

[He loved the wild animals
As if he were their father.]

That he loves the animals like a father implies, of course, that he does not love his people like one. Anyone who would have life or land needs to follow the king's will, the poem continues. William's imposition of his *wille* on the English *land* is the focus of the *Peterborough Chronicle*'s 1085 entry on the making of the famous Domesday Book, in which every acre, every tree, every ox, cow, and pig held by the people is catalogued.

As William reshaped English lands, so his elegist in the *Peterborough Chronicle* reshaped English poetry. If its author lived at the Conqueror's court (as the surrounding prose annal implies), then it is likely that he heard the couplets of Norman French verse and the stanzas of Latin hymns and antiphons. His poem here shows us a writer intent on using the principles of Continental verse against a Continental subject. Linguistic and prosodic choices have political meaning—even in Peterborough Abbey, the monks could recognize the words of Norman imposition and the rhyme and meter of non-English literature. By half a century later, Norman rule had been consolidated and, with it, new words and expressions had begun to percolate up through the grounds of Anglo-Saxon. The *Peterborough*

Chronicle annal for 1137, like that of 1087, offers a sustained response to social change through the nuances of linguistic choice. Like that of 1087, this entry presents a distinctive literary, as well as an annalistic, voice, and it remains one of the most effective pieces of early English prose.

The entry dated 1137 surveys the entire nineteen-year reign of King Stephen (1135–1154) who presided over strife and famine, cruelties and deprivation so great that, as modern readers would well know, no other English king would ever take his name. It begins traditionally, but soon moves into uncharted social and linguistic turf.

> Đis gære for þe king Stephne ofer sæ to Normandi, and ther wes underfangen forþi ðat hi wenden ðat he sculde ben alswic alse the eom wes and for he hadde get his tresor—ac he todeld it and scatered sotlice. Micel hadde Henri king gadered gold and sylver, and na god ne dide me for his saule tharof.

> [In this year the King Stephen traveled over the sea to Normandy, and there he was received because of the fact that they believed that he should be (treated) just as the uncle (i.e., King Henry I) was, and because he (Stephen) had received (i.e., inherited) his (i.e., Henry's) wealth—but he (i.e., Henry) had dispersed it and scattered it foolishly. King Henry had gathered a great deal of gold and silver, but it was not used for the benefit of his soul.]

Like the critique of William in 1087, or for that matter like the elegiacs of *Beowulf*, this entry recalls how worldly wealth does little for the soul. We enter an Old English verbal world, even down to the barely surviving dative case of the opening words. Though there is no ending for *Đis*, the final *-e* in *gære* signals that the scribe still recognized a case at work. Other shards of the old tongue fill his sentences. Even though there are some classic, Old English verb forms (for example, the past tense of the strong verb *faren* is *for*, and the infinitives and plurals of the verbs end in *-en*) the nouns have clearly lost all sense of grammatical gender. The thorns and edths of Anglo-Saxon spelling are still here, but they share company with the new spelling for their sound, *th-*, an influence of Norman scribal habit. And words do remain from old wordhoard—*underfangen* literally means "taken in under" (thus, "received"); *eom* is the word for "uncle"; *wenden*, "they believed," shares the root of the word "wene," still found in regional or archaic English speech.

But that changes when we get to Normandy. For only in Normandy can we speak of Stephen inheriting his uncle Henry's *tresor*: his wealth. A word originally from Latin (*thesaurus*), it appears here, in its Old French form, for the first time in written English, a self-conscious Gallicism in a British landscape.

For the most part, that landscape is syntactically Old English. Traditional *þa/þa* clauses work to indicate temporal correlation:

SUBJECT VERB   VERB SUBJECT
Þa **þe king Stephne** to Englaland **com**, þa **macod he** his gadering æt Oxenford, . . .

[When the King Stephen arrived in England, then he made his assembly at Oxford, . . .]

But in this syntax lie new words, almost like interlopers. For when Stephen returns, he takes his bishops, Roger of Salisbury and Alexander of Lincoln and puts them in *prisun*. This Old French word shows up, in written English, first in the 1123 *Peterborough Chronicle* entry, and then here in 1137. Like *tresor*, it is a new word from the administrative vocabulary of the Normans. And that administrative vocabulary reappears throughout this year's annal, as if the chronicler were offering instruction in the new lexicon of power in the land. Stephen, we are later told, was really ineffective, and his enemies soon realized this:

Þa the swikes undergæton ðat he milde man was and softe and god and na justise ne did, þa diden hi alle wunder.

[When the traitors understood that he was a mild man and was gentle and good and did not inflict punishment, then they all performed atrocities.]

Again, the perfect *þa/þa* pattern, indicating the when/then sequence. Again, the familiar Old English terms taken from the heroic vocabulary (*mild, softe, god*); again, the familiar word for terror. *Wundor* means not just wonder but something atrocious; it is the kind of thing that Grendel did, and in Old English, this noun had an unmarked plural: one *wundor*, two *wundor*. We are in the old linguistic landscape here—except for *justise*. Originally from the Latin *justus*, fair or equitable, the word took on a special meaning in Norman French law, what the *OED* defines as "the exercise of authority or power in maintenance of right." This entry from the *Peterborough Chronicle* is the first appearance of the word in written English.

New words keep popping out of the English matrix here. For when the traitors do their worst, they, too, fill up their *castles*; they put men in *prisun*; they turn their prisoners into *martyrs* (the Greek form of this word was known to the Anglo-Saxons, but the Norman French form comes in for the first time here). Now, the annalist rises to the occasion, offering a list of all the torments in these prisons. The patterns of repetition, the lack of subordination, and the strings of parallels make this description, much like those in Wulfstan's *Sermo Lupi*, a brilliant display of paratactic power.

> Me henged up bi the fet and smoked heom mid ful smoke. Me henged bi the þumbes other bi the hefed and hengen bryniges on her fet. Me dide cnotted strenges abuton here hæved and wrythen it ðat it gæde to þe hærnes. Hi diden heom in quarterne þar nadres and snakes and pades wæron inne, and drapen heom swa. Sume hi diden in 'crucethur'—ðat is, in an ceste þat was scort and narew and undep—and did scærpe stanes þerinne, and þrengde þe man þærinne ðat him bræcon alle þe limes.

> [They were hung up by the feet and smoked completely with smoke. They were hanged by the thumbs or by the head and mail-coats were hung on their feet. They had strings knotted about their head and twisted to the point that it sank into the brains. They (the bad guys) put them (the good guys) in prisons where there were adders and snakes and toads, and killed them in this way. Some they put into a "crucethur"—that is, in a chest that was short and narrow and shallow—and they put sharp stones in there, and crushed the man who was in it until all his limbs were broken.]

Much like Wulfstan's, this is now a vision of hell on earth: a catalogue of tortures, implements, and pains. The opening phrase "me henged" is an old passive construction: *me* is the indefinite pronoun (the unstressed form of the word *man*); *henged* is the third person singular past tense. Literally, the phrase translates as "it was hanged to one." Used in this way, the repeated *me, me, me* rhetorically drives home the tortures to the reader's eye or listener's ear. Repetition is the rule for emphasis: "smoked heom mid ful smoke." The list is the controlling principle. But this is a catalogue not just of tortures but of words, a lexicon of death. Specialized terms jostle with the familiar here. The word *bryniges* is cognate with Old English *byrnie*, coat of mail; but here, it is the Old Norse form of the word. From Old Norse, too, is the word *hærnes*, "brains," and the verb for killing, *drapen*. These, and other forms throughout this entry, reflect the legacy of Scandinavian influence on the dialect of the East Midlands of England. But they also reflect a choice on the part of the annalist: the sense that when he comes to write of torture, he evokes the old, but lasting memory of Viking cruelties upon the English.

Nadres and snakes and pades: each word a history of pain and language. The Old English word *nadder* lost its initial *n* because it so frequently had the indefinite article *a* before it: *a nadder* became *an adder*. *Snake* comes from Old English *snaca*, a word virtually unchanged during the entire life of English. And *pades* are "toads," but the word seems to be a regionalism of the North of England—cognate with forms in German, Dutch, Icelandic, and other old and Modern Germanic languages, yet appearing in English first in this passage from the *Peterborough Chronicle* and, as far as anyone can tell, always perceived as something of an odd term.

The words, as well as the works, come from everywhere: Old English, Scandinavianisms, regionalisms, and even Latin technical terms. *Crucethur*, a word that shows up nowhere else in English, has to be defined as a short, narrow, shallow box (modern editors conjecture that the word comes straight from the Latin, *cruciator*, "torturer"). And when the king's rule disappears and England loses itself in an anarchy of local barons (warlords, really), we are once again granted a lesson in the language of administrative pain:

Hi læiden gældes on the tunes ævre umwile and clepeden it 'tenserie'.

[They imposed taxes on the towns repeatedly and called it "protection money."]

There is a brilliance to this definitional moment here, a sensitivity to the doublespeak of power worthy of George Orwell. *Tenserie* comes from Old French, *tenser*, "to protect." The word shows up in twelfth-century Latin documents (and uniquely in English in the Peterborough annal) to mean exactly what modern readers might think that it means: payment for local protection. There is a sense here not just of a new word being used in writing but a new word being introduced into the populace: as if the warlords were instructing English men and women in the language of power.

New and old words jostle throughout this entry in ways that make politics and language inseparable. French terms from Norman power come in, but Old English phrases, syntax, and idioms remain the expressive baseline of the land. Indeed, when the annalist speaks in his own voice, he is clearly drawing on the diction of the Anglo-Saxon pulpit and the scop. Rhythm and alliteration fill his laments, to the point where one may well wonder if his annal is ventriloquizing some popular or preexisting poem on these miseries.

> Hi hadden him manred maked and athes sworen, ac hi nan treuthe ne heolden. Alle he wæron forsworen and here treothes forloren, for ævric rice man his castles makede and agænes him heolden, and fylden þe land ful of castles.

> [They had done homage to him (i.e., the king) and had sworn oaths, but they did not honor their fealty. They all perjured themselves and abrogated their fealty, for every nobleman made for himself castles and held them against him (i.e., the king), and they filled the land full of castles.]

Notice the alliterative patterns and the assonances: *manred maked*; *athes sworen / forsworen / forloren*. Notice, too, the similar patterns later in the entry, when the annalist describes the attempt of the bishops to excommunicate the traitors:

> oc was heom naht þarof, for hi weron al forcursæd and forsworen and forloren

> [But it mattered nothing to them, for they were all already cursed, and perjured, and lost.]

And, finally, notice the first person voice emerging from this matrix: a voice quite literally crying in the wilderness.

> I ne can ne I ne mai tellen alle þe wunder ne alle þe pines ðat hi diden wrecce men on þis land.

> [I cannot nor may I not tell of all the atrocities nor of all the torments that they did to the wretched men of this country.]

The rhythm of these repetitions is the rhythm of the orator—compare Wulfstan's phrasing from the *Sermo Lupi*, "mænige synd forsworene and swyþe forlogene" (many are perjured and completely perjured themselves).

The English writing of the late eleventh and the twelfth centuries shares with the poetry and prose of the *Peterborough Chronicle* a concern with how a personal, vernacular voice can express the changing social order. At Worcester Cathedral, poets and scribes were still attempting to preserve the old alliterative metrics of the scop. In their laments for learning we may hear the sounds akin to those of Peterborough.

> Nu is þeo leore forleten,   and þet folc is forloren.
> Nu beoþ oþre leoden   þeo læerþ ure folc,
> And feole of þen lorþeines losiæþ   and þet folc forþ mid.

> [Now that teaching is forsaken, and the people are lost.
> Now there is another people that teaches our folk,
> And many of our teachers are dead, and our people with them.]

These lines from a poem known as *The First Worcester Fragment* share with the other writings of post-Conquest England something of an elegiac cast. They share, too, a distinctive vernacular diction. The phrase *forleten and . . . forloren* chimes with the alliterations of the *Peterborough Chronicle*, while the word for teachers, *lorþeines*, evokes once again that kenning-making sensibility that shaped Old English literary life. These are the thanes of lore, much as students were *leorningcnihtas*, knights of learning. While the school system was monastic and its subject matter Christian, the relationships of teacher and student remain modeled on the old Germanic tiers of thane and knight.

Loss is everywhere. The early-thirteenth-century poem known as *The Grave* laments the loss of riches and of bodily strength in ways that recall the elegy on William from the *Peterborough Chronicle*:

> Ne bið no þin hus healice itinbred;
> hit bið unheh and lah þonne þu list þerinne.

> [And now your house is not built high;
> it is short and low, when you lie within it.]

Recall how William, for all of his worldly wealth, wound up with only seven feet of earth; or how the *crucethur* was short and undeep. The word for "built" here is *itinbred*, with the word *timbrian* at its root: to timber, the Old English word for building not in stone. In the thirteenth-century poem *The Latemest Day*, these Anglo-Saxon idioms move almost seamlessly from the alliterative verse forms of the past into a Middle English lyric indebted to Continental models for its rhymed quatrains:

Þi bur is sone ibuld þer þu shald wunien inne,
Þe rof, þe firste, schal ligge o þine chinne;
Nu þe sculen wormes wunien wiþ-inne,
Ne mai ne heom vt driuen wið nones kunnes ginne.

[Your bower is soon built where you shall dwell inside,
The roof, the inner ceiling, shall rest on your chin;
Now worms shall dwell with you inside,
And no manner of ingenuity can drive them away.]

Here, in this little grave, the roof lies so close that it touches the chin. How far are we from *Caedmon's Hymn*, where God's creation lay in being able *heofon to hrofe*, to put a roof on heaven? How far are we, too, from the sounds of Old English: the characteristic initial *hr*-consonant cluster of *hrofe* has now been simplified to the initial *r*- of *rof* (so, too, throughout this period, initial clusters such as *hl* and *hn* were simplified to *l* and *n*: Old English *hlud* became loud; Old English *hnegan* became neigh). Other changes in sound, spelling, and grammar that appear at this time include the loss of the *ge*- prefix for the participle of a verb (in *The Grave* and *The Latemest Day*, it has been reduced simply to *i*-: *itinbred, ibuld*). But perhaps the most notable new thing about this stanza from *The Latemest Day* is its last word. *Ginne* meant cunning, craftiness, or artifice; ingenuity; or a contrivance. It comes from the Old French word *engin*, ultimately from the Latin *ingenium*, and it begins to appear in English texts at the beginning of the thirteenth century.

No kind of *ginne* can cheat death; even the technologies of new Norman power cannot change the all too familiar facts of life's end. When you live and die on English soil, you live and die in English. No imported *ginne* can matter. And yet, for the poet of *The Owl and the Nightingale*, writing at about this same time, *ginne* is power. Here, two birds debate their relative merits in ways that reflect the poet's sensitive awareness of the natural world and his deep learning in the traditions of Latin debate poetry, the philosophical argumentations of the schools, and the lyric modes of Romance-language verse. Written in rhymed couplets, *The Owl and the Nightingale* begins in a supple, Continental manner:

> Ich was in one sumere dale;
> In one suþe diȝele hale
> Iherde ich holde grete tale
> An Hule and one Niȝtingale.

> [I was in a summer valley;
> In a secret, hidden nook,
> I heard a great debate held
> Between an Owl and a Nightingale.]

Though arranged in precise octosylllabic lines and perfect rhymes, all the words in these first four lines come directly from Old English. This is an English landscape, as the Nightingale begins to speak, the poet later tells us, in a corner of a *breche*, a fallow field. This word denotes explicitly the fields, broken up for cultivation, that were the result of William the Conqueror's domestication of the forest. New towns took on new names, each one of which signaled that they were *breches*: Gilbertesbreche, Parkeresbreche, Brechehurne. With each new clearing came, too, a new castle. The Nightingale herself recognizes this, in an early disclaimer to the Owl's accusations of her weakness:

> I habbe on brede & eck on lengþe
> Castel god on mine rise.

> [I have in the length and breadth of my bough,
> A castle, good in every respect.]

Alive to a political landscape manipulated by castellation, she equates her own strength with that of William the Conqueror: "Castelas he let wyrcean." Closer to the date of the poem's composition, the Nightingale's references would recall, too, the castle building and besieging of King Stephen's reign:

> Mid lutle strengþe þurȝ ginne
> Castel & burȝ me mai iwinne;
> Mid liste me mai walles felle
> And worþ of horsse kniȝtes snelle.

[With only a little strength, but through ingenuity,
One may conquer castle and town;
One may bring down walls with deceit
And throw bold knights off their horses.]

But here, the castle falls before the Nightingale's *ginne*. In an English landscape full of newer castles and older burgs, what remains in the aftermath of conquest and anarchy is not so much brute strength as ingenuity. For students, poets, readers, and even singing birds in the two centuries after the Norman Conquest, the question would no longer be that of Bishop Ælfric and his *Colloquy*: "Canst þu ænig cræft?" Instead it would be a question about *ginne*: about the ingenious imagination that could begin to synthesize Old English verbal forms with French nouns and poetic structures to express a unique voice. And in that *ginne* lies the beginnings of the ingenuity of language itself: the skill at finding new words, not to clarify but to occlude, to give the institutions of control new names, to teach the people where the power lies. We see, here, the beginnings of that tension between English and Romance or Latinate vocabulary, and while we are not completely in the world of modern euphemism, we can see the inklings of a time when, as George Orwell had put it, these newer words will fall upon our lives "like soft snow, blurring the outlines and covering up all the details."

CHAPTER 4

From Kingdom to Realm
Middle English in a French World

BY THE MIDDLE OF THE THIRTEENTH CENTURY, the English language of
both script and street was palpably different from the English at the time of
the Conquest. The Old English vowels and consonants had, for the most part,
changed into the forms we now recognize as "Middle English." The grammatical system had simplified; word-order patterns were the primary determiners of meaning in a sentence; and the lexicon was filling with words from
Norman and, later, central French. Though there were many regional dialect
variations, speakers and writers of English two centuries after the Conquest
largely thought of themselves as having a shared vernacular.

The Norman impact lay in more than nouns. French grammar and syntax
had their effect, and by the end of the thirteenth century English idioms (even
if they were made up completely of originally Old English terms) were shaping
themselves to French order. An expression such as "to hold dear" is modeled
directly on the Old French *tenir chier*. "To put to death" comes directly from the
French *metre à mort*. Even though the words in these expressions are English,
the idioms are French. So, too, verbs such as "do," "give," "have," "make," and
"take" came to be used in their French equivalent senses. English idioms such
as "do battle," "give offence," "have mercy," "make peace," "take pains," and
the like are really just translations of French expressions, most of which used
the verbs *avoir* ("have") and *faire* ("do" or "make"). Even as early as the *Peterborough Chronicle*, some of these locutions start to appear (the phrase "na justise
ne did," does not merely borrow the Old French word *justise* but takes the
whole expression *faire justise*, "to punish or inflict judgment," as its model).

Rather than building new words out of the familiar stock of roots or mor-
phemes, as Old English did, Middle English borrowed terms directly from
other languages. The Normans brought new words for learning, commerce,

administration, the church, technology, cooking, and so on. Such words are easily recognizable: they are often polysyllabic, with distinguishing sounds and spellings. Old English and new French words stood side by side, but differed in shades of meaning or connotation. In the early nineteenth century, the novelist Sir Walter Scott developed one of the most famous (if overstated) distillations of this verbal doubling in his analysis of words for food. The Anglo-Saxon raised the food, whereas the Norman Frenchman ate it. Thus our words for animals remain Old English: sow, cow, calf, sheep, deer. Our words for meats are French: pork, beef, veal, mutton, venison.

Of course, Anglo-French linguistic contact was more complicated than that, and the development of Middle English involves far more than the layering of a Gallic veneer on an Anglo-Saxon base. What it does involve is a larger set of social and political relationships among the speakers and writers of three languages (English, French, and Latin) and an emerging sense of nationhood associated not just with a geographical residence but with a vernacular identity. Latin was the language of the Church, French of noble culture and administration, English of the people. But, as Thorlac Turville-Petre has made clear in his detailed study of medieval English literary culture, these three languages were not as clearly stratified as we might think. They existed "not just side by side but in symbiotic relationship, interpenetrating and drawing strength from one another; not just three cultures but one culture in three voices" (Turville-Petre, *England*, 181).

Those three voices show up for the first time, officially and simultaneously, in the 1258 proclamation of King Henry III announcing his adherence to the so-called Provisions of Oxford. Henry had sworn to observe the Magna Carta, that famous document of English legal history in which King John in 1215 had ceded absolute authority to a baronial confederation and a nascent Parliament. But Henry reneged on his promise. He styled himself far more a European than an English monarch, favoring his French relatives in power and preoccupied with maintaining his inheritance from the Angevin royal line. He was widely criticized for promoting non-English courtly and political figures, to the point that his barons stipulated that, "England should in future be governed by native-born men, and that aliens must depart" (*England*, 6). By October 1258, the conflict with Henry reached a breaking point, and the barons compelled him to accept and proclaim his adherence to the Magna Carta, to a thrice-yearly meeting of Parliament, and, most generally, to what appears to us today to be a kind of constitutional monarchy.

The Proclamation that affirmed this agreement was issued in Latin, French, and English—the first time an official, royal document appeared in English since the Conquest. It is a fascinating piece of writing, not just revealing the details of the English language of the mid-thirteenth century but illuminating the relationships of language and national identity emerging at the time. The English text is, scholars have long noted, a translation of the French, and certain facets of the language emerge by comparing the two versions. Just look at the opening sentences:

Henri, þurȝ Godes fultume King on Engleneloande, Lhoaverd on Yrloande, Duk on Normandi, on Aquitaine, and Eorl on Anjow, send i-gretinge to alle hise holde, i-lærde and i-leawede on Huntendone-schire. Þæt witen ȝe wel alle þæt we willen and unnen þæt þæt ure rædesmen, alle oper þe moare dæl of heom þæt beoþ i-chosen þurȝ us and þurȝ þæt loandes folk on ure kuneriche, habbeþ i-don and schullen don in þe worþness of Gode and on ure treowþe, for þe freme of þe loande, þurȝ þe besiȝte of of þan toforen i-seide redes-men, beo stedefæst and i-lestinde in alle þinge abuten ænde.

Henri, par le grace Deu, Rey de Engleterre, sire de Irlande, duc de Nor-mandie, de Aquitien, et cunte de Angou, a tuz sez feaus clers et lays saluz. Sachez ke nus volons et otrions ke se ke nostre conseil, u la greignure partie de eus ki est esluz par nus et par le commun de nostre reaume, a fet, u fera, al honur de Deu et nostre fei, et pur le profit de notre reaume sicum il ordenera seit ferm et estable en tuttes choses a tuz jurz;

(Mossé, Handbook of Middle English, 187–88)

[Henry, by the grace of God King of England, Lord of Ireland, Duke of Normandy and of Aquitaine, and Earl of Anjou, sends greeting to all of his subjects, the learned and the unlearned, in Huntington-shire. You all know well that we want and desire that our counselors, the greater portion of whom that have been chosen by us and by the people in our kingdom, have acted and should act according to the honor of God and fidelity to us, and for the good of the realm, according to the provisions of those aforesaid counselors, that they be steadfast and firm in all things forever.]

The first thing the modern reader notices is the vocabulary. The French *le grace Deu* becomes the English *Godes fultume*. The word *fultume* comes from Old English, where it meant aid, support, or help. It could be used in both secular and sacred contexts: one could help someone else or God could help us. Etymologically, the word has *full* at its root: fullness, completion, a making whole. It passes into Middle English, but it seems clear that by the late thirteenth century, the word was gone, and the Proclamation of 1258 may be, in fact, the last datable appearance of the word in English writing. The French idiom, *par le grace Deu*, would become "by the grace of God," and would efface *fultum* from English. What we see here in the English version of Henry III's Proclamation is, I think, a deliberately old-fashioned English. Throughout the English text, the language seems reluctant to admit French terms. Only the technical terms of power and position appear: *Duk* is French, as is the title *Mareschal*, used later in the text. But "cunte de Angou" is Anglicized to "Eorl on Anjow."

So, too, French verbal idioms take on an Anglo-Saxon flavor. Henry addresses both the clerics and the laymen (*clers et lays*), but this transforms itself into an English pairing redolent of the old, alliterative formulae: *i-lærde and i-leawede*, the learned and the lewd (Old English *lewed* meant not "obscene" but "untutored" or "common"). The English text, by the way, was sent to all the counties in the country, and in this surviving copy it is clear that this was the copy sent to Huntingtonshire.

The opening of the second sentence in French is *Sachez ke*, "you know that." This phrase becomes an Old English-style correlative clause: "Đæt witen 3e wel alle þæt" ("That [fact], let all of you know, [namely] that . . ."). As if to complete the Anglo-Saxon verbal texture of this passage, the French word *conseil*, counselors, becomes the old word *rædesmen*. Hrothgar has his men who give *ræd* (advice) and the famous Anglo-Saxon king we know today as Æthelred "The Unready" was, in fact, known in his own time as *Æthelred unræd* (Æthelred the Ill-advised). Like *fultume*, *rædesmen* is a word clearly passing from the Middle English vocabulary.

More local phrasings abound, for these *rædesmen* were "chosen from among us and from among the people of the land of our country." The English *loandes folk on ure kuneriche* translates the French *le commun de nostre reaume*, but the translation is hardly transparent. The *loandes folk*, the folk of the land, is a phrase that connotes not political brilliance or baronial entitlement but everydayness. It is a phrase less to describe the counselors to the king and more to evoke the audience for this English text. It is a subtle way of bringing the folk to the King's side and affirming their place in the *kuneriche*, the kingdom—a word that defined the country through the ruler (king-dom), unlike the French word *reaume* (realm) that connoted a more abstract and porous sense of rule.

Some of these English words, then, are familiar; some are strange to us now. But a look at the French shows us what would become the common words of politics and public administration: *honur* (honor), *fei* (faith), *profit, ferm et estable* (firm and stable); and, later on, we find *comandons* (we command), *enemi mortel* (mortal enemy), and *tresor* (treasure). These words were clearly part of not just the French but of the Middle English public vocabulary by the middle of the thirteenth century. And yet, the English of the Proclamation translates all of them into what could only be described as an aggressively old-fashioned vernacular:

honur	*treoþe*
profit	*freme*
reaume	*londe*
ferm et estable	*stedfæst and i-lestinde*
comandons	*hoaten*
enemi mortel	*deadlice i-foan*
tresor	*hord*

Just about all of these French words are attested in use by the end of the thirteenth century (the word *tresor* had already appeared in the *Peterborough Chronicle*), and none of them would have been absolutely opaque to an English reader at the time of Henry's Proclamation. For what we have here is not simply a translation of a French document for a wider circulation among a non-French audience. What we have is a political statement about the English language and the English people. By rephrasing official French into an already old-fashioned, deliberately Anglo-Saxon phraseology, this version sends a message. In Thorlac Turville-Petre's terms, both king and barons must have "recognized the value in the propaganda of patriotism of reaching beyond the constituency of royal officials and appropriating (however speciously) the language of the 'loandes folk' in order to involve a wider section of the population in the political program of reform" (*England*, 9).

By the end of the thirteenth century, the politics of English had become explicit. In 1295, King Edward I could accuse the French of trying to rid England of the English language. Chronicles, lyrics, and narrative poems of the early fourteenth century take a special interest in the ways in which English and French, for all their intermingling, still had social associations. In the first third of the fourteenth century, Robert of Gloucester could write that the Normans were the "heyemen" of England and the Saxons the "lowemen." The historian Robert Manning of Brunne, writing at the end of the 1330s, claimed that those who are now "Inglis" were originally "Saxons." And the religious poem, *Cursor Mundi*, written at about the same time recognizes that, even though there are dialect differences in English—a "sotherin Englis" from which the author has turned his story into "northren lede"—"Ingland the nacion" is a place defined by language (see Turville-Petre, *England*, 15–20).

The multilingual quality of British literature at this time, however, crosses many boundaries, and the best and best-known testimony to trilingual medieval England is the set of poems written in the manuscript now catalogued as British Library Manuscript Harley 2253. Compiled sometime in the 1330s or 1340s, this manuscript preserves some of the most exquisite and most famous Middle English lyrics. Its contents have filled anthologies from those of the late eighteenth century to those of our own schoolrooms today. These are beautiful poems, voicing a lyric sensibility that melds vernacular nuance with an attentiveness to the natural and the emotional world.

> When þe nytegale singes þe wodes waxen grene.
> Lef ant gras ant blosme springes in Aueryl, Y wene,
> Ant loue is to myn herte gon wiþ one spere so kene—
> Nyht ant day my blod hit drynkes; myn herte deþ me tene.

> [When the nightingale sings the woods turn green.
> Leaf and grass and blossom spring in April, I know,
> And love has gone into my heart with a spear so sharp—
> Night and day, love drinks up my blood; my heart makes me suffer.]

The poem takes the commonplaces of the European love lyric—the wounding spear of love, the nightingale as symbol of desire, the April turn of season as a turn of heart—and makes them uniquely English. The beloved, later in the poem, is the *lemmon*, the word used throughout Middle English to describe the object of desire (it comes from the Old English *leof*, loved, and *mon*, one; *leofmon* is reduced, over time, to *lemmon* or *leman* by the same principle of syncretism as Old English *hlafweard* became "lord" and *hlæfdige* became "lady"). But that *lemmon* is more than just a lover; she becomes the poet's healer: "A suete cos of þy mouþ might be my leche." A sweet kiss of your mouth might be my doctor. The word *leche* comes from the Old English *læce*, meaning physician or healer (it may, possibly, come from the same root as the word for the blood-sucking animal, the leech, long used in folk medicine). But it took on, in Middle English verse, both a secular and a sacred connotation. Jesus was the "soules leche" throughout devotional poetry, and this poem, in particular, often blurs the line between the passions of carnal love and the Passion of Christ (the blood imagery, the sense of suffering, the physicality of pain here are all part of the religious as well as the amorous diction). But, in the end, the recollections of the Passion or clichés of the European lyric fade before a compelling, local Englishness:

Bituene Lyncolne ant Lyndeseye, Norhamptoun ant Lounde,
Ne wot Y non so fayr a may as Y go fore ybounde.

[From Lincoln to Lindsay, from Northampton to London,
I do not know of so fair a maiden as the one to whom I am bound.]

The Harley 2253 Manuscript is filled with poems of such power and complexity, such sophistication and vernacularity. But it is filled, too, with poems and prose in French and Latin. Often interlarded with one another on the page, these different texts evoke an engaging trilingualism for the manuscript and its intended audience. On one page, in particular, poems in English, French, and Latin follow each other in sequence, and this linguistic meshing takes on a new and deft form in the concluding lines of the last, Latin poem. A love lyric akin in power and naturalism to the English and French poems in the manuscript (it begins, "Dum ludis floribus," when you played among flowers), it ends in a tour de force of scribal brilliance.

Scripsi hec carmina in tabulis;
Mon ostel est en mi la vile de Paris;
May y sugge namore, so wel me is;
ʒef hi deʒe for loue of hire, duel hit ys.

[I have written these verses on my tablets;
My dwelling is in the middle of the city of Paris;
Let me say no more, so things are fine (i.e., leave well enough alone);
If I die for love of her, it would be a pity.]

When this poet writes about the act of writing he does so in Latin: in language reminiscent of such classical epigrammatists as Martial and his medieval scholastic heirs. When he announces his dwelling in Paris—that is, when he affirms that he is a student in the leading university city of the day—he does so in French. And when he announces, in that final couplet, that he may not speak anymore and that he would die of love, he does so in the rich colloquialisms of Middle English.

The story of that Middle English, therefore, must be told as part of a larger story of a multilingual England. For, even though Henry III's Proclamation marks a turning point in the official use of English, French remained the language of the court, of government, of law, and of high culture well into the early fifteenth century. Some of the most famous works of medieval French literature—*The Song of Roland*, the *Lais* of Marie de France—survive in manuscripts written in England. The *Jeu d'Adam*, one of the very first medieval dramatic works in a vernacular, is a French work written in England in the twelfth century. In Robert of Gloucester's words, from the early fourteenth century, "lowe men holdeþ to Engliss" (lowborn men stay with English), and "Vor bote a man conne frenss, / Me telþ of him lute" (unless a man knows French there is little to say about him).

And yet, the French that men and women knew was not some uniform language. The Norman dialect had its own special words and sounds. It differed from the central French, or Parisian dialect which came in with the Angevin kings in the thirteenth century and with new cultural and social affiliations. English people wishing to learn French would have been acutely aware of such distinctions, and one of the most revealing documents of early language pedagogy is the *Traité sur la lange française* by Walter of Bibbesworth. Walter was an English knight who served in Henry III's court in the middle of the thirteenth century, and he composed this *Treatise* for the children of a gentrywoman in order to teach them the language of *husbondrie e manaugerie* (husbandry and management).

Walter's *Treatise* does more, however, than just teach vocabulary or expression. It teaches a conception of language itself: a sense of how the lexicon articulates a social register; of how the grammar of English and French differ; and of how command of spoken and of written language are two different skills. The *Treatise* is in French verse, with some English words written between the lines. Here is a representative selection:

>   *lip   the hare*
> Vous avez la levere et le levere,
> *the pount   book*
> La livere et le livere,
> La levere c'est ke enchost les dens,
> Le levere ki boys se tent dedeins,
> La livere sert de marchaundie,
> Le livere nous aprent clergie

[You have the lip and the hare, the pound and the book; the lip which surrounds the teeth, the hare which hides in the woods, the pound which is used in trade, the book which teaches us clergy.]

Walter aims to train the reader's eye and ear to the different grammatical and phonemic qualities of French. He establishes what modern linguists would call a minimal pair, that is, two words that differ only in one phoneme, in distinguishing *livere* and *levere*. In addition, he establishes the category of grammatical gender as another distinguishing feature: *la livere / le livere; la levere / le levere*. Writing in the middle of the thirteenth century, Walter makes unmistakably clear that the concept of grammatical gender needs to be taught and that it has disappeared from English.

What he also makes clear is that the study of language is an education in culture as well as grammar. The terms he addresses are for parts of the body, hunting, commerce, and learning. This is an education in the social arts, in words for polite conversation, courtiership, and intellectual discourse. His disquisition on the many different words for "red," for example, illuminates the nature of register in discourse (the red hair of a knight, he notes, is *rous*, while his red horse is *sor*, his red shield is *goules*, and his red lance is *rouge*). More than just a lesson book for French, Walter's *Treatise* is a lesson book for *good* French. And by good French he means skill in both speaking and reading. By including the interlineations in the manuscript of his work (you will first find the French and then the English above it, he notes), he builds up a vocabulary of the spoken language designed, in the end, to enhance one's command of the written language.

Walter distinguishes between the spoken and the written, and so did Henry III. His Proclamation opened with a greeting to everyone in his purview, *clers et lays* (clerics and laymen). This phrase shows up in English as *i-lærde and i-leawede*, and I have already mentioned how the English version evokes the old formulaic and alliterative diction to translate the French. But now, read against Walter's contemporary *Treatise*, we can see how Henry's distinction is also one of communicative venue. The clerics and the lay, the learned and the lewd, are the literate and the illiterate. Clerics, quite simply, read. They define themselves, throughout the English and European Middle Ages, as the *literati*, those taught from the books and living with the books. When Walter states, "le livere nous aprent clergie," the book teaches us clergy, he identifies himself with the literate, clerical class—the class trained in the arts of *grammatica*, the schoolroom skills of number, case, and gender, of lexicography and spelling. In fact, that very notion of spelling comes not from Old English but Old French—for the word *spellian* in Old English meant to talk or tell a story or to move with speech (it is the root of the Old English word *god-spell*, the good talk, and thus our Modern English "gospel"). The Old French word *espelir*, by contrast, meant to set out by letters, and it is only late in Middle English that this word converges with *spellian* to produce a verb, *spellen*, that could mean both speak and spell. As far as any one can tell, the earliest attested use of "spell" in English meaning "to form by letters" is in Walter's *Treatise*. There, the phrase, "espau nautrement ki les letters ensemble prent," gets the gloss, *spelieth*.

Walter's is thus an art of spelling in both senses of the word. But even when an Englishman would spell in spoken English, it might not be spelled out in that form. A revealing example of this fissure is the Parliamentary record of 1362. For the first time, Parliament was opened with a speech in English, and even though English had most likely been spoken in Parliament before then, this is the first time that the clerks of the *Rotuli Parliamentorum* (the official record of proceedings) admit it.

> Au quell jour, esteanz nostre Seigneur le Roi, Prelatz, Countes, Barons, & les Communes en la Chambre de Peinte . . . monstre en Englois par . . . de Grene, Chief Justice le Roi, les Causes de Somons du Parlement.

> [On this day, in the presence of our lord the King, the counts, the barons, and the privy counselors of the painted chamber, the King's Chief Justice, Green, announced the causes of the summons to Parliament in English.]

Parliament is addressed in English, but the record is in French—this in spite of the fact that this very same Parliament passed a statute that all court proceedings be henceforth conducted in English (*pledez & monstrez en la lange Engleise*) because the litigants could no longer understand French (*la lange Franceois, q'est trop desconu en la dit Roialme*—"the French language, which has been fully discontinued in the speech of the realm").

But just what was *la dit Roialme?* English does not show up in the parliamentary records until the petition of the Mercers' Guild in 1388; the first post-Conquest English king to have a will in English was Henry IV, who died in 1421; the first English guild to record its accounts in English was the Brewer's Guild, in 1422. Chaucer's contemporary John Gower could write long poems in both French and Latin, clearly expecting them to have as wide a readership as his poetry in English. Even Chaucer himself, some modern scholars think, began his career as a French court poet.

Still, English remained a language of imaginative expression. In addition to such poems as the Harley Lyrics, there were romances, chronicles, saints' lives, prose allegories, devotional works, social satires, manuals of household behavior—just about every conceivable kind of writing could be and was done in English (as, needless to say, they could be and were done in French and Latin, too). There emerged not just a wide use of English but a vernacular sensibility: a way of understanding just what the political and social consequences were of praying, doing business, dreaming, writing, and living in English. Henry III's Proclamation, or the lyric drama of the Harley poems, uses the language for social ends: to make a point about the nature of royal power, to make a point about the nature of the landscape, to make a point about what it means to feel on the road from Lincoln to Lindsey, Northampton to London. English, in other words, became a vehicle of social and emotional movement.

Julian of Norwich, whose *Revelation of Divine Love* was composed in the 1380s, can still move us in her tongue. She transforms a Latinate religious idiom into English; indeed, the word "revelation" becomes, in her text, the English word *schewynge*. Look, for example, at this brief passage from the so-called Short Text of her work.

Botte God forbade that ye schulde saye or take it so that I am a techere, for I meene nought soo, no I mente nevere so. For I am a woman, leued, febille, and freylle. But I wate wele that this I saye. I hafe it of the schewynge of hym that es soverayne techare. Botte sothelye, charyte styrres me to tell yowe it, for I wolde god ware knawenn and my eveynn-Crystenne spede, as I wolde be myselfe, to the mare hatynge of synne and lovynge of God.

[But God forbade it that you should say or believe that I am a teacher, for I do not intend to be so, nor have I ever intended it. For I am a woman, unlearned, feeble, and frail. But I am fully convinced of what I say. I have received it from the revelation of him who is the sovereign teacher. And truly, charity moves me to tell it to you, because it is my wish that God be known and that my fellow Christians prosper, as I would myself, through hating sin more and loving God.]

Such a passage reveals the fluency of Middle English as a theological tongue. Its sentences are short, evocative of everyday speech. Its vocabulary is local, native, even—at times, perhaps, to modern readers—naive. This is, as the editors of the recent volume *The Idea of the Vernacular* put it, a "language of equality," a language that constructs an audience of all English Christians (Wogan-Browne et al., *The Idea of the Vernacular*, 83). In such a language, the very word for the community of Christians is an old-fashioned, Anglo-Saxon-sounding compound: *eveynn-Crystenne*, fellow Christians. There are few words from French or Latin here. *Febille* and *freylle* come originally from the Latin by way of French, but their juxtaposition here, in what reads as an old-fashioned, English alliterative pairing, calls attention away from their etymological origins and toward their native sound. But in this passage, there are two words of distinctively non-English origin, used for powerful effect: God is the "*soverayne* techare," a teacher who is not only the chief instructor of the faith but the very sovereign of doctrine; and the love of this God is very pointedly "charyte," a word that goes back to the *caritas* of Saint Paul, Saint Augustine, and the whole tradition of patristic theology.

Julian's word choice and rhythms are more supple and compelling than, frankly, anything that Geoffrey Chaucer wrote in prose, and she stands as a good foil for those who would claim that Chaucer somehow "invented" English as a literary language. Yes, he did use words in new ways; he did develop a decasyllabic line that would become a metrical standard for English verse; and he did wrest a personal, poetic voice out of the mix of available dialects and idioms. But he did so not in the vacuum of a solitary imagination but on busy streets and crowded docks, in the midst of parliamentary argument and courtly feigning. Chaucer's achievement needs to be assessed against this history of French and English: a history of the learned and lewd, of Aprils and lemmons, of lips and hares and pounds and books.

Overview of Key Changes from Old English to Middle English

Pronunciation

Consonants: OE lost its characteristic consonant clusters

hl, hn, hr became l, n. r: OE *hring* > ring; OE *hlud* > loud; OE *hne-gan* > neigh fn became sn: OE *fnæstian* > sneeze

hw lost its aspiration to become written as w or wh: OE *hwæt, hwa, hwicce* > what, who, which

OE also lost consonants in the middle of words as part of a process known as assimilation.

OE *hlaford* > Early ME *laverd* > late ME *lord*
OE *hlæfdige* > Early ME *levedi* > late ME *lady*

Vowels: among the many changes in the Old English vowel system, two stand out, not just for their own interest but for help in dating sound changes and loan-words.

Lengthening in open syllables: a vowel in an open syllable is one followed by a single consonant or a consonant and another vowel.

OE *nama*, which had a short /a/ became ME *name*, which had a long /a:/

OE *abidan*, which had a short /i/ became ME *abide*, which had a long /ɪ:/

Remember here that vowel length is a quantitative matter: it depends on how long you hold the vowel, not on differences of where you pronounce it in the mouth.

The other important change is that OE long a /a:/ became Middle English long o, which would have been pronounced as /ɔ:/.

OE *ham, ban, swa* > ME *home, bone, so.*

On the basis of rhymes in poetry and loan words, the qualitative change of OE long *a* to ME long *o* must have happened before lengthening in open syllables, otherwise all long *a* sounds in ME would have merged together (that is, we would be saying "nome" instead of "name").

Metathesis: the transposing of two sounds pronounced in sequence. While this is often a function of everyday speech or regional dialect variation (e.g., "psghetti" for spaghetti; "aks" for ask), it permanently affected the pronunciation of some words in the transition from OE to ME:

OE *brid* > ME *bird*; OE *axian* > ME *ask*; OE *þurh* > ME *through*;
OE *beorht* > ME *bright*

Articulative intrusion: the adding of a sound in the course of pronouncing several sounds together. This is also often a function of everyday speech (e.g., saying the word "something" as if it were "sumpthing": saying the word "dance" as if it were "dants"). It also affected permanently the pronunciation of some words in the transition from OE to ME:

OE *slummer* > ME *slumber*; OE *æmtig* > ME *empty*; OE *glisnian* > ME *glisten*;
OE *þunnor* > ME *thunder*

Morphology

The endings of the ME verb remained pretty much the same as in OE, even though the elaborate system of verb classes disappeared. Generally speaking, the infinitive and plural of verbs end in *-en*; the singular third person ends in *-eth*; the singular second person ends in *-st*.

OE distinguished between strong and weak verbs. Strong verbs signaled change in tense by changes in the root vowel: e.g., run, ran; think, thought; drink, drank, drunk. Weak verbs signal the past tense by adding a suffix, usually -ed or -d: e.g., walk, walked; love, loved. Many strong verbs from OE survived into ME, but some did not: for example, knead, help, and wax (meaning "to grow") became weak verbs in Middle English (though, in some texts, the strong forms are also used). All verbs borrowed into English from the ME period onwards are borrowed as weak verbs.

The endings of the ME noun illustrate the loss of the OE case system. Occasionally, there is a final *-e* in some words indicating the dative case (for example, in the phrase "out of toune"). But otherwise, the only remaining markers of case in ME (as in Modern English) are the final -s in plurals and possessives.

With pronouns, ME lost the OE dual (a special form meaning "we two"). It kept, however, the two forms of the second person to distinguish formal and plural from informal and singular. The Middle English pronominal system by the time of Chaucer (late-fourteenth-century, London), is as follows:

I	we	thou	ye	he	she	it/hit	they
me	us	thee	you	him/hi	hir		hem
my(n)	our	thy(n)	your	his	hire		here

With the loss of grammatical gender, ME came to use the word *hit*, or *it* (from the old neuter third person singular) to refer to inanimate objects and concepts regardless of their original OE gender.

ME also saw the rise of interrogative pronouns used as relative pronouns. OE used the definite article as the relative pronoun: *se mon se*, "the man who." This change took several centuries, so many ME constructions may look odd to modern readers:

ME "He which that hath no wyf" = Modern English "He who has no wife."
ME "These folk of which I telle" = Modern English, "These folk of whom I speak."
ME "I that am" = Modern English "I who am."

Vocabulary

The core vocabulary of English comprised the monosyllabic words for basic concepts, bodily functions, and body parts inherited from Old English and shared with the other Germanic languages. These words include: God, man, tin, iron, life, death, limb, nose, ear, foot, mother, father, brother, earth, sea, horse, cow, lamb.

Words from French are often polysyllabic terms for the institutions of the Conquest (church, administration, law), for things imported with the Conquest (castles, courts, prisons), and terms of high culture or social status (cuisine, fashion, literature, art, decoration). Readily identifiable sound features and spellings of French words include:

-ei-, -ey-: obey, air, fair, quaint
-oi-, -oy-: boy, joy, toy, royal, exploit
-ioun, -ion, endings: explanation, relation
-ment, endings: amendment, commandment
-ence, or *-aunce*, endings: eminence, reference
-our, or *-or*, endings: honour, colour, favour

Words which end in -*ous* are adjectives; words which end in -*us* are nouns. Thus, in Modern English, callous is an adjective, while callus is a noun.

Norman French and Central French

The Normans were originally a Germanic people, and they spoke a dialect of French that retained some of the sounds of the Germanic languages. Words from Norman French (or what is also known as Anglo-Norman) came in with the Conquest and are attested from the eleventh through the early thirteenth centuries. Words from Central, or Parisian, French, came in to English beginning in the thirteenth centuries, with kings and courtiers from France itself and with greater intellectual, social, and commercial contact with France.

The Norman dialect had a /w/ sound and spelling for Central French words with a /g/ sound (and a -*gu*- spelling). Note the following:

Wiles	Guile
William	Guillaume
War	Guerre
Warden	Guardian

Norman French had a /k/ sound, spelled with a -c-, for Central French words with a /tʃ/ sound, spelled -*ch*-. Notice the following:

Castle	Chateau
Cap	Chapeau

CHAPTER 5

Lord of This Langage

Chaucer's English

ALMOST FROM THE MOMENT OF HIS DEATH in 1400, Chaucer came to be revered as the inventor of a new, poetic language. His earliest imitators, the poets John Lydgate and Thomas Hoccleve, saw him as "purifying" English from the "rudeness" of the Anglo-Saxon. At the end of the fifteenth century, England's first printer, William Caxton, considered Chaucer the "first founder and embellisher of ornate eloquence in English," while at the end of the sixteenth century, the poet Edmund Spenser could praise his forebear as "the well of English undefiled." Throughout the seventeenth and eighteenth centuries, poets, historians, and critics found in Chaucer the first stirrings of a literary vernacular, and nineteenth- and twentieth-century academics granted him nothing less than revolutionary status: "he decided to invent a literary English," writes one, while for another, Chaucer "began a revolution in poetic diction."

Just what did Chaucer do to garner such obeisance? Compared with his contemporaries, he does seem to have brought into literary English a wide range of loan words from French and Latin. But he did more than simply enlarge the vocabulary of the language. He often juxtaposed terms from Old English against those of French and Latin, creating, in the process, striking literary effects. He often placed words strategically in the poetic line for heightened emphasis, rhymed words in often memorable ways, and, on occasion, stretched syntax and word order almost to their breaking point.

More than these technical achievements, Chaucer was acutely conscious of linguistic difference as a social, historical, and even philosophical problem. He reflected on language change and dialect variation, presented characters who manipulate the world through their vernacular, and set up the figure of a poet who is himself an innovator in the uses of language. Language is always a theme for Chaucer's poetry, and Chaucer himself took up the persona of a writer preoccupied with new words and vernacular command. As the scholar Christopher Cannon has recently shown, Chaucer's borrowings, distinctive usages, and juxtapositions of old and new words "help Chaucer's English to gather the quality of novelty to itself and to present that novelty as constitutive of its own making." In other words, Chaucer does not so much "invent" a new English as much as he invents the pose of someone who invents a new English.

In this pose lies the brilliance of Chaucerian English. Like many later writers—Milton, Wordsworth, Dickens, Twain, or Norman Mailer—he is able to create the impression of linguistic innovation, not so much by genuinely coining new words or new phrases (as Shakespeare really did) but by making us feel as if he did so. "Chaucer's English," therefore, does not simply connote the details of London Middle English of the later fourteenth century but the personal transformation of those details into an imaginative, linguistic space.

Nowhere is that transformation more brilliantly accomplished than in the famous opening of the General Prologue to the *Canterbury Tales*.

Whan that Aprill with his shoures soote
The droghte of March hath perced to the roote,
And bathed every veyne in swich licour
Of which vertu engendred is the flour;
Whan Zephirus eek with his sweete breeth
Inspired hath in every holt and heeth
The tendre croppes, and the yonge sonne
Hath in the Ram his half cours yronne,
And smale foweles maken melodye,
That slepen al the nyght with open ye
(So priketh hem nature in hir corages),
Than longen folk to goon on pilgrimages,
And palmeres for to seken straunge strondes,
To ferne halwes, kowthe in sondry londes;
And specially from every shires ende
Of Engelond to Caunterbury they wende,
The hooly blisful martir for to seke,
That hem hath holpen whan that they were seeke.

(1.1–18)

[When it happens that April, with his sweet showers, has pierced the drought of March to the root, and bathed every vein in that fluid from whose power the flower is given birth; when Zephyr also, with his sweet breath, has inspired the tender crops in every wood and heather, and the young sun has run half his course through the sign of the Ram, and little birds make melody who sleep all night with their eyes open (so Nature stimulates them in their hearts), then people desire to go on pilgrimages, and professional pilgrims desire to seek strange shores; and they wend their way, especially, from the end of every county in England to Canterbury, in order to seek the holy, blissful martyr who had helped them when they were sick.]

This passage is many things: an invocation, an exordium, a call for audience attention, and a display of poetic craft. Its line of sight moves from the heavens to the earth, focusing down from the zodiacal empyrean, through the clouds of meteorological reality, to the tops of the trees, to the earth itself. And once we hit the ground, the sentence then moves from the outer to the inner: from the peripheries of "every shires ende / Of Engelond" to the telos of the pilgrimage to Canterbury. Two parallel contractions, one vertical, the other horizontal, bring the world of everyday experience into sharp focus.

That focus, though, is calibrated metrically and lexically, and Chaucer emerges in these opening lines as a linguistic innovator. Words such as *engendred* and *inspired* would have been, by the late fourteenth century, part of the new vocabulary taken from the Romance languages, while words such as *vertu* and *melodye*—long in the Middle English lexicon—appear in distinctive ways. The histories of words come to the fore (*vertu*, for example, appears in all its etymological force from the Latin *vir*, masculine prowess). Figuration takes precedence over denotation (the word *melodye*, for example, evokes, as it did for many in the later fourteenth century, a sense of heavenly bliss or mirth). The Anglo-Saxon and the French contend (the nature that pricks these birds to melody, for example, gets them in their *corages*—their very francophone hearts).

Juxtaposed against these learned and Romance words is an English landscape. *Holt* and *heeth*, two old and here alliterating words, emblematize that landscape into which Zephyr's new winds blow. And against that mythological west wind comes the zodiacal figure of the Ram: not "Aries," but the ordinary animal. The *palmeres* on their *pilgrimages* (both originally Old French terms) "seken straunge strondes / To ferne hal-

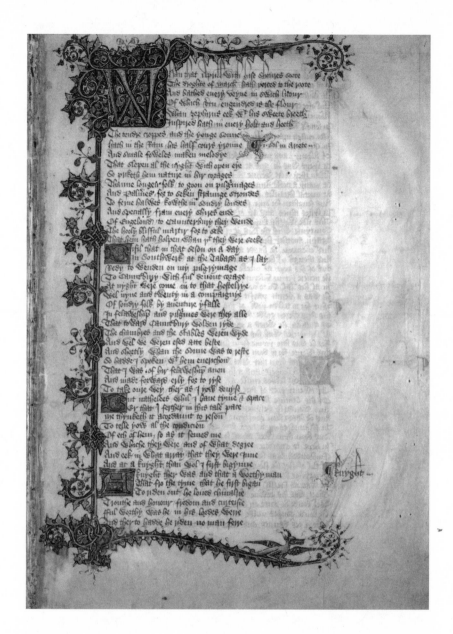

FIGURE 5.1

Geoffrey Chaucer, *The Canterbury Tales*, the opening page of the Ellesmere Manuscript. The Huntington Library, MS Ellesmere 26 C, fol 1r. Reproduced by permission of the Huntington Library.

wes, kowthe in sondry londes"—every word there, ultimately, from Old English. And, at the sentence's conclusion, the last couplet reaffirms the Englishness of this experience. Though Beckett remains here a *martir* (a French word that entered English almost from the moment of the Norman Conquest), he stands surrounded by English modifiers: *hooly* and *blisful*. Finally, in the last line, we may find a formal reassertion of a native English prosody and idiom: "That hem hath holpen whan that they were seke." The strong alliterations on the *h-* words slow the pace of reading down. They force the performer (for this is, as far as we can tell, a poetry that was read aloud) to articulate, to feel the repetitions soon to be felt again in the concatenating "that they." Chaucer deploys the resources of his rich vocabulary and his metrics to suggest a politics to literary form. There is a sense of a resurgent English vernacularity here—a poem in decasyllabic couplets that apposes words of English and French origin; a poem in which the alliterative idiom can rear up; a poem in which, for all the learning of astrology or the sophistications of science, there is still an old familiar holt and heeth.

The General Prologue is an essay in the arts of language. It establishes the poem's narrator as a describer of the world, a portraitist of people, and a philosopher of language. For his job, as he puts it at the Prologue's close, is to retell the pilgrim's tales faithfully: to "reherse" each word, according to the teller. Fidelity to source remains his primary concern, for if he were to falsify, expand, or invent something and attribute it to someone else, "he moot tell his tale untrewe" (1.736). Plain speaking is the order of the day—"Crist spak himself ful brode in holy writ" (1.739)—and Plato's authority dovetails with the scriptures to affirm: "The wordes moote be cosyn to the dede" (1.742). Words should reflect the things they denote. The relation of word and deed echoes a sustaining medieval debate about *verba* and *res*. From Saint Augustine, through Macrobius, Boethius, the scholastics, and the nominalists, philosophers of language and behavior recognized the complexities among intention and expression, word and object. "Every word," Macrobius had argued, "has a true meaning," but the circumstances and intentions of the utterer could possibly impede the true expression of that meaning. Some held that the speaker's will to say was more important than what was said, and many recognized that words may have effects that writers or speakers did not intend. Here in the real world, words cannot have a one-to-one correspondence to the things they denote or to the wills of their speakers. Instead, there is but a rough association—cousinhood rather than, say, brotherhood.

Chaucer's narrator recognizes that potential slippage between the utterance and the idea while at the same time trying to be faithful to both. And yet, for all his claims not to find "wordes newe" in his retellings, it is Chaucer the poet who emerges from the General Prologue as precisely that finder of new words—indeed, the Middle English word *find* means both "discover" and "invent," and when Chaucer's early imitators call him the "first finder" of our language, they mean exactly that he invents it. The opening of the General Prologue really does find a new way for the vernacular, much as it finds a way for fictive pilgrims, and it is essential to see just what the linguistic landscape was in late-fourteenth-century London through which Chaucer found that way.

The London Middle English of the later fourteenth century was a lightly inflected language that had developed distinctive patterns of word order, had appropriated a large and growing French and Latin vocabulary, and developed a system of pronunciation based, largely, on the East Midlands dialect (but which had elements of other, regional sounds and forms). Verb endings, as in Old English, marked the infinitive, and the first, second, and third persons in both the singular and plural. Noun endings did not indicate grammatical gender, nor did they largely indicate cases (though there were a few exceptions). They did distinguish singular from the plural, most often using the final -s for plural, though Chaucer's Middle English also preserved (as our Modern English does, to some extent) some plural forms inherited from Old English. These include sets of words that formed their plurals by changing the root vowel of the word: foot, feet; goose, geese; mouse, mice. They also included words that formed their plural with an -*en* ending: child, children; brother, brethren; ox, oxen. And there remained a few words that did not distinguish singular from plural (those that survive in modern English include *sheep* and *fish*, though in Chaucer's Middle English there would have been others, including the Old English word *wonder*).

Word-order patterns were the primary determiners of meaning and effect in a sentence. The normal pattern, Subject + Verb + Object, may be illustrated by the sentence: "He takes hys leve." The inversion of Verb and Object could be used for emphasis ("I him folwed"), while Subject and Verb could be inverted for asking a question ("Gaf ye the child any thing?"). Chaucer's Middle English could use multiple negation for emphasis (in fact, English speakers and writers multiplied negation well into the eighteenth century, when grammarians believed it to be illogical). Thus, we may see, in the description of the Knight from the General Prologue, the following, staggering quadruple negation: "He nevere yet no vileynye ne sayde in al his lyf unto no manner wight" (He never, to this point, in any way said anything bad in all of his life to any kind of person).

As in Old English (and, in fact, as in the English language well into the time of Shakespeare), Chaucer's Middle English distinguished between singular and plural and informal and formal second-person pronouns. Such forms as *thou, thy, thine,* and *thee* were singular and informal; such forms as *you, your,* and *ye,* were plural and formal. This distinction worked in literature and in society much as it does in modern French, German, Italian, or Spanish—that is, to mark personal relationships of power, intimacy, age, social status, and affection. There are times in Chaucer's poetry (as there are throughout medieval and Renaissance literature) when the meaning of a scene depends wholly on the subtleties of pronouns. In the "Clerk's Tale" from the *Canterbury Tales,* for example, the Italian despot Walter is dismissing his long suffering, yet patient wife, Griselda, after years of marriage (he is testing her, but cruelly). Turning to her husband, Griselda says: "Remembre yow, myn owene lord so deere / I was youre wyf, though I unworthy were" (4.881–82). She speaks to him in the formal *you* form. When Walter responds, telling her to go and take only the old smock she is wearing, he dismisses her in the *thou* form: "'the smok,' quod he, 'that thou hast on thy bak, / Let it be stille, and bere it forth with thee'" (4.890–91). But when he finishes her testing and accepts her, finally, as his beloved, Walter uses the *thou* forms of intimacy: "Thou art my wyf, ne noon oother I have" (4.1063).

Social relationships define themselves throughout the *Canterbury Tales* in *you* and *thou* forms: the Host and the Clerk address each other with *you* forms of respect in the Prologue to the "Clerk's Tale." But at the close of the "Pardoner's Tale," the Pardoner angers the Host, not just by inviting him to buy one of his bogus relics but by addressing him in the *thou* form: "Come forth, sire Hoost, and offer first anon, / And thou shalt kisse the reikes everychon" (6.943–44). When the Host brutally responds (also in the *thou* form), it takes the Knight to come in and restore both social and dramatic balance—but he does so by maintaining hierarchies through pronouns. He speaks to "ye, sire Hoost," but to the Pardoner he says " I prey thee, drawe thee neer" (6.964–66).

At moments such as this one, Chaucer reaches deep into the grammatical resources of his language to make social and dramatic claims (claims lost on modern readers unaware of the old pronouns). But here, as elsewhere, there is no single kind of English that is emblematically Chaucerian. No individual passage, however extended or extensive, can convey the range of register, vocabulary, dialect, and idiom that he deploys throughout his writing. Chaucer evokes the high style of the Francophile court, the coarseness of the commoner, the Latinism of the scholar—and everything in between. Take the Prologue to the "Clerk's Tale." The Host has called upon the Clerk to tell a story, and he responds by announcing that he will recount a tale told to him by the Italian poet, Francis Petrarch. The story of patient Griselda that follows is Chaucer's version of the narrative told by Petrarch in Latin but before him by Boccaccio in Italian. The Clerk praises his source, however, in terms that, for the first time in English, synthesize the language of poetic praise as developed in the European vernaculars.

> I wol yow telle a tale which that I
> Lerned at Padowe of a worthy clerk,
> As preved by his wordes and his werk.
> He is now deed and nailed in his cheste;
> I prey to God so yeve his soule reste!
> Fraunceys Petrak, the lauriat poete,
> Highte this clerk, whos rethorike sweete
> Enlumyned al Ytaille of poetrie . . .
>
> (4.26–33)

[I intend to tell you a tale that I learned in Padua from a worthy clerk—his worthiness proved by his words and deeds. He is now dead and nailed in his coffin. I pray to God that He give his soul good rest. Francis Petrarch, the laureate poet, was the name of this clerk, whose sweet rhetoric illuminated all of Italy with poetry.]

As happens throughout the *Canterbury Tales*, English and European, old and new, jostle for effect. Petrarch is here a clerk (from the Latin, *clericus*) from Padowe (Padua, the first time this Italian city shows up in English writing). His worthy status (from the Old English, *weorþ*) has been proved (from the Latin), "by his wordes and his werk," an Old English alliterative pairing. Once we get to hear Petrarch's name, however, just about everything that follows is a new imported word: *laureate*, from the Latin *laureatus*, recalls Petrarch's crowning as the poet laureate in Rome; *rethorike* is, of course, *rhetorica*, one of the medieval liberal arts; *enlumyned* comes from *illuminatus*, and appears here for the first time anywhere in English; and *poetrie*, from the Latin *poetria*, connotes for Chaucer literary writing in Latin by a dead author (the term Chaucer uses consistently for vernacular writing in English, or writing by living authors, such as himself, is *making*). The character of Chaucer's Clerk displays his erudition in the range of these terms, while the poet Chaucer puts into practice the very "heigh style" for which Petrarch had been known.

Elsewhere in Chaucer, his high style sets out to naturalize in English the flow of a European intellectual or courtly voice. In *Troilus and Criseyde*, a poem rich with courtly gestures and itself a translation of Boccaccio's *Il Filostrato*, Chaucer can sound almost classical in his allusions and his polysyllables.

> O blissful light of which the bemes clere
> Adorneth al the thridde heven faire!
> O sonnes lief, O Joves doughter deere,
> Plesance of love, O goodly debonaire,
> In gentil hertes ay redy to repaire!
> O veray cause of heele and of gladnesse,
> Iheryed be thy might and thi goodnesse!

(*Troilus*, 3.1–7)

[O blissful light, whose clear beams adorn the beautiful third planetary sphere! O beloved of the sun, O Jove's dear daughter, love's delighted, O excellent gracious one, ready to go, indeed, into gracious hearts! O true cause of health and of happiness, may your might and your goodness be praised!]

In this and the previous example, new words call attention to the speaker's position of power in relationship to his addressee (in the "Clerk's Tale," it is an authoritative poet; in *Troilus and Criseyde*, it is a god). As far as we can tell, this is the first time that the verb *adorn* is used in English writing, and it introduces a string of loan words: *cler, plesance, debonaire, gentil, repaire, verray, cause*. You had to be immensely well read in late-fourteenth-century England to know these words, let alone to use them effortlessly in vernacular poetry. Indeed, Chaucer may even be playing on the etymology of *debonaire*, which came from the French, *de bonne aire*, of good disposition, but also of good "air"—he does the same thing in his translation of Boethius's *Consolation of Philosophy*, when he calls Zephyrus the "deboneire wynde."

If Chaucer can evoke the high style of a European romancier, he can equally well satirize the pretentiousness of loan words, as in the "Tale of Sir Thopas." Here, the poor pilgrim Chaucer has been called upon to tell a tale, and what he tells is so god-awful that the Host must interrupt it with the criticism: "Thy drasty rymyng is nat worth a toord!" Turdlike must be those stanzas in which fancy, polysyllabic, French terms stand out like lumps:

> Listeth, lordes, in good entent,
> And I wol telle verrayment
> Of myrthe and of solas,
> Al of a knight was fair and gent
> In bataille and in tourneyment;
> His name was sire Thopas.

("Tale of Sir Thopas," 7.712–17)

[Listen, lords, with good intention, and I will truly tell you something of pleasure and solace, concerning all about a knight who was fair and of of noble birth, in battle and in tournament; his name was Sir Thopas.]

Just what kind of poet would say of his hero that his face was white "as pandemayn" (that is, *pain de main*, handmade or very fine bread)? And by the time we get through the catalogue of herbs and spices filling the forest (lycorys, cetewale, clowe-gylofre, notemuge), or the delicacies at the knight's table (mazelyn, spicerye, gyngebreed, lycorys, comyn), we too may grow as impatient as the Host. "Myne eres aken of thy drasty speche," he complains, and that is precisely the point. For this is a poetry of the ear, a poetry designed to satirize the pretensions of courtly romance by having the complicated sounds and syllables of Gallic terms jangle much like the bridle of Sir Thopas's horse.

Chaucer's is always a poetry of the ear—in part, because it was performed; in part, too, because it is designed to capture the sound of the speech of people from a range of social strata. For in addition to the high style, there are stretches of colloquial dialogue that reach deep into the recesses of the obscene: "Derk was the nyght as pich, or as the cole, / And at the window out she putte hir hole" ("Miller's Tale," 1.3731–32). And in the "Reeve's Tale," Chaucer can present so reasonable a facsimile of the Northern Middle English dialect that modern linguists have relied on this tale for its evidence of regional pronunciation at the time: "By God, need has na peer. / Hym boes serve himself that has na swayn" (1.4026–27).

We think of Chaucer as a poet of facility and flair, but he was also a prose writer whose translations and adaptations of earlier material were in some ways even more appreciated in his own time than the poetry. His translation of Boethius's *Consolation of Philosophy* (known as the *Boece*) takes the Latin text, by way of an intermediary French translation, and seeks to develop a vernacular English philosophical diction. Take, for example, this passage from book 5, metrum 4 of the *Boece*, where Lady Philosophy is setting out the Stoic theory of sense impressions:

> [The Stoics] wenden that ymages and sensibilities (that is to seyn, sensible ymaginaciouns or ellis ymaginaciouns of sensible thingis) weren enprientid into soules fro bodyes withoute-forth (as who seith that thilke Stoycienis wenden that the sowle had been nakid of itself, as a mirour or a clene parchemyn, so that alle figures most first comen fro thinges fro withoute into soules, and ben emprientid into soules): . . . ryght as we ben wont somtyme by a swift poyntel to fyc- chen letters emprientid in the smothnesse or in the pleynesse of the table of wex or in parchemyn that ne hath no figure ne note in it.

> [The Stoics believed that images and sense impressions (that is, impressions gained through the senses or impressions of things that can be sensed) were imprinted into souls from bodies outside of themselves (after the manner of those who say that these same Stoics believed that the soul was naked in origin, as if it were a mirror or a blank piece of parchment, so that all figures had to first come from things outside into souls, and thus be imprinted into souls): . . . just as we are in the habit at times of making letters impressed into the smooth surface or plain covering of a wax tablet with a fast moving stylus or pen, or on to a parchment surface that has no letter nor marking on it.]

Here, in a passage that segues from Boethius's own text to asides from learned commentaries, Chaucer's English seems to survive in only the barest of grammatical scaffolding for a lexicon heavy with French and Latin polysyllables.

By contrast, his *Treatise on the Astrolabe*—a synthesis of medieval astronomical and astrological teaching inherited from Greek and Latin, Arabic, and European teaching—simplifies a technical language for the work's addressee, Chaucer's ten-year-old son, Lewis. This treatise, Chaucer states, "wol I shewe the under full light reules and naked wordes in Englissh, for Latyn canst thou yit but small, my litel sone." Chaucer speaks in the *thou* forms as a father to a son. The old idiom for knowing a language—using the form of the verb "can"—shows up here, as do other old vernacularisms: the use of *full* to mean "very"; the use of *light* to mean "simple"; the word *small* to mean "a little bit" (this last idiom shows up again, centuries later, when Ben Jonson would chide Shakespeare for his "small Latin and less Greek"). The English will be *naked* here, a word Chaucer uses elsewhere to mean unadorned, straightforward, simple: the "naked text" in his translation of the *Romance of the Rose* means without gloss or explanation; in the Prologue to the *Legend of Good Women*, he will aver his intention as "the naked text in English to declare / Of many a story," that is, to narrate without asides or embellishment (Prologue, G-version, 86). In these terms, there is little naked about the *Boece*, as its sentences fill themselves with terms from French and Latin, with asides from commentaries, and with repetitions designed to rephrase a technical language into something equally technical (the only thing naked in the passage I had quoted earlier is the soul that the Stoics thought was empty of ideas at birth).

The Prologue to the *Treatise on the Astrolabe*, in addition to establishing the framework for instruction, offers a lesson in language itself.

Now wol I preie meekly every discret persone that redith or herith this litel tretys to have my rude endityng for excused, and my superfluite of wordes, . . . And Lowys, yf so be that I shewe the in my lighte Englissh as trewe conclusions touching this mater, and not oonly as trewe but as many and as subtile conclusiouns, as ben shewid in Latyn in eny commune tretys of the Astrelabie, konne me the more thank. And preie God save the king, that is lord of this langage, and alle that him feith bereth and obeieth, everich in his degree, the more and the lasse. But consider wel that I ne usurpe not to have founden this werk of my labour or of myn engyn. I n'am but a lewd compilator of the labour of olde astrologiens, and have it translated in myn Englissh only for thy doctrine.

[Now I intend to pray humbly to every individual person that reads or hears this little treatise to excuse me of my coarse writing and the overabundance of words. . . . And Lewis, if it should happen that I reveal to you in my easy English the conclusions concerning this material in as true a fashion as any ordinary treatise shows in Latin—conclusions not only as true, but as many and as subtle as in those treatises—then you can thank me the more. And I pray to God to save the king, who is lord of this language, and to save all of them that have faith and obey, each one according to his social rank, the greater and the lesser. But recognize truly that I have not taken over the authority for this work, nor originated any of it through the activity of my imagination. I am nothing but a simple compiler of the work of old astrologers, and I have translated it into my English only for your instruction.]

Chaucer sets out to explain, and if at times that explanation requires some extra verbiage, so be it. It seems significant in these sentences that when Chaucer writes about the basics he does so in basic English, and when he invokes a pedagogical difficulty or a claim for social status, he does so in words borrowed from French or Latin. He prays *meekly*, but the people he addresses are *discreet*: judicious, prudent, courteous (a word from a French courtly vocabulary; think ahead to Shakespeare's Falstaff: "The better part of valor is discretion"). He apologies for his "superfluite of wordes" (and *superfluity* appears to have come into English only in the 1380s—it is a word that calls attention to itself, a bit of self-conscious superfluity). Chaucer seeks to write "light English," but when he writes about what lies in his Latin sources, he refers to "subtile conclusiouns." And when he prays to God to save the king, he makes him "lord of this langage," and in the process gives a powerful political cast to writing in the vernacular.

This is the point of the *Treatise*, more than any technical education in the arts of astrology. For the first time ever, English is the language of the king (though the exact phrase, "the king's English," does not appear until Shakespeare). And for the first time, Chaucer establishes a literary authority in the vernacular as a political problem. Lest we think that he has made all this up, he avers that he has stuck closely to his sources. He is "but a lewd compilator," not a usurper. Chaucer's is one of the very first uses of this word, according to the *Oxford English Dictionary* (s.v., *usurp*, vb.), and it brilliantly brings together politics and language in a way that takes us back to Henry III's Proclamation and to the whole history of Anglo-French courtly commerce. As my earlier chapters illustrated, English was gradually coming into political prominence by the close of the fourteenth century. True, parliamentary records were still kept in French, but the language of its arguments was mandated as English. History was coming to be written in the language; John Wycliff and his followers were translating the Bible into English; Julian of Norwich was composing complex theological texts in it; and, in 1388, Parliament was petitioned in English, for the first time, by the Mercer's Guild.

And yet, French was still there. There is no surviving parliamentary petition in English after 1388 until about 1413. Richard the II (the king who was lord of Chaucer's "langage") lived little in the language (his successor, Henry IV, was, as I had mentioned previously, the first post-Conquest king to leave a will in English). During the Rising of 1381—perhaps the most disruptive social event of the English Middle Ages and one so threatening that Chaucer, along with his poetic contemporaries John Gower and William Langland, could not get away from writing about it—the insurgent groups (made up of peasants, artisans, and some local professionals) made much of their command of English and of the official lack of it. In the words of Steven Justice, whose study *Writing and Rebellion: England in 1381* illuminates this vernacular insurgency, the political and public uses of English were acts affirming "that those who read only English—or even could only have English read to them—had a stake in the intellectual and political life of church and realm" (30). What Justice calls "the linguistic specialization of official culture," that is, its conduct in French and Latin, "was a resentment suffered for generations" (70).

So in a world of an insurgent English, where French remained royal and official and yet was in some sense under siege, Chaucer's avowals at the close of the Prologue to the *Treatise on the Astrolabe* have a profound political and linguistic effect. Richard II did not work his lordship in English, and usurpation was a threat to all. Indeed, but a few years after Chaucer put the *Astrolabe* together, Henry Bolingbrooke took up—some would have said usurped—King Richard's throne. That is the very word used by the poet of a mid-fifteenth-century account:

> To have in mynde callyng to Remembraunse
> The gret wrongys doon of oold antiquitey,
> Unrightful heyres by wrong alyaunce
> Usurpyng this Royaume caused gret adversitey;
> Kyng Richard the secounde, high of dignytee,
> Whiche of Ingeland was Rightful enheritoure,
> In whos tyme ther was habundaunce with plentee
> Of welthe & erthely Ioye withouyt langoure.
>
> ("A political retrospect," dated to 1462)

[To have in mind calling into remembrance the great wrongs done in ancient times, unrightful heirs who, by making bad alliances usurped this realm and caused great adversity; King Richard the

Second, great in his dignity, was the rightful inheritor of England,
in whose time there was great abundance of wealth and earthly joy
without distress.]

Here, in this awkward stanza of late Middle English verse, we can see
something of the legacy of Chaucer's language and the politics of words.
For in a poem praising the rights of a deposed English king, we find far
more French words than English. This is a diction of the polysyllable,
what late-medieval writers would call "aureate," or golden, language and
would praise (or sometimes blame) Chaucer for inaugurating. The shim-
mering high-concept words—remembrance, antiquity, alliance, adversity,
dignity, inheritor, abundance, languor—evoke not just a political but a
linguistic former age: an age of Francophile inheritance. This is no naked
text in English.

And, for that matter, neither is Chaucer's. Even when he is at his most
straightforward, his most Saxon, his most monosyllabically simple, Chaucer is never without ambiguity or double edge. The ironies of the *Astrolabe*
remind us that if Richard II was really no lord of the English language,
Chaucer was. His paternity over the diction and the forms of English literature was well acknowledged (he came to be called the "father" of English
poetry within only decades of his death). Even if he did not coin many
new words, he deployed an emerging vocabulary in a new and critically
effective way. Even if he used the resources of Middle English available
to him, he used *all* those resources, writing in the registers, the dialects,
and the idioms of an entire English-speaking nation. Even if at the close
of the Prologue to the *Astrolabe* Chaucer avows that he has done nothing
original—that he has not *founden*, that is, invented, anything—and even if
he claims this stance throughout his literary works, it is clear that he transformed the legacy of Latin, French, Italian, and English literature available
to him into a unique synthesis of styles.

Over a century after the *Astrolabe* was written, English authors came to
use the word "usurp" to mean appropriating words from other languages.
Sir Thomas Elyot notes in his *Book of the Governor* (1531) that he has been
"constrained to usurpe a latine word" where none exists in English. For
the next three centuries, according to the *OED*, words were "usurped" for
English—as if writers were in some sense conquerors of the linguistic
imagination. Chaucer, it may be said, usurped a nation of new words, and
in the process, made himself a lord of language that no king—rightful or
usurping—could become.

CHAPTER 6

I Is as Ille a Millere as Are Ye
Middle English Dialects

WHEN I ARRIVED AT OXFORD IN THE FALL OF 1976, I was assigned to a tutorial in Middle English dialects. I had enrolled in Course II of the English Honours School, a degree program centered on the history of the English language, medieval literatures, and what was then and there called "linguistic theory." Expecting to read deeply in Old and Middle English poetry, I was baffled at the structure of instruction and, in particular, at the attention paid to early English dialects. My bafflement was only enhanced at the meeting of my first tutorial with the distinguished scholar of late-medieval English religious prose, Anne Hudson. "Do you know your don," she seemed to ask me, in a ringingly inflected voice I could not reproduce without recourse to the International Phonetic Alphabet. "My don?" I answered. Well, I thought *she* was my don (the word "don," in Oxford parlance, referred to a college tutor in the university—a term that emerged in the seventeenth century ultimately from the Latin, *dominum*, "lord, or master," by way of the Spanish honorific, *Don*). "No, no, I mean Richard Your Don, *The Handbook of Middle English Grammar.*" Oh, Richard Jordan, the German philologist, whose *Handbuch der mittelenglischen Grammatik* of 1925 had appeared in an English translation just two years before I began my studies. Of course, to my American ears, he was Richard "Dzórdan"—accent on the first syllable, *j* pronounced like a *j*.

Such was my introduction to the dialects of English: to the ways in which the language harbored often mutually incomprehensible pronunciations, to the lies of spelling. In the course of my tutorial, however, I learned more than how to pronounce the names of German philologists after the fashion of British academics. I learned that the English were possessed by dialects:

that forms of speech determined region, class, level of education, and gender with a precision almost unheard of anywhere else. (I also learned, in passing, that George Bernard Shaw's Henry Higgins was himself modeled on Henry Sweet, the brilliant nineteenth-century English philologist who, among other things, systematized the early West Saxon dialect of Old English and was instrumental in the founding of the Early English Text Society, the *Oxford English Dictionary*, and the discipline of historical philology itself.) Dialectology was, in many ways, a form of social history. But it was also a practice demanding such precision, such skill at making distinctions among vowel sounds and consonants, and such technical facility with transcription, that it had become, in mid-twentieth-century Oxford, *the* empirical discipline of the humanities. It was the way in which a British academic could command resources of an almost scientific skill, the way in which the study of English could be elevated on a par with genetics, nuclear physics, or—Oxford being Oxford—even classics.

Middle English provided such scholars with a rich and unique diversity of dialects, recorded in the manuscripts of poetry and prose from the twelfth through the fifteenth centuries. In the book that I was assigned to read that first year of my studies, B. M. H. Strang's *History of English*, the author (a professor at Newcastle-upon-Tyne) defined that uniqueness:

> What is unprecedented, and unparalleled since [the Middle English period], is that this tiny nation produced such writers, especially poets, in such abundance, and that they each wrote individually, not merely in style, but in language. The forms of English in which their writings are preserved vividly demonstrate that in addition to the successive varieties identified by Professor Samuels [M. L. Samuels, then the leading scholar of English dialect history], there were many other kinds of English which had a rather fixed tradition of writing. Because they conformed to standards and were recognizable as standard, and because their currency was less than nationwide, we might call them cultivated regional, or regional standard.
>
> (220)

Middle English, Strang continued further on, "is *par excellence*, the dialectical phase of English, in the sense that while dialects have been spoken at all periods, it was in Middle English that divergent local usage was normally indicated in writing" (224).

Strang's assessment—which distilled half a century of scholarly opinion and which has held up to the present day—is about more than simple regional variation. It is about the fact that such variation could become the basis of a "cultivated standard." Cultivation implies learning, literacy, and aesthetic culture. Standard implies a hierarchy of values and the institutions in place to sustain them. And writing implies that medieval scribes not only wrote as they heard but that they could (and in fact did) translate texts from other dialects into their own, and that there were, within regional dialect areas, certain agreed-upon forms of spelling. Literary culture for the Middle English period, in this assessment, was literate culture, and the purpose of literary writing was, to some degree, to record the local voice of verbal artists of the region.

Now, all of this made sense when I read such "cultivated regional" texts as, say, *The Cursor Mundi* from the north, *The Bestiary* from the East Midlands, *The Song on the Execution of Simon Fraser* from the West Midlands, *The South English Legendary* from the south, or *The Ayenbite of Inwit* from Kent. In each of these texts, ranging from the late thirteenth to the mid-fourteenth centuries, we can see how scribes recorded local pronunciations and regional differences in grammar and idiom. But all of this made little sense when I came to Chaucer's "Reeve's Tale" from the *Canterbury Tales* or to the *Second Shepherd's Play* from the mid-fifteenth-century group of religious dramas known as the Wakefield Cycle. In these two works, regional differences appear not as cultivated written standards but, instead, as representations of either country-bumpkin-ness or affectation. These literary evocations of regional and class dialects have as their purpose social satire and humor. Their goal is to reveal how differences in language point to differences in culture; how the north and south of England, in particular, stand as opposing poles of politics and power; and, perhaps most broadly, how the diversity of human speech reveals something of the transitoriness of earthly life—that language is a mutable thing, and that, in a post-Babel world, our inability to understand one another leads to social strife (as St. Augustine put it, in his *City of God*, "*linguarum diversitas hominem alienat ab homine*," the diversity of languages alienates man from man).

John of Trevisa, writing in the middle of the 1380s, understood this principle. In his Middle English translation of Ranulf Higden's history, known as the *Polychronicon*, Trevisa commented on the different forms of English spoken at his time.

Also Englischmen, þey3 hy hadde fram þe bygynnyng þre maner speche, Souþeron, Norþeron, and Myddel speche (in þe myddel of þe lond), as hy come of þre maner people of Germania, noþeles, by commyxstion and mellyng furst wiþ Danes and afterward wiþ Normans, in meny the contray longage is apeyred, and some useþ strange wlaffyng, chyteryng, harryng and garryng, grisbittyng. Þis apeyryng of þe burþ-tonge ys bycause of twey þinges. On ys, for chyl-dern in scole, a3enes þe usage and manere of al oþer nacions, buþ compelled for to leve here oune longage, and for to construe here les-sons and here þinges a Freynsch, and habbeþ, suþthe þe Normans come furst into Engelond. Also, gentilmen children buþ y-tau3t for to speke Freynsch fram tyme þat a buþ y-rokked in here cradel, and conneþ speke and playe wiþ a child hys brouch; and oplondysch men wol lykne hamsylf to gentilmen, and fondeþ wiþ gret bysynes for to speke Freynsch for to be more y-told of.

Hyt semeþ a gret wondur hou3 Englysch, þat is þe burþ-tonge of Englyschmen and here oune longage and tonge, ys so dyvers of soun in þis ylond; and þe longage of Normandy ys comlyng of anoþer lond, and haþ on maner soun among al men þat spekeþ hyt ary3t in Engelond. Noþeles, þer ys as meny dyvers maner Frensch yn þe rem of Fraunce as ys dyvers manere Englysh in þe rem of Engelond.

Al the longage of the Norþhumbres, and specialych at 3ork, ys so scharp, slyttyng and frotyng, and unschape, þat we Southeron men may þat longage unneþe undurstonde. Y trowe þat þat ys bycause þat a buþ ny3 to strange men and aliens þat spekeþ strangelych, and also bycause þat þe kynges of Engelond woneþ alwey fer fram þat contray.

[Now the English, even though they originally had from the begin-ning three kinds of speech, Southern, Northern, and Middle (in the middle of the country), as they came from three groups of people from Germania [i.e., Germanic-speaking Europe], nonetheless, by mixing together and meddling first with the Danes and then with the Normans, in many people the native language has been corrupted, and some use strange *wlaffyng, chyteryng, harryng and garryng grisbit-tyng*. This corruption of the native language is due to two causes. One is because children in school, contrary to the habit and manner of all other nations, are compelled to forsake their own language and construe their lessons and [name their] things in French, and they have done so since the Normans came first into England. The second is because the children of gentlemen are taught to speak French from the time they are rocked in their cradle, and the child can speak it and play with his toys in it. In addition, socially ambitious men want to present themselves as if they were gentlemen, and they try with great effort therefore to speak French in order to be thought better of.

It seems a great marvel just how English, which is the native language of the Englishmen and here our own language and tongue, is so diverse in sound in this island. And the language of Normandy, which comes from another land, nonetheless has one way of sounding for all men that speak it correctly in England. Still, there are as many different forms of French in the realm of France as there are different forms of English in the realm of England.

The whole language of the Northumbrians, and specially that of York, is so sharp, cutting and scratching, and unshapely, that we Southern men may scarcely understand it. I believe that this is because they live near strange people and aliens that speak strangely, and also because the kings of England always stay far away from that part of the country.]

This is a long, remarkable, and complex commentary on the state of English at the time of Chaucer. But we can distill it into three points: first, that English dialects have a history keyed to the original settlement patterns of the Anglo-Saxons; second, that language is socially stratified and that the prestige speech of a given group (in this case, French) will remain stable across English dialect boundaries; and third, that the dialect in the north of England is unique and that the reasons for this uniqueness are both sociolinguistic (the northerners are in contact with speakers of other languages, notably Celtic and Scandinavian dialects) and political (they are far from the center of power and culture).

These three points have remained the main lines of inquiry into Middle English dialectology. The Old English dialect boundaries, like those of the Middle English period, were determined by particular natural and manmade barriers. North of the Humber River was Northumbria, since the seventh century a distinctive linguistic and social group. The old Roman road that ran from London north through the Midlands bisected English speakers into what would be called East and West Midland. The Thames river separated Southern English speakers, while, in the southeast, the Kentish coast remained the site of another distinctive group. Middle English dialect regions can be thus defined by history and geography, but they are also principally defined by how Old English sounds changed into later form. What happened to the Old English long *a* (written phonetically as /aː/) is a key determiner of dialect. In all of the dialects except that of Northumbria, the sound was, linguists would say, raised and rounded. It became a kind of "aw" sound (written phonetically as /ɔː/), and almost always spelled with an "o." Thus, Old English words such as *ban, ham, la, swa, twa, fra,* and *halig* became *bone, home, lo, so, two, fro,* and *holy.* In Northumbria, this sound change did not happen; thus the Northern Middle English forms of these words stayed with the long *a.* Other Old English sounds changed in distinctive ways according to region. In the East Midlands, Old English short *a* followed by a nasal and a consonant (for example, in the words, *land, hand, band*) became a short *o: lond, hond, bond.*

Old English regional dialects had different sounds, too, that passed into their Middle English descendants. In the north, the influence of Scandinavian languages led to pronunciations of *k* and *sk* for what, in the south, would be *ch* and *sh.* Thus, in Middle English the Southern and Midland words *church, shirt,* and *each* would be, in the Northern dialect, *kirk, skirt,* and *ilk* (each of these Northern words, by the way, eventually passes into modern English, along with many other forms, due to migration patterns and contact among dialects; our Modern English word "milk," by the way, is a northernism, with the southern form "milch" surviving only in the technical term "milch cow"). The Scandinavian influence in the north affected vocabulary, too. Words such as *ill, ugly,* and *muggy* come into English originally through the Northern dialect. Other features of Northern-dialect speech that would have marked it as distinctive—some inherited from Old English, some influenced by Scandinavian contact—include the use of the *th-* forms for pronouns. In the Scandinavian languages, the third person plural would have been *thei.* In Old English, and in the Midland and Southern dialects of Middle English, this word would have been *hey* (similarly, *them* would have been *hem; their* would have been *hir*). For a speaker of Modern English, the northern forms seem familiar (again, a function of migration patterns and dialect contact in the late Middle English and early Modern English period). But for people of Trevisa's or Chaucer's day, these forms would have seemed odd. Odd, too, would have been the ending of the present participle: *-and* in the north, in contrast to *-end* in the Midlands and south. Odd to both them and us would be the final *-sh* sound as *-s,* and the raising of the *-e-* sound before the *-ng* conso-

Northumbrian

West
Midland

East Midland

Southern

Kentish

MAP 6.1

The major Middle English Dialects. A basic, coarse-grained map dividing England
into the five major dialect regions, ca. 1200–1500.

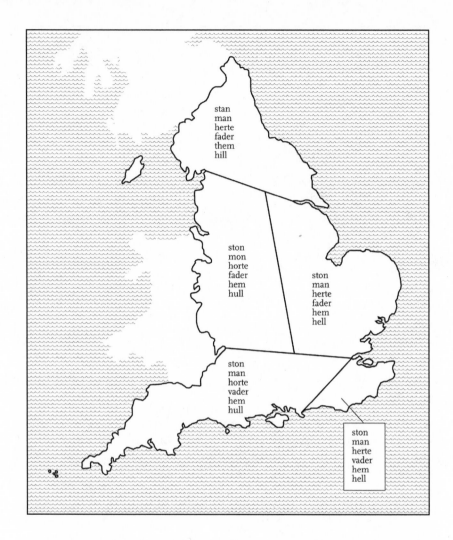

MAP 6.2

Middle English dialect variation according to key words and sounds. A finer-grained map, dividing England into linguistic regions based on the Middle English pronunciation of earlier Old English sounds and forms of the third-person plural pronoun: "stone," *stan-ston* > OE /a:/; "man," *mon-man* > OE /a/; "hill," *hill-hull-hell* > OE /y/; "heart," *horte-herte* > OE /œ/; "them," *them-hem*; "father," *fader-vader* , OE /f/.

nant cluster. Thus, the combination of these two sounds would produce the word "Inglis" for "English."

The rough and slicing sounds of Trevisa's northerners can now be understood, somewhat more precisely, as a function of their distinctive phonology and morphology. These sounds and endings, too, contribute to the humor of Chaucer's "Reeve's Tale," a story of sexual predation and commercial duplicity that focuses on the exploits of two northern students studying at Cambridge. At one point, one of the students turns to the other and addresses him:

'Symond,' quod John, 'by God need has na peer.
Him boes serve himself that has na swayn.

[Simon, said John, by God need has no peer.
He best serves himself who has no servant.]

He goes on, commenting on the milling of the grain that they have brought to the mill:

Our manciple, I hope he will be deed,
Swa workes ay the wanges in his heed.

[I expect that our manciple (i.e., the chief victualer of the Cambridge college) will be dead,
so ache the teeth in his head.]

. . . .
. . . se howgates the corn gas in.
Yet saugh I nevere, by my fader kyn,
How that the hapur wagges til and fra.

[see how the grain goes in.
But I swear by my father's family, I never saw
the hopper of the mill wagging to and fro like that.]

. . . .
I is as ille a millere as ar ye.
[I am as bad a miller as you are.]

. . . .

I have herd seyd, 'Man sal taa of twa thynges
Slyk as he fyndes, or taa slyk as he bringes.'

[I have heard it said, 'Of two things, one should take
Such as he finds, or take such as he brings.']

Chaucer has evoked all of the central features of the Northern Middle
English dialect (or, at the very least, those that the southern, or the London, ear would hear). There is the maintenance of the Old English long
a: *fra* (for *fro*), *gas* (for *goes*). There is the *s* for the *sh* sound (*sal* for *shall*).
There is the *k* for *ch* (*slyk* for *swich*, Modern English "such"). In the north,
the forms of the verb "to be" were different, too, from the south and Midlands. Thus, one said "I is" instead of what a Chaucer or Trevisa would
have said: "I am" (or even, going further south, "Ich am"). The third-
person singular in the north ends in *-s* rather than in *-th* (thus the form
goes rather than *goeth*); the plural of the verb ends in *-s* rather than in *-en*
(*workes*, rather than *worken*). And the Scandinavian vocabulary is there:
boes (for the word "behooves"), *til* (for "to"), *taa* (for "take"), and *ill* (of
course, for "ill").

Chaucer's is not a phonological transcription but a literary evocation—a kind of extended dialect joke, emphasizing the most obvious of
Northern Middle English sounds and forms. But writers in the north of
England could make fun of southerners, too. In the *Second Shepherd's Play*
from Wakefield (near York), the villainous and deceitful Mak, a shepherd,
pretends to be a noble visitor from the court; in fact, he has been steal-
ing sheep. Mak's attempt at Southern speech conforms to no single and
specific dialect. Instead, his lines are full of forms which appear in the
Southern, Kentish, and the Midland dialects. What we have in this scene
is a character's imagined version of Southern speech—a kind of "stage
Southern," if you will, full of not just sounds but a rich, courtly, Gallicized
vocabulary. The following scene is a dialogue between the three shepherds
and Mak:

2s: Mak, where has thou gone? Tell us tithing.
3s: Is he commen? Then ilkon take hede to his thing.
MAK: What? Ich be a yoman, I tell you, of the king;
    The self and the some, sond from a greatt lording,
    And sich.

Fie on you! Goith hence
Out of my presence!
I must have reverence:
Why, who be ich?

1s: Why make ye it so qwaint? Mak, ye do wrang.
2s: But, Mak, list ye saint? I trow that ye lang.
3s: I trow the shrew can paint, the dewill might him hang!
MAK: Ich shall make complaint, and make you all to thwang
    At a worde,
    And tell evyn how ye doth.
1s: Bot, Mak, is that sothe?
    Now take outt that Sothren tothe
    And sett in a torde!

[Mak, where have you gone? Tell us something.
Has he arrived? Then let each and every one pay attention to this
    event.
What? I am a yeoman, I tell you, of the king;
The very selfsame one, sent from a great lord, and such a one.
Fie on you. Leave my sight
Out of my presence!
I must have reverence:
Why, who am I?
Why are you speaking so oddly, Mak? You do us wrong.
But Mak, do you want to be like a saint? I believe you long to be so.
I believe the shrew can deceive, may the devil hang him!
I shall make a complaint, and have you all be flogged
At my word,
And I will report what you are doing.
But Mak, is that really true?
Now, take out that Southern tooth
And stick it in a turd!]

This passage reveals many things: it shows the complex stanzaic patterns
of the northern English cycle plays, with their interlocking rhyme schemes;
it shows the brilliant humor of the regional imagination; and it shows a
sensitivity to dialect and social class.

    Mak uses sonic and verbal feints to sustain his pretence. He uses "Ich"
for the Northern first person "I" (though not consistently), and he uses the

be forms of the verb: "Ich be" is the equivalent of the "I is" in the "Reeve's Tale." Mak attempts to reproduce a Southern and Midlands form *swich*, but he does so only partly by using the word *sich* (the Northern form would have been *swilk* or *slik*, as it is in the "Reeve's Tale"). Specific Midlandisms are the *-th* endings on the verbs *goith* and *doth*. In fact, the play's spelling of the verb "goith" indicates that Mak is stressing the long o that would have been long *a* in the north (recall in the "Reeve's Tale," *gas* for what should be "goeth"). Such a spelling indicates the overdone lengthening and rounding of this sound—it is a kind of eye dialect, really, a written evocation of a sound. And, of course, there is the fully Frenchified vocabulary: *presence, reverence*. Against this bogus dialect, the northernisms of the two shepherds stands out: *wrang* and *lang* show the characteristic long *a* (for "wrong" and "long"); their verbs end in *-es* and *-s*, not in *-th*; and their *-k-* sound in *ilkon* marks them as the Northerners they are.

This little scene demonstrates that northerners could have some fun at the expense of the "king's English," for Mak claims to be a royal messenger. That the First Shepherd tells Mak to take his southern tooth and stick it in a turd is but the crudest of ways of telling him to drop the pose and fess up. If Chaucer and Trevisa imagined northerners as doltish or barbaric, the northerners could paint the southerners as affected, effete, and elitist.

And so, Trevisa's recognition of the social stratification of language bears itself out in this scene from the medieval drama—indeed one wonders how much of Trevisa's kind of sentiment is in the mind of the playwright half-a-century later: that "þe kynges of Engelond woneþ alwey fer fram þat contray." We, as modern readers, live far away from that country, but some things seem familiar to us. From our perspective, Northern Middle English seems phonologically conservative (that is, it preserves Old English sounds), but it seems morphologically advanced. Many of the forms that would become standard English appear first in the north, notably the borrowed Scandinavian *th* forms for the pronouns, rather than the *h* forms; the use of the *is/are* forms of the verb to be, rather than the *be* forms; and the third-person singular verb endings in *-es*, rather than in *-eth*. These forms entered the mix of what would become Modern English through migration patterns from the north into London and, in particular, the rise of those Northern-dialect speakers (and writers) in the scribal professions. From our perspective, too, Southern dialects seem to have sounds that pass recognizably into Modern English, but they seem morphologically, and at times lexically conservative. This conservatism is most evident in the Kentish *Ayenbite of Inwit*, written by Dan Michael of Northgate in 1340. It ends with the following claim:

Þis boc is Dan Michelis of Northgate, y-write an englis of his oʒene hand. Þet hatte: Ayenbite of inwyt. And is of the bochouse of saynte Austines of Canterberi . . . .

Vader oure þet art ine hevens, y-halʒed by þi name, cominde þi riche, y-worþe þi wil ase in hevene: and in erþe. bread oure eche-dayes: yef ous to day. and vorlet ous oure yeldings: as we vorleteþ oure yelderes. and ne ous led naʒt: into vondinge. and vri ous fram queade. zuo by hit.

[This book is that of Dan Michael of Northgate, written in English by his own hand. It is called: Ayenbite of Inwit. And it came from the library of Saint Augustine's of Canterbury. . . .

Our father that art in heaven, hallowed be thy name, thy kingdom come, thy will be done, in earth as it is in heaven; give us this day our daily bread, and forgive us our sins, as we forgive those who have sinned against us, and lead us not into temptation, and free us from evil. So be it.]

Here, in Kent, we see distinctive features. Most striking is the voicing of the *f-* and *s-* sounds into *v-* and *z-* sounds. "So be it" becomes *zuo by hit*; "father" is *vader*; the Old English word for "forgive," *forletan*, is *vorlet*; "free" is *vri* (to my knowledge, by the way, the only example of this dialect feature that passes into Modern Standard English is in the word for the female fox, "vixen"). The present participle ends in *-inde* ("coming" is *cominde*). But there is also the old vocabulary. A word like *bochouse*, "book house," is, of course "library," but, here it stands like an old kenning, a strange relic of an ancient time. So, too, words such as *vorlet*, instead of "forgive," and *yeldings* (really the word "guilts," for the term "sins") recall the Anglo-Saxon idiom, as do phrasings such as "cominde þi riche" (thy kingdom come) and the opening "Vader oure" (the order "father our," instead of "our father" is a classic Anglo-Saxonism). And, finally, there is the title of this work. The *Ayenbite of Inwit* is the "again-bite of inwit," what a later medieval world would call *The Prick of Conscience*. For what is "conscience" but *inwit*, a brilliant kenning that recalls the inner lives of Beowulf's companions or the struggles of the Anglo-Saxon saints.

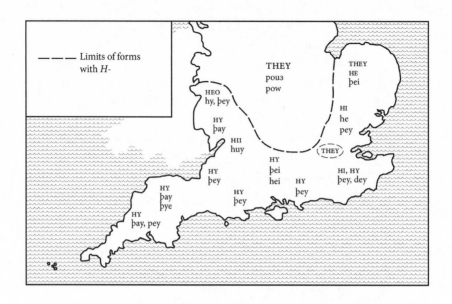

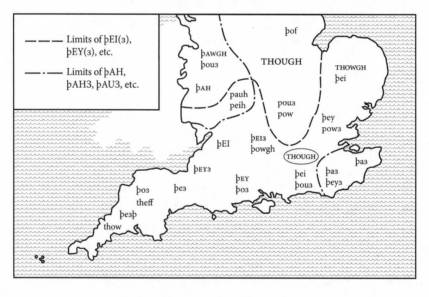

MAP 6.3

Middle English dialect variation according to the forms of particular words. A fine-grained map, based on manuscript evidence for regional variation.

Source: Reproduced from Samuels, *Linguistic Evolution*.

From the far north to the far south, English varied, and in London many of these forms would mix as sons of provincials traveled to seek fortunes, as men married women far from home, as traders came and went along the city streets. The London English of the time of Chaucer takes, as its base, an East Midland Middle English, but marks of the north and south and west show up in many texts written in the metropolis. John Gower, Chaucer's friend and lawyer and perhaps his sole poetic peer in London, came from Kent, and there are Kentishisms in his writings. From Kent, too, came William Caxton, England's first printer, born in the 1420s, resident in the Low Countries until the mid 1470s, and then back to England to set up his print shop in Westminster. Nearly a century after Chaucer's death, he recognized that the language "now vsed varyeth ferre from that whiche was vsed and spoken what I was borne." And he notes, too, that "comyn englysshe that is spoken in one shyre varyeth from a nother." Diachronic change and synchronic variation, as the linguists would say. Chaucer knew this as well, as he had noted, in his *Troilus and Criseyde*, that words that once had "prys" (value or meaning) now seem "wonder nyce and straunge." At that poem's close, he worries that some scribe will "mysmetre" his lines "for defaute of tonge"—that is, rewrite them into a different dialect, thus causing them to fail to scan or rhyme as Chaucer intended.

Middle English remains the most variable of languages. Indeed, in the end, it may not be a language at all but rather something of a scholarly fiction, an amalgam of forms and sounds, writers and manuscripts, famous works and little-known ephemera that we can roughly date, locate, and classify. Dialecticians have minced Middle English up so finely that their maps can show us almost town-by-town variation: what were the forms of the third-person, feminine pronoun; how did the Old English *y* develop; where are the borders of the Scandinavian vocabulary, forms, and sounds? Such research has the value not just of recovering the speech and writing of specific times and places; it illustrates the building blocks of language change itself. For at the heart of dialectology lies the relationship between synchronic variation and diachronic change: do languages change over time because of contact among different forms? Such is the largest question asked by modern scholars and by medieval writers.

As for me, I have spent years trying to crack the codes of Middle English dialects. Reading the work of scholars such as M. L. Samuels or Angus MacIntosh, or plowing through the chapter by James Milroy in the *Cambridge History of the English Language*, I remain daunted by detail. This is a discipline of fineness and finesse, not unlike grinding fine flour from coarse grain. In the face of such technical facility, I feel as I felt thirty years ago: like some provincial student at a major British university, gaping at the workings of technique and turning to friend, only to say, "I is as ille a millere as are ye."

CHAPTER 7

The Great Vowel Shift and the Changing Character of English

GOOGLE THE "GREAT VOWEL SHIFT." Though there are almost fifty thousand returns, the information is remarkably consistent. The Great Vowel Shift, you will learn, was the defining moment in the history of English pronunciation. It made modern English "modern." It was the systematic raising and fronting of the long, stressed monophthongs of Middle English, and it took place roughly from the middle of the fifteenth through the end of the seventeenth centuries. This was the change that made the language of the age of Chaucer largely opaque by the time of Shakespeare. While scholars of English from the Renaissance onward had been aware of these changes, it was not until the rise of empirical historical philology in the nineteenth century that a way was found of explaining them as a single phenomenon. And it was not until 1909 that the great Danish linguist, Otto Jespersen, codified these philological researches into a concise statement of what happened and why it was important. "The great vowel-shift," he wrote in his *Modern English Grammar*, "consists in a general raising of all long vowels," and in 1933, in his *Essentials of English Grammar*, he restated this definition with the claim: "The greatest revolution that has taken place in the phonetic system of English is the vowel-shift." So influential were these statements, and so maximal were they in their phrasing, that they made their way into the *Oxford English Dictionary* as the first two entries for the phrase "vowel-shift," under the word *vowel*. If anyone, in short, knows anything about the history of the English language, it is the Great Vowel Shift.

From the classroom to the Web site, Jespersen's account (or some version of it) has held sway for a century. But what, exactly, happened to the sounds of English in the period from Chaucer to Shakespeare? What is the evidence of this occurrence, and can we come up with explanations—not just for the shifts in sound but for the larger, social acceptance of a new way of speaking "standard" English? Even though professional linguists have recently questioned the systemic and causal nature of Jespersen's account, why does it still possess us?

The question that possesses me is how we represent the sounds of English visually. Linguists define vowels according to their place of articulation in the mouth. They create charts, tables, and pictures that somehow make real the evanescence of the spoken word. What makes those words real, too, are the systems of writing that we use, and in an age before standardized spelling, English writers could reveal the sounds of speech changing before their eyes. For Middle English scribes, as we have seen, written evidence could mark the boundaries of dialect. Their handiwork provides us with the clues for what modern linguists call synchronic variation: the varieties of language over space. For later writers, written forms provide us with the clues for diachronic change: shifts in sound, usage, grammar, and vocabulary over time.

Unlike the historical sound changes I noted earlier, the Great Vowel Shift was not a set of local differences in speech sounds or a collection of individual distinctions between earlier and later forms of English. It was a systemic change: a change in an entire sound system, in the course of which each element of that system had an effect on, or was the result of, the change in any other element of that system. That system was the long, stressed monophthongs of Middle English. "Long" means that the vowels were held for a longer time than others; it is, in Old and Middle English, a matter of quantity, not of quality. "Stressed" means that the vowels had to be in a word's syllable that received major stress (usually, this meant the root syllable of the word). "Monophthongs" are vowels that contain only one, continuously produced sound: to put it in the terms of physical articulation, it means that the tongue and the lips remained in the same position during the production of the sound.

But the notion of systemic change also implies cause and effect. Each of these long stressed monophthongs may be said to have occupied a place in the mouth. Vowels could be high or low—that is, pronounced with the tongue high in the mouth or low in the mouth. And they could be front or back—that is, pronounced either in the front of the mouth (toward the lips) or the back (toward the throat). Linguists have come up with ways of representing the place of these vowels schematically, and much of the business of explaining the Great Vowel Shift has, in fact, gone on by coming up with visual representations of its stages (see figure 7.1). Otto Jespersen imagined this sequence as a kind of chain (see figure 7.2). Any movement of one link in this chain affected all the other links, and while Jespersen and his successors argued over what moves came first, something of a standard account soon emerged. According to this account, the first thing that happened was that the high front and back vowels, the /i/ and the /u/, became diphthongs. This means that their pronunciation changed from a pure or single sound to a double one. Over time, it appeared, these vowels added a kind of semivowel or glide to their pronunciation. In Modern English, we say something like ahh—ee for the sound descended from Middle English -i-, and aah-ooo for the sound descended from Middle English -u-. Linguists represent these modern sounds phonetically as /ai/ and /au/. By this account, Middle English words such as *bite, mite, my*, and so on changed from pure, high front vowels to diphthongs. So, too, Middle English words such as *hus, mus, lus*, and so on, changed from pure, high back vowels to diphthongs.

This change, it was argued, took a long time and passed through many different variations. But what it did, even initially, was in effect move the two high vowels out of their position. It created a kind of phonetic space, a vacuum that needed to be filled by other vowels. And so, according to the standard account, the mid-vowels of Middle English were raised. Thus the sound /e/ became /i/ and the sound /o/ became /u/. Then, the low back vowel /a/ rose to fill the position left by /e/. This also happened in many stages, but the overall effect was that Middle English words such as *name, came*, and *gate* passed through a sequence of pronunciations until they reached their modern form. Finally, the long open o sound in Middle English /ɔ/ became a long, close o /o/.

All histories of the English language—from Jespersen's of 1909, through the textbook of Albert C. Baugh and Thomas Cable (from the first edition of 1957 to the fifth of 2002), to the chapter on "Phonology and Morphology" in volume 3 of the *Cambridge History of the English Language* (published in 1999)—give some version of this process. Depending on the level of technicality, textbooks cut the distinctions finer and finer. Drawing on their examples, we can come up with a schematic presentation of the vowels from Chaucer's time to that of Shakespeare's (see figure 7.3). These charts offer valuable information. They tell us, for example, why it is that certain words rhymed in the past and do not today (for example, why Shakespeare, writing in about the year 1600, could rhyme *nature* and *creature*, or *play* and *sea*); they help us understand the nuances of literary language; and they indicate that the Great Vowel Shift, whatever it was, took centuries to run its course.

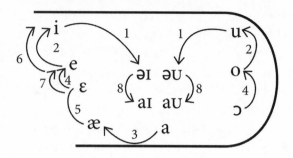

Step 1: i and u drop and become əɪ and əʊ
Step 2: e and o move up, becoming i and u
Step 3: a moves forward to æ
Step 4: ɛ becomes e, ɔ becomes o
Step 4: æ moves up to ɛ
Step 6: e moves up to i
    A new e was created in Step 4; now that e moves up to i
Step 7: ɛ moves up to e
    The new ɛ created in Step 5 now moves up
Step 8: əɪ and əʊ drop to aɪ and aʊ

FIGURE 7.1
The Great Vowel Shift

The order of these steps is largely conjectural, but it remains the standard for most histories of the English language. The illustration schematically represents the human mouth, with the front at the left and the back at the right. The positions of the vowels, as represented using the International Phonetic Alphabet, are roughly their positions in the mouth. The arrows indicate the movements of the vowel shift from Middle to Modern English. Numbers on the visualization correspond to numbers in the steps below.
Source: http://alpha.furman.edu/~mmenzer/gvs/what.htm.

But what these charts also offer is the realization that the Great Vowel Shift is something to be visualized. We need to see it in the mouth; we need, somehow, to spatialize these sounds in relation to one another. We also need to see these sounds on the written page. During this period men and women continued to write as they spoke. As urban merchants or provincial gentry learned to read and write for economic and social advancement (indeed, as it became clear that literacy was the pathway to such advancement), a culture of writing developed that took those public skills to private arenas. Secular schools and private tutors fostered a new vernacular literacy. The word "character" came to stand for both the shape of letters and the inner quality of a person.

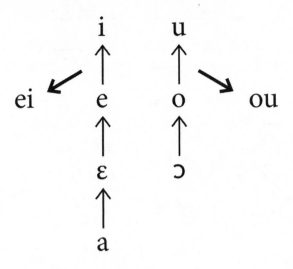

FIGURE 7.2

Jespersen's schematic diagram of the Great Vowel Shift. Jespersen imagined the vowels ranged in a kind of chain. Pressure on any one point of the chain pulled, in effect, the other vowels in the chain.

In this new literate environment, the fifteenth and the sixteenth centuries are a kind of golden age of English personal-letter writing. Families that stretched from provinces to cities kept in touch by letters. Lovers met by missives. Gifts came to be accompanied by personal inscriptions. To meet this rising social need, manuals of letter writing proliferated. They taught parents and children, lovers, diplomats, and business people how to shape themselves in writing. The letter was the place of private, as well as of public, declaration. A new intimacy developed through these epistolary skills, and the great humanist Erasmus codified these social shifts and literary traditions in his manual, *De conscribendis epistolis* (*On Writing Letters*, composed from the 1490s to the 1520s). In a particularly revelatory passage, Erasmus associates the character of handwriting with the character of the writer, and he reveals that even though the letter is a written form, it has the quality of a performance.

For this ought to be the character of the letter (*epistolae caracter*): as if you were whispering in a corner with a dear friend, not shouting in the theater, or otherwise somewhat unrestrainedly. For we commit

1400	1500	1600	Modern English	KeyWords
i	ei	ɛi	ai	bite
e	i	i	i	meet
ɛ	ɛ	e	i	meat
a	a	ɛ	ei	mate
u	ou	ɔu	au	out
o	u	u	u	boot
ɔ	ɔ	ɔo	əo	boat

FIGURE 7.3

The Great Vowel Shift, illustrated according to the changing pronunciation of representative words, ca. 1400–1700.

many things to letters, which it would be shameful to express openly in public.

What is, then, the character of English? How do writers express not just their personalities or their intentions but their sense of themselves as vernacular characters? Throughout the fifteenth and the sixteenth centuries, large English families such as the Pastons, the Celys, the Stonors, and the Lisles kept in touch over generations through the art of letter writing, and what they committed to their pages is the evidence for the changing character of the vernacular.

The Pastons in particular provide brilliant examples at all these levels. Most specifically, the spellings in their letters illustrate how members of the family used the conventions of Middle English spelling to represent changes in pronunciation that we now see, in retrospect, as features of the Great Vowel Shift. Thus, throughout their mid-fifteenth-century letters, we may find in spellings such as *myte* for the word "meet," or *hyre* for the word "hear," the use of *y* to indicate the high front vowel /i:/. Such spellings evidence that the old, Middle English open and close *e* (the phonemes /e:/ and /ɛ/) would have been raised and fronted. Spellings such as *abeyd* for the word "abide" indicate that the Middle English /i:/ sound has become a diphthong (probably pronounced, at this time, as /ei/). The word "our" is often spelled *aur*, "out" appears as *owt*, and "house" appears as *hows*, all indicating that the Middle English high back vowel /u:/ has diphthongized. Spellings such as *mayd* for the word "made" have been taken to indicate that the Middle English long back vowel /a/ has been raised and fronted (at this point, probably pronounced as a kind of diphthong, something like /ɛi/ or /ei/).

Behind these ad hoc spellings we can see people coping with their language changing in their own lifetimes. More than just illustrating details of linguistic use, these letters reveal writers measuring their writing against new standards of speech or spelling. They represent encounters with vernacular authority. But to appreciate their understanding of vernacular authority more broadly—to hear these writers, as it were, whispering in the corners to friends and family—we need to look closely at their letters in full. Take, for example, Agnes Paston, the brilliant and affluent matriarch of the family, who wrote to her son John in a letter dated October 29, 1465. It has the rich simplicity of a biblical homily, tempered by allusions to the poetry of Chaucer and popular proverb. It hews closely, as many of the Paston letters do, to the conventions of medieval vernacular epistolarity: the greetings, the signatures, the forms of address are all formulaic (and, indeed, were found in many of the manuals of letter-writing circulating at the time). Still, it remains a deeply personal appropriation of the conventions of written English.

Sonne, I grete ʒow wele and lete ʒow wete þat, for as myche as ʒoure broþir Clement leteth me wete þat ʒe desire feythfully my blyssyng, þat blyssyng þat I prayed ʒoure fadir to gyffe ʒow þe laste day þat euer he spakke, and þe blyssyng of all seyntes vndir heven, and myn, mote come to ʒow all dayes and tymes. And thynke verily non oþer but þat ʒe haue it, and shal haue it with þat þat I fynde ʒow kynde and wyllyng to þe welfare of ʒoure breþeren.

Be my counseyle, dyspose ʒoure-selfe as myche as ʒe may to haue lesse to do in þe worlde. ʒoure fadyr sayde, 'In lityl bysynes lyeth myche reste.' Þis worlde is but a þorugh-fare of woo, and whan we departe þer-fro, riʒth nouʒght bere with vs but oure good dedys and ylle. And þer knoweth no man how soon God woll clepe hym, and þer-for it is good for euery creature to be redy. Quom God vysyteth, him he louyth.
And as for ʒoure breþeren, þei wylle I knowe certeynly laboren all þat in hem lyeth for ʒow.

Oure Lorde haue ʒow in his blyssed kepying, body and soule.

Writen at Norwyche þe xxix day of Octobyr.

By ʒoure modir A. P.

[Son, I greet you well, and I want you to know that, on account of the fact that your brother Clement had me know that you desire faithfully my blessing, that blessing that I prayed your father to give you on the last day that he ever spoke, and the blessing of all saints under heaven, and my own, may come to you at all days and times. And believe truly that none other than you have it, and shall have it as long as I find you kind and inclined to the welfare of your brothers. Take my advice: act in such a way as you may have less to do with world. Your father said, "In little public activity there lies great ease." This world is nothing but a thoroughfare of woe, and when we leave it, we take nothing with us but our good and bad deeds. And no man knows how soon God will call him, and for that reason it is good for everyone to be ready. Whomever God visits, he loves. And as for your brothers, they will, I know, work hard such that everything they do will be for you. May our Lord have you in his blessed keeping, body and soul. Written in Norwich on the 29th day of October.]

At the linguistic level, Agnes's letter is a mix of seemingly advanced and conservative forms. First off, it appears that the language is moving to accept the *you* forms as the standard second-person pronoun. Throughout the Paston correspondence, in fact, everyone addresses one another using this old, formal form. The few exceptions are reserved for moments of true anger or contempt, and reading through the correspondence we can sense not that this is a particularly formal family but that *you* forms of the second person were becoming, by the close of the fifteenth century, the normative, or unmarked forms of address. Some of Agnes's spellings, too, indicate changes in pronunciation or particulars of local dialect (for example, spelling "blessing" as *blyssyng*, and "much" as *myche* suggests that the short -*e*- and the short -*u*- sounds of Middle English were similar in her speech). She is also spelling the word "right" as *riȝth* to indicate the new pronunciation without the velar fricative (the sound indicated by linguists as /x/ and found in, say, modern German *Ich*). But this letter also shows some old-fashioned forms. The third-person pronoun is *hem*, rather than *them*; plurals of verbs end in -*en* (*laboren*); and there is a markedly un-French vocabulary in this letter (*counseyle* stands out as one of the very few words of obvious French origin).

What we might say is that this letter is an essay in vernacularity itself: an engagement with the everyday Englishness of English as it comes through proverb and quotation. "In lityl bysnes lyeth mych reste." Agnes introduces this maxim as a saying of the boy's father, but these are the words not just of the father of the family but the father of English poetry. In Chaucer's little poem, "Truth" (by all accounts the most widely circulated of his lyrics in the fifteenth century), he advises: "Gret rest stant in little besiness." (I note, in passing, that in one textual tradition of "Truth," the word "Gret" is replaced by "Meche": MS Corpus Christi Oxford 203.) And in the "Knight's Tale" from his *Canterbury Tales*, Chaucer has Egeus, the old father of King Theseus, give the son this advice for living:

> This world nys but a thurghfare ful of wo,
> And we been pilgrymes, passynge to and fro.

These lines find their echo in Agnes's advice, too. So at her most parental, then, she turns to some of the most famously parental and advisory of Chaucer's lines, not simply to give counsel to her son but to appropriate the voice of vernacular counsel itself: the voice of Chaucer.

Now, compare Agnes's straightforward and affirmative vernacularity with the complex syntax and polysyllables of Agnes's son John, who writes on June 27, 1465, to his own wife, Margaret (whom he addresses as "cosyn"), about their son. Here is an excerpt from his letter.

> *Item, as for yowre sone: I lete yow wete I wold he dede wel, but I vnder-*
> *stand in hym no dispocicion of polecy ne of gouernans as a man of*
> *the werld owt to do, but only leuith, and euer hath, as man disolut,*
> *with-owt any prouicion, ne that he besijth hym nothinge to vnderstand*
> *swhech materis as a man of lyuelode must nedis vnderstond. Ne I*
> *vnderstond nothing of what dispocicion he porposith to be, but only I*
> *kan think he wold dwell ageyn in yowr hows and myn, and ther ete and*
> *drink and slepe.*

[Item: as for your son—I want you to know that I wished he acted well, but I find in him no habit of good sense nor any sense of self-control as a man of the world ought to have, but he only lives, and he always as, as a dissolute man, without any foresight, and he acts in such a way that he clearly does not understand anything of such matters as a man who makes a living should understand. Nor do I understand anything of what kind of person he sets out to be, but I can only think that he wants to live again in your house and mine and eat, and drink, and sleep there.]

There is more of interest here than sound shift. When John writes about the behavior of a "man of the werld," he uses the resonant vocabulary of French legalism: "I vnderstand in hym no dispocicion of polecy ne of gouernans." His son may live, but he does so "disolut, with-owt any prouicion." He claims not to understand "what dispocicion he porposith to be," but he can only imagine that he would simply like to live in their house and only "ete and drink and slepe." He goes on to reflect on just what makes a good upbringing, recognizing that every poor man who has brought up his children to the age of twelve expects to be helped and gain profit from them and every gentleman hopes that his servants would aid in that growth. As for your son, he writes to his wife, "ye knowe well he neuer stode yow ne me in profite, ese, or help to valew of on grote." These sentences arc from elaborate French to basic English. They set up high expectations, only to dash them. From the rich polysyllables of politeness, we end with the blunt monosyllables of failure: eat and drink and sleep. From the claims of parental expectation ("euery gentilman that hath discrecion"), we wind up with a child who isn't worth a groat.

But there are difficulties, too, for in this letter (written in John Paston's own hand), we can see the writer struggling with language, looking for the right expression, seeking the correct character of description. One particularly telling example appears in the line about his son. Norman Davis, in his standard edition of the *Paston Letters and Papers*, prints the text:

As a man disolut, with-owt any prouicion.

The word *disolut* (dissolute) appears, in his edition, in half brackets, indicating that it is an interlinear addition to the letter. Davis's notes make clear that John first wrote "as a man fownd of." Apparently, John was going to write that his son was a man fond of something (or maybe even fond of nothing). But he crossed that out, and over it wrote "disolut." Then he wrote "hauing nothing" next to it, but crossed that out, too. John's self-correcting replaces familiar, vernacular expressions with newer terms of French or Latin origin. Instead of being fond of something, John's son is "dissolute," a word that first appears in the early fifteenth century, originally from the Latin, *dissolutus* (untied, set apart). The use of the word meaning "unrestrained in behavior," or "wanton," is not attested until 1460, while the sense of being morally loose or debauched (what the *OED* calls "the current sense") is not attested until 1513. Clearly, John Paston's use is very new, a word emerging into vernacular consciousness. So, too, the everyday phrase "hauing nothing" becomes "with-owt any prouicion." *Provision* came from the Latin, by way of the French, and originally connoted the ability to see ahead, to plan for the future. From this sense, the word's meaning extends to embrace those things that we provide for the future (i.e., provisions). The word emerges, according to the *OED*, in the first third of the fifteenth century but does not take on its modern, extended meaning until the end of the century. Again, for Paston writing in 1465, it is a new word.

John Paston has, in these lines, effectively translated a commonplace, vernacular expression into an exotic, new vocabulary. What he is saying is that his son lives from day to day, without making any plans for the future—and he says it in a language whose imported newness, whose polysyllabic technicality, not only damns the son but elevates the father. His letter, in short, is a study in character: a self-presentation of his own, as well as a damning criticism of his son's. John comes off, here, as a figure of both social and linguistic authority, a man of the word as well as of the world.

And such is the character of English. For the changing shape of the vernacular, by the close of the fifteenth century, was as a language of men and women of the world: people of learning, commerce, literacy, and experience. Why did the Great Vowel Shift happen? The best explanations seem to me to be less about the word than about the world. As French began to disappear as the prestige language for England, some form of English itself had to emerge as the social standard. As dialects came into contact in the cities, different pronunciations vied for social prominence. The sounds of English may have changed in the fifteenth and sixteenth centuries as part of a larger, social process of replacing a lost prestige *language* with a prestige *dialect*—a dialect not keyed to region but to social class, to education, or to wealth. As Matthew Giancarlo puts it in a recent critique of the philological debates around the Great Vowel Shift: "The 'standardization' described by the GVS may simply have been the social fixation upon one variant among several dialectical options available in each case, a variant selected for reasons of community preference or by the external force of printing standardization and not as a result of a wholesale phonetic shift."

We want, it seems, to hold on to the Great Vowel Shift not as a myth of nineteenth-century philologists but as a fact of English history. We want to see it—along with the Norman Conquest, say—as a defining phenomenon that makes English what it is today. Our histories of the English language, in the end, are histories in search of character: the character of speech, as well as speakers, the essence of our linguistic communities.

England's first printer, William Caxton, recognized this. Few were as worldly as Caxton. Born in Kent in the early 1420s, he became a successful cloth merchant (a mercer), did business in the Low Countries, rose to social and financial prominence in the circles of the Burgundian court, and eventually took on the new trade of printing as a source of further economic gain. He returned to England in the mid 1470s to set up his printing press in Westminster, the seat of English government, and he was soon printing both literary and official documents for commissioning patrons as well as individual book buyers. Towards the end of his life, in 1490, he came to print an English translation of a French prose version of the *Aeneid*, known as the *Eneydos*. Into what version of the language should he translate it, he asks himself? "Certainly our langage now vsed varyeth ferre from that whiche was vsed and spoken what I was borne." The Great Vowel Shift was changing English in a lifetime. And dialects were still competing for mutual comprehension. He goes on, in the Preface to the *Eneydos*:

> For we englysshe men ben borne vnder the domynacyon of the mone, which is neuer stedfast but euer wauerynge wexynge one season and waneth & dyscreaseth another season. And that comyn englysshe that is spoken in one shyre varyeth from a nother. . . . [It] happened that certain marchauntes were in a shippe in tamyse [i.e., on the Thames] for to haue sayled ouer the see into selande and for lacke of wynde, they taryed ate forlond, and wente to land for to refreshe them: And one of theym . . . cam in to an hows and axed for mete: and specially he axed after eggys; And the goode wife answered, that she coude speke no frenshe. And the marchaunt was angry, for he also coude speke no frenshe, but wolde haue hadde egges and she vnderstode hym not. And than at laste a nother sayd that he wolde haue eyre, then the good wyf sayd that she vnderstod him wel.

> [For we Englishmen are born under the control of the moon, which is never the same but always wavering—waxing at one time and waning and decreasing at another time. And the common English that is spoken in one county varies from that of another. . . . It happened that certain merchants were in a ship in the Thames River planning to sail across the Channel into Zeeland, and because of a lack of wind they had to wait on the coast, and so they went onto land to refresh themselves. And one of them . . . came to a house and asked for food;

in particular, he asked for eggs. And the good woman of the house answered that she could speak no French. And the merchant was angry, because he could speak no French, but he wanted eggs and she didn't understand him. At last, another man said that what he wanted was "eyre," and then the good wife said she understood him clearly.]

The word "eggs" had become, in the London standard of the late fifteenth century, the accepted plural form. But it was, in its dialect origin, a Northern form. The word "eyren" was the plural form descended from Southern Old English, and it remained the accepted word in parts of rural Kent (where these sailors have run aground). "What sholde a man in thyse dayes now wryte, egges or eyren?" Caxton asks. It is "harde to playse euery man by cause of dyuersite & chaunge of langage."

The point of Caxton's musings is to recognize that English is a language of the world: that we must get by in our speech, whether our goal is to buy eggs or translate literature. Much like John Paston's letter on his son, Caxton's preface to the *Eneydos* is an essay on relationships of character and language. And, like Paston, Caxton makes his verbal choices carefully. His book will be, in the end, "not for euery rude and vnconnynge man to see but to clerkys and very gentylmen that vnderstand gentylnes and science." The changing nature of the English language in the fifteenth century pressured those old relationships of character and language, and that character had as much to do with the written look as with the spoken sound of English.

Tracing *-ea-* and *-ee-* Spellings in the Great Vowel Shift.

Words that are now spelled with an *-ea-* and pronounced with the /i/ sound come from Middle English words that had the sound /ɛ:/. Linguists call this a long open *e*. This sound was raised and fronted in the course of the Great Vowel Shift. Words of this kind include *meat, feat, beat, sea,* and so on.

Words that are now spelled with an *-ee-* and pronounced with the /i/ sound come from Middle English words that had the sound /e:/. Linguists call this a long close *e*. This sound was also raised and fronted in the course of the Great Vowel Shift. Words of this kind include *meet, feet, beet, see,* and so on.

It is important to note that these two groups of words did not rhyme in Middle English poetry. It is also important to note that certain words that do not rhyme today did rhyme at various times during the course of the Great Vowel Shift. Thus, Shakespeare can rhyme the words *nature* and *creature*; they were both probably pronounced with the /ɛ:/ sound. He can also rhyme the words *play* and *sea*, also probably on /ɛ:/ or on /e:/.

In the course of the Great Vowel Shift, only four words (and one proper name) that had the long open *e* and were spelled -*ea*- did not change their pronunciation. They were *great, break, steak, yea,* and *Reagan.* No one seems to know why.

CHAPTER 8

Chancery, Caxton, and the
Making of English Prose

"IN THE MODERN AND PRESENT MANNER OF WRITING," wrote John Hart in his *Orthographie* of 1569, "there is such confusion and disorder, as it may be accounted rather a kind of ciphering, or such a darke kinde of writing, as the best and readiest wit that euer hath bene could, or that is or shal be, can or may, by the only gift of reason, attaine to the ready and perfite reading thereof, without a long and tedious labour" (2). By the middle of the sixteenth century, English writing had effectively divorced itself from speech. True, personal communication still went on in a haphazard way, with spellings and word forms often in ad hoc imitation of the sounds of regional or personal pronunciation. But the professionals of English scribal life (and, by the early sixteenth century, the printers) had developed systems of orthography that split script from speech. English, in essence, was becoming opaque to itself. For while the changes of the Great Vowel Shift had made the writers of the medieval past unreadable to those of the early modern present, the conventions of spelling had made speakers of the present mute to anyone who did not know the language. In John Hart's words, the inability to "write as we speake" has left English with "no fit Carracts, markes or letters" through which to present our "voices, soundes or breaths" (6).

Among the many changes wrought on English writing from the time of Chaucer to the time of Hart, the development of "Chancery Standard" had the most vivid and most long-lasting effect. Originating in the household of the medieval English kings, Chancery emerged out of the mix of domestic administration to come to control the production of official documents by the middle of the fourteenth century. It was a kind of "Secretariat of State" (in the words of the great historian, T. F. Tout), which not only produced texts but trained scribes to write them. From the 1380s until the 1450s, Chancery taught a house style of spelling, grammatical forms, lexical usage, and idiom that characterized the papers coming out of many of the royal offices (those of the Signet, the Privy Seal, even of Parliament itself). Chancery, too, taught a house style of handwriting, originating in the scripts used for European business and politics and adapted for quick letter formation in English. The very look of English was changing.

But in that look lay certain values: clarity and speed, directness and flow. Letters and official documents needed to be written quickly and legibly. The prose of those documents needed to be understood by readers coming from different regions of the country or with different levels of literacy. And, as most of the documents in Chancery English were really kinds of letters—addresses, petitions, legal requests—that prose needed to be unambiguously direct. The writings that emerge out of this time hold up, it might be said, a public and official mirror image to the private selves of people like the Pastons. Behind them lies a conception of vernacular character and the character of the vernacular.

Chancery English also had an impact on the rise of printed documents in Britain. When Caxton set up his printshop in Westminster, he located his business not in the commercial part of London (the old City) but the site of court. Caxton adopted Chancery-style spellings and word forms when he came to print not just official or intellectual texts but literary ones as well. His early volumes of the English authors Chaucer, Gower, Lydgate, Malory, and others, calibrated themselves not to the older spelling habits of the scribe but to the newer conventions of Chancery. Caxton's achievement was to take a standard of official writing for a literary standard. In this move, he made literature, in turn, fit entertainment and instruction for the public man—the "clerkys and very gentylmen" to whom he had addressed the *Eneydos* in 1490.

The scholar John Hurt Fisher has done more than almost anyone to call attention to the place of Chancery in the making of modern English, and his researches have made available a wealth of sources little known to students of a generation ago. In his *Anthology of Chancery English*, Fisher lays out the details of the language, characterizes forms of writing, and edits and publishes a collection of letters, papers, and parliamentary proceedings, all of which illustrate English at its most official in the fifteenth century. One of the best and most succinct examples of this kind of document, and one of the best for illustrating features of Chancery English, is a petition of William Walysby, treasurer to Queen Katherine (the mother of Henry VI), of 1437. Like many of these kinds of texts, this is a sort of letter: salutation, greeting, exposition, explanation, valediction, attestation, and signature all follow in sequence according to set rules. Fisher presents the text as follows:

R h nous auouns graunte

Please it to the Kyng oure souerain Lord of youre Benigne grace to graunte to youre humble seruant and Oratoure sir William Walysby Tresorer with the Quene youre moder the denerye of hastynges in the dyose of Chichester the which Prestewyke Clerke of youre parlement late had on who sowle god assoile And youre saide Oratour shal pray god for you.

[in another hand] letter ent feust faite a Westministre le viije. jeur de November. 1an &c xve.

[King Henry we have granted this

May it please the king our sovereign lord out of your benign grace to grant to your humble servant and orator, Sir William Walysby, Treasurer with the Queen, your mother, the deanery of Hastings in the diocese of Chicester, which appointment the clerk of your parliament had recently had, may God bless his soul. And your said orator will pray to God for you.

This letter prepared at Westminster on the 8th day of November, in the 15th year (i.e., of the reign of Henry VI).]

Even though this is an English document, the opening annotation is in French, as is the dating at the end. The fluidity of style and syntax of this petition owes much to the patterns of French legal prose. In fact, much early English prose before the time of Chancery seems largely unreadable. Chaucer's *Treatise on the Astrolabe* is hard to parse (and was most likely equally so for his contemporaries), and many bits of Middle English prose seem caught up on grammatical confusions, shifts of form, or too much repetition. Fisher compares the fluency of texts such as the Walysby petition with earlier prose exemplified by the 1388 petition of the Mercers:

And lordes, by yowre leue, owre lyge lordes commaundment to simple & unkonnyng men is a gret thing to ben vsed so famuler-ilich withouten need, for they, unwyse to saue it, mowe lightly ther ayeins forfait.

The reader struggles to discern just what the words "they" and "it" refer to. In the middle of the sentence, the use of the phrase "withouten need" implies a certain grammatical relationship; but by the sentence's end, the phrase "theyr ayeins" implies a different one. This is technically known as anacoluthon, the shift in grammatical structure in midsentence, and it still characterizes English prose well into Caxton's day. Notice, for example, his remark in the *Eneydos* Preface: "the mone, which is neuer stedfaste but euer wauerynge wexynge on season and waneth & decreseth." Caxton shifts from participial phrasing to simple, active verbs, apparently without much concern. But it all makes this hard to read.

By contrast, the Walysby petition, and most of the Chancery documents of its kind, are models of directness. Relative clauses are regular here. The references are unambiguous. Simple Subject–Object–Verb word order is in control. Even though expressions such as "the which" and "your saide ora-tour" are archaic to us, their references are clear. The only obvious howler, at least to modern readers, is the phrase, "shal pray God for you," which is most likely an old dative construction without the necessary preposition (it should be, in other words, "shall pray to God for you," but this is most likely a formula and not fully representative of current usage).

From this passage, too, we can find features of the Chancery Standard. First, there is the beginning of the spelling -*ig*- used for the long /i/ sound from French. The word "benign" is spelled *benigne* (but notice that this form is not consistent; the word "sovereign" is spelled phonetically, as *souerain*). Notice too, here, the spelling *saide*, at heart the modern English spelling for the past tense of the verb "to say." The Middle English spelling would have been *seide*. This may seem an arbitrary and a minor feature, but it indicates that Chancery scribes were being taught to spell according to conventions, rather than according to personal pronunciation or historical precedent. Another example of this new spelling convention is the form *had*, where Middle English would pretty consistently have offered *hadde*. Infinitives have lost their -*en* ending and are now indicated by having an unmarked form of the verb following the preposition *to*. Thus, we see the phrase "to graunte," not "graunten."

As I read through the range of materials in Fisher's *Anthology*, other fea-tures of Chancery spelling and usage emerge. Old, nonphonetic spellings seem to be preserved by choice: *high, ought, slaughter, right, though, nought*. We know from other examples of fifteenth-century writing (most notably, the Paston letters), that the -*gh*- spelling was no longer pronounced as the Middle English velar fricative /x/. The Pastons themselves often spelled such words in ways that reflected the new pronunciation. But the Chancery scribes did not.

For all its claims to standardization, however, Chancery does preserve some regional dialect forms. But it does so in unexpected ways. It is clear that at least some of Chancery's scribes came from the north of England. Such young men would have been part of the great, fifteenth-century migration of the children of gentry, commercial, or rural families to the metropolis. Their regional preferences appear, and soon become codified, in Chancery Standard. Thus, the ending of the adverb takes on the Northern-dialect form, -ly, rather than the Midlands or Southern form, -lich. A good example of this shift in process is illustrated in the 1429 petition of William Pope, which begins: "Vnto þe kynge oure full souerain lorde, Biseches full lowelich and mekelich youre humble seruant" (Fisher, Richardson, and Fisher, 154). *Lowelich* and *mekelich* are striking here; but at the end of the petition, the scribe is writing *fully*, and not "fulliche." Chancery scribes also preferred the Northern ending of -s over the Midlands and Southern -eth for the third-person singular of verbs. In the petition from which I just quoted, we can see how, even in the same phrase as the scribe uses the Midlands -lich adverbial ending, he uses the -s form for the third-person singular (*Biseches*, instead of "Bisecheth").

Caxton, as I have noted, drew on Chancery English for his forms and spellings. "We English men *ben* borne," he writes in the *Eneydos* Preface, a signature use of the Chancery form of the verb "to be" (and a Northernism). He uses -ly endings for his adverbs, drops the old prefatory ge- or y- for participles (also a Chancery habit), and he generally relies on a Subject–Object–Verb word order. He uses spellings consistent with Chancery habit: *almyghty* (for "almighty"); *lyke* (for "like," and not the Midlands *lich*); *right*, or *ryght* (preserving the -gh- as Chancery scribes did); and *souerayn* (notice here, as in the Walysby petition, the convention of not spelling the word with the -gn-).

By adapting a Chancery model for his printed English, Caxton not only helped to promulgate an official writing standard for wider dissemination. He also effectively translated Middle English literature for his own time. Look, for example, at the opening of Chaucer's *Canterbury Tales* in Caxton's 1483 edition:

Whan that Apryll with hys shuris sote
The droughte of marche hath percyd the rote
And bathyd euery veyne in suche lycour

Of whyche vertue engendryd is the flour
Whanne Zepherus eke with hys sote breth
Enspyrid hath in euery holte and heth
The tendyr croppis / and the yong sonne
Hath in the ram half hys cours y ronne
And smale foulis make melody
That slepyn al nyght with opyn eye
So prykyth hem nature in her corages
Than longyn folk to gon on pylgremages
And palmers to seche straunge strondis
To ferue halowys couthe in sundry londis
And specially fro euery shyris ende
Of engelond to Cauntirbury thy wende
The holy blysful martir for to seke
That them hath holpyn when they were seke

For any reader of the poem schooled in the editions based on the great Ellesemere Manuscript, Caxton's lines will seem just slightly off. For example,
Caxton prints, in line three, *suche lycour*, rather than "swich licour," and his
choice is a Chancery one (*such* or *suche* was the preferred form in Chancery
documents to *swiche*). While Caxton does preserve the older, Middle English
plural verb ending in *-n* (*slepyn, longyn, holpyn*), he neglects to do so in the
line, "And smale foulis *make* melodye"—again, a Chancery habit. His plural
nouns end more frequently in *-is* than in the older *-es* (*shouris, croppis, foulis,
strondis*), also a feature of many Chancery documents. And, on occasion,
Caxton substitutes the newer, Chancery inspired (and ultimately Northern
dialect–derived) *them* for the older *hem* form of the third-person plural pronoun (he has, "That them hath holpyn," while the Ellesemere Manuscript
and the most reliable early texts have, "That hem hath holpen"). But there
are other features of his text, even in these few opening lines, that cannot
be explained simply as Chancery forms. Chaucer's line that establishes the
astrological dating for the poem's opening—"Hath in the ram his halve
course yronne"—seems, in Caxton, both to misscan and misread: "Hath in
the ram half hys cours y ronne." So, too, the final line of the first sentence
seems off in Caxton: "That them hath holpyn when they were seke." In
these two examples, Caxton's lines seem, for lack of a better term, more
modern than Chaucer. While they may not scan as precisely as the lines
derived from the Ellesemere scribe, they avoid Middle English idiom in
favor of a phrasing that, from our perspective, simply looks more modern.

And it is precisely this modern look of Caxton that raises the issue. For by modernizing his texts, Caxton did make earlier literatures more readable for current audiences. But what he did, too, in the process, was efface historical forms. This is the paradox of Chancery and Caxton's English: the preservation of old spellings that no longer matched pronunciation; but, at the same time, the displacement of forms familiar from the Midlands Middle English of the age of Chaucer. This paradox, as well, governs the look of Caxton's books. For Caxton based his typefaces not on new forms of letters but on the handwriting of the Flemish scribes who had produced the manuscripts he used and read in Europe. English print looks like handwriting, and early printed books were as handsome or as artistically designed as manuscripts.

More than any technical innovation, or really even more than any focused linguistic standard, Caxton's achievement lies in the development of English prose. The prologues and epilogues he wrote for his editions wrest narrative and criticism out of observation and hearsay. His Preface to the *Eneydos* is really a set of stories. Sitting alone, he discovers the book of the *Eneydos* lying among the piles that clutter his shop. He tries to translate its French, but is unsure about the dialect and diction into which the book should go. He turns to the abbot of Westminster, an authority both ecclesiastical and linguistic, who shows him some books in "olde englysshe" in his possession: they "were more lyke to dutche than englysshe." Then we get the reflections on language change and variation; the story of the mercers trying to buy eggs in Kent; and the claims for his own choice of English here. In the end, however, Caxton must turn to another authority, the poet John Skelton, "late created poete laureate in the vnyuersite of oxenford," as the one who will "ouersee and correcte" the production of the *Eneydos*. Caxton closes the preface with a commendation to the newly born Prince Arthur, Prince of Wales, and to King Henry VII himself.

The work is done, the printed books have all been made, and Caxton, nearing the close of his life, surveys his past when something new appears. The story told here is a story that begins at the beginning of all literary history, with Virgil and the classics, and it takes us to the present moment of a living poet laureate. We move from the city to the country, from the church to the court, from the print shop to the university, from Kent to Oxford. Caxton's prologues and epilogues are full of stories (his preface to the 1483 reprinting of the *Canterbury Tales* recounts how one of his customers brought one of his own father's manuscripts of the poem back to Caxton, in order for the printer to prepare a new and corrected edition). Such prose may be personal, but it bears all the legacy of Chancery. For as we read through many of its petitions and documents, wills, claims, and legal actions, we can see English public narrative emerging from the private life. The Pastons told tales, too, but most of their letters read like inventories: lists of points, each signaled by the word "item," that the letter writer wishes to address. The model for this kind of familiar letter is, in fact, the household list: the personal account, the record of events, or costs, or services. But for the scribes of Chancery, or for Caxton, the world was always there.

And it is there for us as well. If Caxton comes upon a text at random, so, too, I might do so. Coming upon Fisher's *Anthology*, I find a text as rich with language and adventure as Caxton's *Eneydos*. In 1437, Isabell, the wife of John Boteler of Lancashire, was brutally raped and abducted by a certain William Pulle, and she petitioned Parliament to punish him. In the hands of the Chancery scribe who wrote it, this petition becomes more than a legal document. It reads as an essay in the arts of narrative.

To the right sage and full wise Comunes of this present parlement

Besecheth meekly your right sage and wyse discrecions Isabell that was the wife of Iohn Boteler of Beausey in the shire of Lancaster Knyght to consider that where one william Pulle late of wyrall in the Shire of chestre Gentilman the moneday next afore the fest of Seynt Iame the Appostell last passed the seid Isabell being ate Beausey aforesaid with force and armes in riotouse manere with grete number of other mysdoers the house of the seid Besecher ate Beausey aforesaid breke ageynst the peas of our soueraigne lorde the kyng And there the seid Besecher felonousely and most horribly rauysshed and her naked except hir kirtyll and hir smoke ledde with hym into the wilde and esolate places of wales of the whiche rape he tofore the kynges Iustices ate lancastre is endited And in wales aforesaid and in other secrete places her kept till nowe late that itt liked the kyng oure soueraigne lorde of his special grace ate the besechyng of diuers of the ffrendes of the seid Besecher shewyng to hym the seid grete and horrible felonye and offences to giff in commaundement aswell by his commission vndir his grete seal as by his letters of his piuey seal. as well to diuers lordes as to other to take and bring the seid William Pulle and other of the seid mysdoers into the presence of oure seid soueraigne lorde. And also to take the seid Besecher and her to putte into safe warde into the tyme that itt liked the kyng in other wise for her to ordeigne wheruppon the seid William Pulle perceyuyng the seid commaundement hym withdrewe and absented into desert and other secrete places in wales and other Countrees where the kynges writt renneth noght: so that he in no wise by the seid Commissioners as yitt may be take notwithstondyng that the seid Commissioners haue done thair diligence hym to haue take in alle that thay in any wise godely might doo. And so itt is that Thomas Stanley knight one of the seide Commissioners nowe late ate Birkhede in the seid Shire of Chestrre the seid Besecher fonde and her brought to Chestre and putte in warde. Please itt to your seid wise discrecions considering these premises to pray the kyng our soueraigne lorde to oredeigne by auctorite of this present parlement a writt of proclamation oute of his Chauncellarie of lancastre direct to the Shirref of the same Shire to do proclayme in the tovne of lan- castre ate euery marketyday within two wekes next folowyng aftir the date of the seid writt that the seid wlliam Pulle Rauysshour appier afore the Iustices of our seid soueraigne lorde of his Countee palen- tine the next Session there to be holden next aftir the seid proclama- cion made to answer of the seid felonyes wherof he afore the seid Iustices is endited by what so euer name the seid William be called or endited the seid writt to be returned ate the seid Session before the seid Iustices And if he appier not ate the seid Session: that than he stand atteint of high Tresoun by the same auctorite. Considering that the seid rauysshyng is done in more horrible wise and with more heynouse violence than any hath be sene or knawen before this tyme And that the seid William Rauysshour is and of long tyme hat be outelawed of felonye for mannes dethe by him foule murdred and slayn not charging the execution therof And that for the love of god and in werk of charitee.

[To the very thoughtful and wise gathering of this present parlia- ment: Isabell, who was the wife of John Butler of Beausey in Lancast- ershire, beseeches meekly your very thoughtful and wise discretion, to consider (the following case): that of a certain William Pulle, formerly of Wirrall in Chestershire, a Gentleman, on next Monday before the feast of Saint James the Apostle has passed—(that he) attacked the said Isabell living at Beusey forcibly and with arms in a riotous manner and with a great number of other criminals in her own house in Beusey; that he broke the peace of our sovereign lord the king; and that there he feloniously and most horribly raped the said beseecher (Isabel) while she was naked except for her skirt and smock, and then led her with him into the wild and desolate places of Wales, and of which rape he is accused before the king's justices at Lancaster. And in this same Wales and in other secret places he kept her until recently, when it pleased the king our sovereign lord—on account of his special grace and through the beseeching of many different friends of the said beseecher showing to them the aforesaid great and horrible felony and offences—to command, by the authority of his great seal and also by letters written under the office of the Privy Seal, to several different lords and some others to take and bring the said William Pulle and the other said misdoers into the presence of our aforesaid sovereign lord. And (the king) also (commanded) that the said beseecher be taken and put into safe keeping until the time that it pleased the king or until she saw fit to have it different; whereupon the said William Pulle, hearing about this commandment, disappeared and withdrew into deserted and other secret places in Wales and in other lands where the king's power did not extend—(and he did this) so that he would not be apprehended in any manner by the said commissioners, even though these said commissioners have done everything in their power to apprehend him. And for this reason Thomas Stanley, knight, and one of the said commissioners now recently of Birkhede in Chestershire, found the said beseecher and brought her to Chester and put her in safe keeping. May it please your (i.e., Parliament's) wise discretion in considering these activities to pray to the king our sovereign lord to order by the authority of this present parliament a writ of proclamation coming out of his Chancery of Lancaster directly to the sheriff of this same shire to proclaim in the town of Lancaster at every market day over the two weeks following the date of this said writ that the said William Pulle rapist appear before the justices of our said sovereign lord of his county palentine (i.e., local justices with royal privileges) the next session to be held there after the said proclamation made in response to these said felonies, so that he—by the name of William or whatever other name he is called by or charged by—be called before the said session, according to the said writ, and before the said justices. And if he does not appear at the said session, then let it be that he stands charged with high treason by the same authority, because this said rape was done in a more horrible manner and with more heinous violence than any other that has been seen or known about before this time. And let it be that the said William rapist be outlawed, both now and for a long time, on the charge of felony for the death of a man foully murdered and slain, not charging the execution of it. And let all of this be done for the love of God and as an act of charity.

For any reader, medieval or modern, this is a difficult document. Its sentences are long and grammatically confusing; its vocabulary is highly specialized; its patterns of reference (*the said* this, *the said* that) anticipate the easily parodiable legalese of the modern court. Nonetheless, we can make sense of it and, even more, recognize its verbal accomplishment.

William Pulle abducts Isabell and takes her into the wild and desolate places of Wales. He rapes her, brutally, while she is naked except for her skirt and smock. He then tries to hide out in other deserted and secret places in Wales and in other areas where the king's power does not reach. The power of this story lies in the ability of English prose both to present a legal matter and to tell a tale. Look at the judgmental vocabulary here: *riotouse, felonousely, horribley, wild, desolate, secrete.* The word "felonousely" appears in English, as far as the *OED* can tell, for the first time in this very document: while "felonous" appears in use from Chaucer on, it is clear that what this Chancery writer has done is nothing less than coin a new term (I note in passing, too, those characteristic Chancery *-ly* adverbial endings throughout). "Horribley," too, though first appearing in the mid-fourteenth century, takes on by the early fifteenth a sense of bodily distress, of something so awful as to make one shiver. "Riotouse" connotes, throughout late Middle English, the sense of wanton living, of dissipation. Now, compare these relatively new, polysyllabic words, with the old monosyllables of dress. Isabell is "naked except [for] hir kirtyll and hir smoke." There is an almost biblical purity to these lines, a vernacular straightforwardness that recalls Griselda's protestation in Chaucer's "Clerk's Tale," when she faces her husband Walter's feigned ire:

"Naked out of my fadres house," quod she,
"I cam, and naked moot I turne agayn,
. . . .
But yet I hope it be nat youre entente
That I smoklees out of youre paleys wente."

["Naked out of my fathers house," she said,
"I came, and naked I must return again,

. . . .

But still, I hope that it be not your intention
That I leave your palace without my smock."]

William Pulle becomes something of a devil here, a creature not just of sheer sexual violence but of desolation, wilderness, and hiding. He retreats to his secret places, "wilde and desolate places" that cannot but evoke the desolation of the great myths, romances, or epics of the English tradition— the wastes of Grendel's mere, or the rough landscapes of the mid-fifteenth-century *Desert of Religion*:

He fand hym in deserte land . . . in wilderness,
Whare all walkes þat wilde es.

[He found himself in a deserted land . . . in wilderness,
Where everything that walks is wild.]

And, at the petition's end, when William Pulle stands "atteint of high Tresoun," it is because he has ravished Isabell "with more heynouse violence than any hath be sene or knawen before this tyme." The word "heynouse," from the French root, *haine*, or "hatred," is, again, a relatively new word by the 1430s. It signals here, like so many other of this petition's terms, a Francophone legal vocabulary; but, too, it signals how the writer must reach outside of the commonplace vernacular for words to express what must have been a far from commonplace transgression.

Much like Caxton's Preface to the *Eneydos*, this is a story of the center and the margins. It distinguishes the local from the foreign, the familiar from the wild. It searches for authority, much as Caxton would search for his (kings and their aegis remain ever present in these texts, either as patrons and commissioners, or as sites of power—it is significant that William Pulle seeks out those secret places "where the kynges writt renneth noght"). Both of these texts are romances of language, adventures into the never-before-seen-or-heard. And, as I read the two of them together, I cannot but be struck that both are, in some sense, about ravishment: the rape of Helen, or the secret tryst of Dido and Aeneas. Of course, William Pulle is no Paris or Aeneas, but for every culture, violence against women remains the test of political control and legal authority, of language and expression.

Chancery records fill themselves with such tales, as do Caxton's writings, and we can see throughout the fifteenth and the early sixteenth centuries a grappling with the resources of English prose to make things clear: to cut through wildernesses of the word to reach a meaning. And for John Hart, with whose *Orthographie* I began this chapter, written English has become itself a wilderness. That sentence with which I began brilliantly evokes the confusions that he finds. Notice the repetition, the elaborate augmentation of tense, phrase, and idiom. Hart's words, "euer hath bene coulde, or that is or shal be, can or may," create a kind of conjugation of confusions, a very grammar of despair. Hart claims that "by opening the windowe whereby is light giuen to decerne betwixt perfection and barbarousness, so as euery reasonable creature vniuersally . . . may be a perfite iudge howe euerye language ought to be written" (2). Let there be light. And later in his treatise, he remarks how "tongues haue often changed," and therefore "reason should correct the vicious writing of the speach" (13). English spelling is, quite simply, against the "law of nature" (17).

Hart's *Orthographie* has been studied for its attempt to create a kind of phonetic spelling system and, in turn, for its detailed account of just how educated English men and women spoke in the mid-sixteenth century. But I want here, in closing, to attend to Hart's charged idiom itself. His is a judgmental call for clarity, a story about acting against nature, about barbarous behavior, about what makes English English and its people people. Like the petitions to a Parliament, or like Caxton's preface to the *Eneydos*, Hart's *Orthographie* seeks correction in corruption ("corrupt" remains one of his most favorite terms of opprobrium).

And yet, this is a story not about the rape of women or the loss of empires, but about spelling. The scribes of Chancery had an indelible impact on English spelling, and Caxton's press did much to disseminate their habits. But they also had an impact on the rise of English prose and on the ways of finding language that would cut through obfuscation into clarity. I think, in some way, that Isabell's petition resonates with such a search—or, at the very least, that the Chancery scribe who scripted it reached deep into the resources of English to create a drama of discernment and decision. So, too, did Caxton, and so, too, did Hart. In their writings, we may find both the invention of an English prose and the invention of a self: a self blown back to Kent and lost in dialect; a self armed with the rigors of reason to cut through vice in spelling. Speakers of English live, as Caxton noted, "under the domynacyon of the mone," and in this sad, sublunary world, it may be futile to control or fix our tongue, to outlaw felonies of language, or to do more than make the long, but I hope not tedious, labor to expose the secret places in our history of ciphering.

CHAPTER 9

I Do, I Will

Shakespeare's English

SHAKESPEARE. THE VERY NAME EVOKES THE ACME of the English language. Even people who have never seen his plays know phrases such as "sound and fury," "the most unkindest cut," "ripeness is all," and, of course, "to be, or not to be." His tragic characters have helped the modern age define just what it means to be a human being. His comic episodes make audiences laugh four centuries after their first performance. His sonnets still stand as the benchmarks of love poetry. More than any other writer in the language, Shakespeare used the resources of English to their full. He coined nearly six thousand new words; he juxtaposed terms from the Anglo-Saxon and the learned Latin for striking effect; he wrestled with the syntax of everyday speech until it almost broke.

Linguistic change, of course, goes on not simply at the level of the big new word or the dramatic metamorphosis in syntax or pronunciation, but in the space of unsuspecting little phrases. Shakespeare helps make the English of the modern world, but he does so often through the nuances of detail and of diction. This chapter, therefore, looks at Shakespeare's language great and small. It illustrates the ways in which he drew on the linguistic resources of his time to shape dramatic episodes and lyric poetry of powerful effect. But it also focuses on just how Shakespeare stands on the cusp of English linguistic modernity: how his language looks back to earlier forms (at times, to forms archaic even in his own age) while at the same time using words and idioms new for his audiences. The vocabulary, grammar, and pronunciation of his lines are the basis of this chapter. But Shakespeare's language is made up of more than just these elements. His is a rhetorical language, a way of speaking and writing shaped by the educational traditions of Renaissance England and the public arenas of politics and the pulpit.

I begin with something little. In the exchange between Prince Hal and Falstaff in act 2, scene 4 of *Henry IV, Part 1*, the young prince and his old friend take turns playacting as each other. They banter back and forth as they agree to try on new roles. "Do thou stand for me, and I'll play my father," says Hal. Falstaff, in Hal's guise, sets out to praise himself, while Hal acts the imperious king. Finally, in one of the great set-pieces of dramatic oratory, Falstaff (playing Hal, of course) gives what may be the grandest self-eulogy in all of English literature, concluding with the plea: "but for sweet Jack Falstaff, kind Jack Falstaff, true Jack Falstaff, valiant Jack Falstaff, and therefore more valiant being, as he is, old Jack Falstaff, banish not him thy Harry's company, banish not him thy Harry's company. Banish plump Jack, and banish all the world." To which Hal—in his father's voice, or perhaps now his own—simply replies: "I do, I will."

These four words are, paradoxically, both the oldest and the most modern English any audience would have heard in the 1590s. The verb "to do," though coming from a root deep in the old Germanic past, was taking on new uses in the sixteenth century. Instead of serving simply as a full verb (meaning to act or make something), it was becoming what we now would call periphrastic: that is, it could be used to stand for another verb, it could be used in tandem with another verb for emphasis, and finally, it could be used to form a question. In Old and Middle and in early Modern English, questions had been asked by inverting the order of the subject and the verb. "You love me" is a statement; "love you me" is a question. By the sixteenth century, it was possible to ask the question "do you love me?" and the answer would be, "I do." When Hal thus says to Falstaff, "Do thou stand for me," he is using the verb *do* in its new emphatic sense. And when he says, at the close of their exchange, "I do," he is similarly using the verb in a new way—now, as the replacement for Falstaff's verb "banish." "I do" means "I banish."

But Hal also says "I will." Like the verb "to do, " "to will" (common to all the Germanic languages) was taking on new uses. Once restricted to full verbal status—meaning to want or to will something to happen—it came to be used to indicate the future tense in conjunction with other verbs, but always with a sense of personal desire (the verb "shall," also used to indicate futurity, still carried with it a sense of obligation). Will you love me? I will.

Marriage rituals remain among the most archaic forms of speech in all languages. They preserve old forms, granting to the rite a dignity of linguistic formality. But in the sixteenth century, the changes in the rituals of birth and death, marriage and divorce, came with the changes in the English Church, as it moved from Catholicism to new Protestant forms following King Henry VIII's break with Rome in the 1530s. The language of the Church changed too—indeed, one of the central tenets of the Reformation was the shift to the vernacular in holy services and the translation of the Bible into the languages of the populace. In 1549, Archbishop Thomas Cranmer put together a new Book of Common Prayer for the church under Henry VIII's successor, his son Edward VI. Over the next five decades, through various revisions and reprintings, this book served as the base text for the English Protestant religious rite. Its language is familiar to us, still, today. "Dearly beloved friends, we are gathered together here in the sight of God, and in the face of this congregation, to join together this man and this woman in holy matrimony." And when the priest turns to the man and asks, "Wilt thou have this woman to thy wedded wife," the man shall answer, "I will." And when he turns to the woman and asks the same question, she shall answer, "I will."

I begin with this moment in a Shakespeare play and in the Book of Common Prayer to illustrate the subtle ways in which the English language changed during the sixteenth century. Shakespeare's scene resonates with marriage rites. Prince Hal and Falstaff, taking on their roles, play out a comic scene of power. But it turns all serious when Hal takes on the pledges of the marriage rite: pledges, in his mouth, that become claims not of uniting but of separating. Hal offers up, in essence, not a marriage but a divorce.

Shakespeare's plays and poems ripple with these nuances of usage, as he absorbs what was changing in the English of his day into the power of his fiction. But Shakespeare was acutely conscious of the older forms of speech. Take, for example, the second-person pronoun. As I illustrated in my chapters on Old and Middle English, there were two second-person-pronoun forms throughout the history of the language. *You* forms were formal and plural; *thou* forms were singular and informal. These were grammatical and social categories, and in Shakespeare's time they still had force.

The scene between Prince Hal and Falstaff indicates just how the drama of exchange plays out in pronouns. When Hal asks Falstaff to play himself, he says: "Do thou stand for me." Whatever roles they play, Hal should call Falstaff *thou*, both because they are intimate friends, but also because Falstaff remains, whatever their games, the Prince's social inferior. Playacting as his father, Henry IV, Prince Hal speaks to his son (now played by Falstaff): "Now, Harry, whence come you?" He speaks in the formal, a king to a prince. But when this play king chides his errant son he shifts into the *thou* form: "Swearest, thou, ungracious boy?" He condescends, complains, demeans. The imagined son here moves to a lower rank before the anger of the father. And when Falstaff, playing the prince, addresses the play king, he responds in kind: "I would your grace would take me with you." *You* forms signal deference and respect—an attitude Falstaff clearly forgets toward the end of his speech, when he begs Hal, playing Henry IV, not to banish Falstaff from "thy Harry's company." The lapse in pronouns signals Falstaff's lapse in decorum.

A more highly developed version of this drama of the pronoun appears in *Richard III*, in an exchange between the aspirant usurper and the woman he craves, Lady Anne. Richard interrupts Anne on her way to Henry VI's funeral. She had been married to the old king's son, Edward, and Richard has murdered both men. Richard raises the question of just what had caused their deaths, and Anne shoots back:

ANNE: Thou was't the cause, and most accurst effect.
RICHARD: Your beauty was the cause of that effect:
    Your beauty, that did haunt me in my sleepe,
    To vndertake the death of all the world,
    So I might liue one houre in your sweet bosome.
ANNE: If I thought that, I tell thee Homicide,
    These Nailes should rent that beauty from my Cheeks.
RICHARD: These eyes could not endure y^t beauties wrack,
    You should not blemish it, if I stood by;
    As all the world is cheared by the Sunne,
    So I by that: It is my day, my life.
ANNE: Blacke night ore-shade thy day, & death thy life.
RICHARD: Curse not thy selfe faire Creature,
    Thou art both.
ANNE: I would I were, to be reueng'd on thee.
RICHARD: It is a quarrel most vnnaturall,
    To be reueng'd on him that loueth thee.

They go on, in this vein, until she finally spits on him in disgust (at which point Richard, at his most unctuous, replies: "Neuer came poison from so sweet a place").

Richard is trying to woo Anne; she is spurning him. She opens with a contemptuous, condescending *thou*, as to a servant. Richard responds with a socially correct, formal *you*, indicating he is addressing a superior. Anne and Richard exchange *thou* and *you* forms in the next section. But at the final line of this passage, Richard shifts to *thee,* and in so doing he announces his intention to love Anne. Here it is the *thee* of closeness. He offers not an insult, but a sign of hoped-for intimacy. She, however, keeps to the contemptuous *thou.*

These subtleties would have explained the personal dynamic to contemporary audiences. They are now lost to us. Lost, too, is the sound these lines would have had for the late sixteenth century.

ðəʊ wast ðə kaus ænd mɔst akərst ɛfɛkt
jur bjutɪ was ðə kaus əf ðæt ɛfɛkt
jur bjutɪ ðæt dɪd haunt mi ɪn məɪ slip
tu ʊndərtɛk ðə dəθ əv al ðə wɔrld
so əɪ məɪt lɪv on əʊr ɪn jur swit bʊzm

The most important thing to notice about this transcription is that it reveals that the Great Vowel Shift had not fully sorted itself out by the end of the sixteenth century. The older, Middle English long high vowels, /u:/ and /i:/, had not completely become the modern diphthongs /au/ and /ai/. The schwa sign in my transcription of words like *thou* and *my* indicates this partial diphthongization. So, too, the older, Middle English long vowel /a:/ had not fully moved up to its modern position /e:/. A word like *undertake,* therefore, would probably have had a long /ɛ:/ sound. Even though sound changes had distinguished Shakespeare's English from that of Chaucer's, some words were probably still pronounced as they had been in Middle English. The words *cause* and *haunt* still had their old diphthongs [au], and had not changed into that *-aw-* sound of Modern English.

Some words are harder to place. The word *world* may have been pronounced with its old, Middle English vowel, or with a higher vowel. What we have here is evidence of the instability of vowels before *-r.* This phenomenon has long vexed historians of English and still helps to characterize regional dialects to this day. Depending on where you are from, you may or may not distinguish the sounds in the words *Mary, merry,* and *marry.* In the spoken English of the sixteenth and seventeenth centuries, the *-er-* spelling may have been pronounced /ɪr/ or /ar/. This instability is still reflected in the spelling of certain words. *Person* and *parson* are now spelled differently to signal the differences in meaning, but for centuries they were homonymns. We speak of *vermin* infesting a house, but in certain American dialects a person who acts like vermin is a *varmint.* This difference in pronunciation and spelling is a legacy of this early Modern

English instability. So, too, is the distinction between a university and the sports team that plays for one: varsity. British speakers say the word *clerk* as if it were "clark" and *Berkeley* as if it were "Barkley."

Other features of Shakespearean pronunciation include the pronunciation of the word *one*. Descending from the Old English word *an*, "one" was the stressed form of what would become, in unstressed positions, the indefinite article *a*. Our modern pronunciation with the initial glide [wun] did not appear until the eighteenth century. Another old pronunciation is for the word *houre*. Speakers dropped their *h*'s after words that ended in a consonant. We still signal something like this today: should one say "a historian" or "an historian"? An archaism in our speech lies in the line: "Myn eyes have seen the glory," where the *-n* ending on *myn* signals the vowel sound following the word. Chaucer makes the same distinction: "my wit," but "myn heart." It is clear, then, that in Shakespeare's time, "hour" was pronounced without the initial *h*.

If Shakespeare's lines sound odd to the modern ear, they certainly look odd, especially as I present them in their old spelling taken from the First Folio edition of the plays, printed in 1623 (see figure 9.1). Some of the features of this spelling seem a little weird but are perfectly understandable: there is the long form of the *s*; major nouns are capitalized; and many nouns have a final *-e* on them. Other features are more fascinating and reflect not so much the habits of speech but the conventions of the early printing press. The letters *u* and *v*, for example, seem interchangeable: until we realize that, historically, they were not. Before printing, texts were written out by hand, and letters such as *u* and *v*, *w*, *i*, *m*, and *n* were made by making short, vertical lines and then joining them together (these little lines were called minims). In many forms of medieval and early modern script, this habit made letters such as *u* and *n* almost indistinguishable, and it could be confusing if a *u* and an *i* were in close proximity. So, a convention developed of writing a *v* next to an *i* and a *u* in all other contexts. Early printers somewhat altered this convention by using a *v* at the beginning of a word and a *u* in the middle of the word. Thus, we see the familiar spellings for *cause* or *beauty*, but *vnnaturall* and *vndertake*. But we also see *reueng'd* and *loueth*.

Another oddity of this text, and one that similarly looks back to older, medieval manuscript traditions, is the form y^t. This symbol represents the word "that". As we had seen in Old and Middle English, the letter thorn, þ, drawn from the ancient runic alphabet, was used to indicate the *-th-* sound. This habit was continued in the late-medieval and the early-modern periods, really as a form of abbreviation. Written quickly, the thorn became indistin-

An. Thou was't the caufe, and moft accurft effect.

Rich. Your beauty was the caufe of that effect :
Your beauty, that did haunt me in my fleepe,
To vndertake the death of all the world,
So I might liue one houre in your fweet bofome.

An. If I thought that, I tell thee Homicide,
Thefe Nailes fhould rent that beauty from my Cheekes.

Rich. Thefe eyes could not endure ÿ beauties wrack,
You fhould not blemifh it, if I ftood by ;
As all the world is cheared by the Sunne,
So I by that : It is my day, my life.

An. Blacke night ore-fhade thy day, & death thy life.

Rich. Curfe not thy felfe faire Creature,
Thou art both.

An. I would I were, to be reueng'd on thee.

Rich. It is a quarrell moft vnnaturall,
To be reueng'd on him that loueth thee.

FIGURE 9.1

William Shakespeare, *Richard III*; from the First Folio edition (London: Hemmings and Condell, 1623).

guishable from a *y*, so that *y*^t is really *th* plus *t*, with the *a* implied. This little bit of history may seem hopelessly pedantic; yet it is the explanation for that mainstay of the cute: Ye Olde Shoppe. The definite article was never "ye." But it *was* "þe." And so, over time, it began to look like "ye." This is a confusion of letter forms and spelling, not of grammar.

In little words like these lie larger patterns of linguistic change. But I must not neglect the big words. Shakespeare was a master of the grand vocabulary. Acutely sensitive to learned Latinate formations, but at the same time alert to the Anglo-Saxon roots of English, he coined words and phrases at a rate unmatched by any previous or subsequent author. Sometimes, he takes a relatively new word in the language and transforms it. The word *assassin*, for example, comes originally from an Arabic term meaning a "hashish eater." Members of certain sects would get high on their hash before committing violent deeds, such as the public killing of a public figure. The term floated into European languages with the Crusades, but rarely out of its specific, Middle Eastern context. Only in the first third of the sixteenth century does it appear, in English (and spelled *Ascismus*) to mean someone who would kill for money. And only in the first years of the seventeenth century does it start to appear, in its modern spelling, to refer generally to a killer of a public figure. Shakespeare takes it, puts the familiar Latinate *-ion* ending on it, and transforms it into a noun, for the first time, in a soliloquy from *Macbeth* (written probably in 1605 or 1606) that rings with verbal innovation.

> If it were done when 'tis done, then 'twere well
> If it were done quickly. If th' assassination
> Could trammel up the consequence, and catch
> With his surcease success, that but this blow
> Might be the be-all and the end-all—here,
> But here upon this bank and shoal of time,
> We'd jump the life to come.

$$(1.7.1–7)$$

At the most basic level, Macbeth contemplates killing Duncan. If it were over and done with when the killing was done, if there were no consequences to the act, then fine—but, as Macbeth will go on to reflect, these kinds of actions have long consequences. But at another level, Macbeth's words twist tough around the tongue. New terms, wild images, strange metaphors all concatenate to mime the snarelike logic of his meditation.

First, the repetition: done, done, done. Recall, now, how the verb *do* was taking on new uses in the late sixteenth and early seventeenth centuries. Shakespeare deploys it here to mark the ambiguities of action: first, to mean the act of doing the killing itself; then, to mean over and done with; then, the act again. All the words in these first one-and-a-half lines are Anglo-Saxon words: short, old, only deceptively clear. And then the new word, "assassination," recorded here for the first time in any writing, and with that word the door opens, as it were, for verbal strangeness. A trammel was a kind of fishing net. The word first appears as a verb, meaning to bind up a corpse, in the mid-sixteenth century. Shakespeare is the first to use it figuratively—to bind up . . . what? The consequence? Look at the figurative diction here: the assassination is the act that would bind up in a net the consequences of the action, not letting anything escape. And then the next clause: if the assassination could ensure success with "his surcease" (that is, the murder of Duncan). "Surcease" comes from the word "cease." It appears in the late sixteenth century as a new coinage meaning an act of bringing to an end. But it also must stand, here in Macbeth's speech, for its sound as much as its sense. Read these first three-and-a-half lines aloud and hear the repetitions, the alliterations, the tongue-twisting (try saying "with his surcease success" three times). And then keep reading, as the mouth falls back into Anglo-Saxon: "that but this blow / Might be the be-all and the end-all." How familiar these words sound, how obvious their meaning. And yet, Shakespeare made them up. "Be-all and end-all," like phrases such as "bated breath" (*Merchant of Venice*), "salad days" (*Antony and Cleopatra*), "what the dickens" (*Merry Wives of Windsor*), "my mind's eye" (*Hamlet*), and nearly countless others are Shakespeare's gift to our modern sense of the colloquial.

But as Macbeth's first sentence ends, we move to yet another area of the Shakespearean. This is the language of the copula, the world of *and* that fills the mouths of tragic heroes. "This bank and shoal of time." Shakespeare takes metaphor—here, the idea of time as a river—and splits it down the middle. We stand on the sandbanks and the shallows of time's river. One word is not enough, just as one word would not suffice for Hamlet ("slings and arrows of outrageous fortune"). Standing upon those banks and shoals, "we'd jump the life to come." The word *jump* first appears in the sixteenth century, probably as an onomatopoetic coinage. People are jumping all over the place by the year 1600, but in this passage from *Macbeth* the word clearly means something other than "to take a leap." It must mean something like "risk" or "hazard," but it also has to carry the familiar, literal sense. We're standing on the shore, getting ready to jump. If life is a river, then we're ready to dive in.

All these complexities spin out of my initial query into *assassination*. How many other places can we find where Shakespeare coins a word and, in the process, leads us into English literary and linguistic history? There are too many for me to record here. *Accommodation, barefaced, countless, courtship, dwindle, premeditated, submerged*—these are just a few of his new words. His characters are linguists of the imagination. And all of it is not high-born. Witness this magisterial moment of dissing from *King Lear*, when Kent confronts the self-important Steward. He is, in Kent's words,

A knave, a rascal, an eater of broken meats, a base, proud, shallow, beggarly, three-suited, hundred-pound, filthy worsted-stocking

knave; a lily-livered, action-taking knave; a whoreson, glass-gazing, superfinical rogue; one-trunk-inheriting slave.

(1608 text; 2.2.13–17)

As in Macbeth's soliloquy, the real subject of this passage is not the external world but the speaker's inner imagination. Action is speech here, as throughout Shakespeare—a bringing together of old bits and pieces of vocabulary into new compounds. It is as if Shakespeare reaches back into the old techniques of Anglo-Saxon versemaking, to come up with new compound nouns and adjectives, each one a miniature (and often alliterating) metaphor (how marvelous, by the way, to learn that "lily-livered" is Shakespeare's and not the bon mot of the Western varmint).

Shakespeare's characters do go on, spinning their selves out of a language old and new. And there is no character who shapes himself in language as much as Hamlet. For if Shakespeare has been seen as the apex of linguistic usage, then it is Hamlet that remains the exemplar of the modern character. His speeches have bequeathed to us rafts of figures that now border on cliché. Nothing, perhaps, is so familiar to us as the great soliloquy:

To be, or not to be: that is the question:
Whether 'tis nobler in the mind to suffer
The slings and arrows of outrageous fortune,
Or to take arms against a sea of troubles,
And by opposing end them.

(3.1.56–60)

But was this really what Shakespeare had written? These lines come from a tradition of texts grounded in the 1604 publication of the play (the so-called Second Quarto edition) and in the First Folio of 1623. But in 1603, another version of *Hamlet* appeared—what scholars today call the First, or "Bad" Quarto: a short, seemingly garbled text, perhaps the record of an actor's memory, perhaps the record of an earlier Shakespearean assay. Whatever the origins of this version, the "To be or not to be" soliloquy is very different.

To be, or not to be, I there's the point,
To Die, to sleepe, is that all? I all:
No, to sleepe, to dreame, I mary there it goes,
For in that dreame of death, when wee awake,
And borne before an euerlasting Iudge,

From whence no passenger euer retur'nd,
The vndiscouuered country, at whose sight
The happy smile, and the accursed damn'd.

Right from the start, there is a difference. Hamlet's "question" comes from the Latin *quaestio*, and in the Renaissance schoolroom such questions would have been the topics for debate. His opening words signal, then, not so much a crisis of the soul as a command of the classroom. Resolved: to be or not to be. Take either side. Here, Hamlet takes up the debate himself, arguing in good rhetorical fashion each side of the argument. But for the speaker of the First Quarto version, this is not a question but a point. The ambiguities, the doubts, the back-and-forth rhetorical patterns of the more familiar version absent themselves here. Instead, we get a set of statements. Every line ends with a bit of punctuation; there is virtually no enjambment, as there is throughout the Second Quarto/First Folio version, and where such a device creates something of a formal tension between the controlling patterns of the verse line and the flow of Hamlet's language. The First Quarto soliloquy comes off, especially to those of us reared on the "better" version, as confused, as ungrammatical, as silly.

But more than simply seeming better, the Second Quarto/First Folio version has become a benchmark in the history of English itself. The editors of the *Oxford English Dictionary* relied on it precisely as this benchmark, often citing it as the first example for a word or idiom. Read on in the soliloquy: "to say we end the heart-ache and the thousand natural shocks / that flesh is heir to." The *OED* defines the *heartache* as "pain or anguish of mind," and gives this passage as the first use in English. "It is a consummation devoutly to be wished." Look up *consummation* in the *OED*, and under definition 4, "fulfillment, goal," the dictionary gives this passage as the first use in English. "Aye, there's the rub." The *OED* has Shakespeare as the coiner of this phrase, and the dictionary's subsequent quotations illustrate an afterlife of Hamlet in the mouths of later poets, politicians, and poseurs. And when we come to the "undiscovered country, from whose bourne no traveler returns," we can find in *bourne* a lexicon of Shakespeare's influence. For definition 3, "the limit or terminus of a race, journey, or course," the *OED* notes: "Shakespeare's famous passage probably meant the 'frontier or pale' of a country; but has been associated contextually with the goal of a traveller's course."

Shakespeare is the most quoted author in the *OED*, and from these few examples we can see how Hamlet's great soliloquy not only provides evidence for word use but also makes Shakespeare, and this play, the epicenter of the history of the language—as if modern character and modern English both emerged with *Hamlet*. We have, in essence, made our literary and linguistic history arc through the stars of Hamlet's words. "To be or not to be" becomes not just a query about life but a statement about vernacular identity, about Englishness itself. And when we hold up these two radically different versions of the play and its soliloquy, we must ask ourselves which one is real, which one is truly Shakespearean or truly Hamletlike: which one we might let be and which one not to be.

I must stop somewhere, and as I survey the range of plays and poems, one last scene catches my eye. Throughout *Henry V*, the Princess Katherine tries to learn English. She banters with her nursemaid-tutor Alice, mangles word and sound, cannot quite get the sense of words. At the play's end, when King Henry seeks her hand, he would love her in English. But there is too much difference between them, and whatever one might try to say, language can always go amiss. "O bon Dieu!" Katherine exclaims in French. "Les langues des homes sont pleine de tromperies."

> KING HENRY: What says she, fair one? "that the tongues of men
> are full of deceits."
> ALICE: Oui, dat de tongues of de mans is be full of deceits.
> Dat is de princesse.
>
> (5.2.118–22)

The spelling on the page evokes the accent on the stage. Language is a deceitful thing. We say one thing and mean another, and when language changes, old terms that once had meaning may now seem strange. As Henry himself says, in another one of those brilliant Shakespearean coinages, when people try to speak each other's language, it comes out "most truly-falsely" (5.2.190). *Henry V* is a play of many things, but it is most assuredly a language lesson for a world whose words were changing meaning. Shakespeare tutors his audiences in the ways of English, much as I have tried here to teach something of the richness of his tongue. For Princess Katherine, confronted by an eloquent King Henry, all she can say is, "I cannot speak your England" (103). But this is more than mere grammatical error. To speak a language is to speak a nation. Prince Hal, the younger figure of this same king, knew that, for when his Falstaff would attempt to sway him with his "tromperies," he cuts through with four words that do not marry but divorce him from his friend. "I do, I will." Such are the ways of speaking England in Shakespeare, and such are some of the ways we still do now.

CHAPTER 10

A Universal Hubbub Wild

New Words and Worlds in Early Modern English

DURING THE SIX DECADES OF SHAKESPEARE'S LIFE, more words entered the English language than at any other time in history. Science and commerce, exploration and colonial expansion, literature and art—all contributed to an increased vocabulary drawn from Latin, Greek, and the European and non-European languages. While the lexicon of Old English took only 3 percent of its vocabulary from elsewhere, nearly 70 percent of our modern English lexicon comes from non-English sources (Lass, *Cambridge History*, 3:332). Recent statistical analyses of loan words throughout history affirm, too, that the bulk of this borrowing came in the late sixteenth and early seventeenth centuries: the spike in the graph of figure 10.1 reveals, more vividly than any textual examples I could give, just what was happening to English in the age of Shakespeare.

Most histories of the language are content simply to list these words— as if their attestation were enough to show how English changed. So what if you could say *mustache* or *probability* (from French), or *cannibal* or *yam* (from Spanish), or *smuggler* (from Dutch), or *raccoon* (from North American Indian)? So what if you could *osculate* instead of *kiss*, be *dexterous* instead of *handy*, be *malignant* instead of *bad*? So what if you could put a prefix or a suffix on a word and make it new: *sense* becomes *nonsense*; *civilized* becomes *uncivilized*; *gloom* becomes *gloomy*; *laugh* becomes *laughable*? The history of the expanding English vocabulary is about more than numbers. It is about the idea of numbers: about a rhetorical and social ideal of amplification, about a new fascination with the copiousness of worldly things, and about a new faith in the imagination to coin terms for unimagined concepts. English at this time, in effect, defines itself as a word language, and the business of much sixteenth- and seventeenth-century scholarship

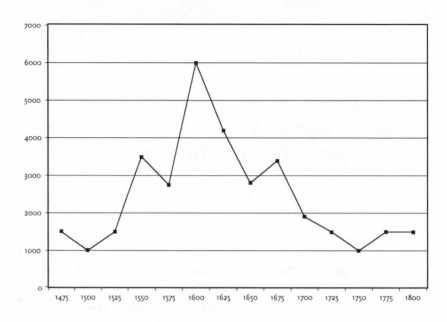

FIGURE IO.I
Increases in New Words Over Time

This chart illustrates the influx of new words (coinages, borrowings, and compounds) into English during the course of the early-modern period. Data is based on the records of the *Oxford English Dictionary*.
Source: Adapted from material in Nevalainen, "Early Modern English Lexis and Semantics," 339.

becomes the business of defining. Dictionaries emerge as guides to this new lexical landscape, as if language were a brave new world akin to that of the explorers or the colonists. By 1658, Edward Philips could affirm this link between the verbal and the voyaging in the title of his *New World of Words*, a dictionary that affirmed not simply the voracity of English for new terms but the imperial aspirations of England. As Philips put it in his preface, "There are not many nations in Europe, some of whose words we have not made bold with." There was a politics to this prolixity. Forty years before Philips, Joseph Bullokar could note, in the preface to his *Expositor*: "it is familiar among best writers to vsurp strange words." Recall that word usurp in Chaucer's *Astrolabe* or Thomas Wilson's *Arte of Rhetorique*: the arts of language are the arts of power.

There remains among the welter of these dictionaries and our textbooks a still unanswered question. Why do certain words survive in language and why do others disappear? *Impede* and *expede* show up in the seventeenth century, but only *impede* lives on. *Adapted* survives, but not *adepted* (meaning "attained"). *Commit* and *transmit* were coined and stayed on, but *demit* (meaning "send away") vanished. *Adnichilate* (to reduce to nothing) is gone; *eximious* ("excellent") is lost to time; *temulent* ("drunk") forgotten. The only time I ever heard the word *invigilate* (meaning to "watch over") is when I sat my Oxford exams and someone had to look over our shoulders (invigilate) to make sure we did not cheat. The study of the English vocabulary is therefore a study of choices, a study of social and imaginative contexts in which words vie for usage and acceptance.

And in such contexts, too, words vie almost within themselves for meaning. What characterizes the English of the Renaissance is not only the wealth of words but the wealth of word meanings. Polysemy, the term used to describe many meanings for a single word, is paramount at this time. Old words were taking on new meanings, and for a period of time, all coexisted. Words such as *uncouth* or *silly* that originally had specific, limited meanings in Old English ("unknown" and "blessed," respectively) came to connote broad patterns of social behavior. Words drawn from technical disciplines also began to take on figurative connotations. Words from commerce could apply to social life; words from physical experience could refer to emotional conditions. This process, known as extension in lexis, may lead to confusion, but it enables the imagination. "Brazen" in Old and Middle English meant "made of brass," but by Shakespeare's time it meant "impudent." To "bristle" in the fifteenth century meant to stand up stiffly; by the middle of the sixteenth, it meant "to become indignant." To "broil" in the age of Chaucer meant to burn, but for Shakespeare it could mean "get angry."

An explanation for these kinds of changes remains as elusive as an explanation for why certain words survive and others pass away. But if precise answers elude us, we may still see the workings of verbal choice in society and the imagination. Renaissance English culture had many aspects, but the two that I would single out here for their impact on the language are theatricality and copia. The England of the Tudors was a place of theater: from the richly staged royal entries and elaborate ceremonies of power, through the many local plays and pageants that filled civic life, to the growing professional theater companies that settled themselves in such innovative spaces as the Globe and the Swan. Politics was theater and theater was politics. All the world, as Shakespeare had put it in *As You Like It*, was a stage.

Along with theater was rhetoric. Arts of eloquence had long been taught in both religious and secular schools, and the classical traditions of forensic oratory had long formed the basis of such later medieval and Renaissance activities as preaching, diplomacy, lovemaking, and courtiership. Rhetoric had devices—tropes or figures that enabled both persuasion and display. *Amplificatio* was one of the most vital of these tropes. Originally, it was just a way of making speeches longer and more detailed. But for sixteenth- and seventeenth-century England, in particular, it became something of a cultural motif. For the worlds of Henry VIII or Queen Elizabeth, the ruler's body, voice, and power were all amplified. Great buildings, great speeches, and eventually, great empires would grow. And like the sumptuous dress that clad the courtiers of such monarchs, the English language itself could be clad in what the rhetorician George Puttenham called, in his 1589 *Arte of English Poesie*, "rich and gorgeous apparel." We could, he argued, "polish our speech and as it were attire it with copious and pleasant amplifications and much varietie of sentences, all running vpon one point and one intent" (3.20.255). And yet, not everyone was happy with such excesses. The Lord Keeper, Sir Nicholas Bacon, opened Parliament on April 2, 1571, by criticizing the excesses of earlier times, and his speech evokes the copiousness of the earlier age of Henry VIII while at the same time critiquing the gaudiness of his own, Elizabethan period. It is a brilliant speech, worth quoting at length as an exemplar of Renaissance political oratory.

> It hath bin in tymes paste that prince's pleasures and delightes have been commonly followed in matters of chardge as things of necessity, and now (God be praised) the relieving of the realme's necessity is become the prince's pleasure and delight: a noble conversion, God continue it, and make us, as we ought to be, earnestly thankfull for it, a princely example shewed by a soveraigne for subiectes to follow. To discend in some perticulers, what neede I to remember to yow how the gorgeous, sumptuous, superfluous buildings of times past be for the realme's good by her Majestie in this time turned into necessary buildinges and uphouldinges; the chardgeable, glittering, glorious triumphes into delectable pastimes and shewes, the pompes

and solempe ambassadors of chardge into such as be voide of excesse and yet honorable and comely. This and such like were draweinge dames be able to dry upp the floweinge fountains of any treasurye, these were quills of such quantity as would soone make the many pipes to serve in tyme of necessity such an expendit is hardly satisfied by any collector.

Bacon's language flows with all the features of Renaissance rhetoric: repetitions, patterns of echo and response, strings of polysyllabic words. His speech both speaks about and mimes a spew of things, as if the body politic were engorged and in need of relief—the phrase "the relieving of the realme's necessity" has a positively intestinal connotation to it, while the image of a new, political world "voide of excesse" connotes the voiding of an overcharged body. Indeed, the repetition of the word "chardge" and its forms here (meaning, in this case, a burden caused by a result of taxation or payment) resonates with the other, Renaissance meaning of the word: to feed to excess (Thomas Wilson, in his *Arte of Rhetorique* of 1553, had told a story of a gentleman who, "being overcharged at supper with overmuch drink . . . should vomit the next day in the Parliament House"). Bacon's speech is rife with polysemy, with words of both corporeal and corporate connotation that make it a story of a body politic disgorging the excesses of an earlier age.

For all the praise of copia, some rhetoricians of the sixteenth century found the body of English, much like the body politic, expanding out of control. Thomas Wilson, in his *Arte of Rhetorique*, offered up as evidence a letter supposedly written by a gentleman seeking patronage, but most modern readers think that Wilson made the letter up, presenting not historical evidence but parody. Still, it remains a brilliant evocation of the verbal intoxication many clearly felt in the mid-sixteenth century:

Ponderyng expendyng, and reuolutyng with my self your ingent affabilitee, and ingenious capacitee, for mundane affaires: I cannot but celebrate and extolle your magnificall dexteritee, aboue all other. For how could you have adepted suche illustrate prerogatiue, and dominicall superioritee, if the fecunditee of your ingenie had not been so fertile, and wounderfull pregnaunt.

This letter may exemplify an overuse of highly learned, Latinate words. But it also takes as its own theme the matter of expansion. The writer praises the potential patron's *ingent affabilitee*, his great affability and his ingenious capacity. The addressee is *magnificall, illustrate* (illustrious), *dominical* (lordly). His *ingenie*, or intellect, has *fecunditee*; it is fertile and wonderfully pregnant. These are all words about amplification: all words about increasing, growing, giving birth. The power of the addressee expands, much as his mind does. Wilson's exemplary letter is about more, then, than simply parodying highfalutin language. It is about the ways in which Renaissance courtiers live in a world of copia: how one might seek new words to match the greatness and the grandeur of a courtly life.

But for the everyday man or woman, expansion lay not in the halls of power but the streets of commerce. Ships were coming in from everywhere filling the markets with new foods, new ornaments, new fascinations. Words, much like objects of the market or the loading dock, became such fascinating things—indeed, they became almost like the fetishes that would be filling captains' cabins or collectors' cabinets (the word "fetish," by the way, entered English in the early seventeenth century by way of the term *fetiço* that the Portuguese traders had been using to describe the amulets and totems of the African coastal peoples).

As a guide to such new words, new dictionaries would be made. Joseph Bullokar's *Expositor* of 1616; Henry Cockeram's *Dictionairre* of 1623; Edward Phillips's *New World of Words*; Nathaniel Bailey's *Dictionary* of 1730—these were some of the major lexicons made in response to the expanding vocabulary. Each one lists, on its title page, the many disciplines from which it draws. Indeed, each title page stands as something of a syllabus of study: a collection of the arts and sciences of the new schoolroom, an assembly of the things of all this world. Language is now much like Creation itself, as if God had ranged life according to the alphabet. Cockeram's *Dictionairre*, for example, ranges itself in three parts: the first containing hard words, new to English; the second containing the "vulgar" or familiar terms, together with their synonyms; the third containing all the mythological and newly found creatures throughout the world. This is a book of everything, from social culture, to economic advancement, to exploration.

It is worth pausing over Cockeram's claims to see how dictionaries of the early Modern period become shapers of the character of English and the character of English men and women. His first part has what he calls "the choisest words . . . now in vse, wherewith our language is inriched and become so copious." Enrichment, copia, choice: English is something of a marketplace, a bazaar of words whose purchase will enhance the look and status of the user. For, in Cockeram's second part, the vulgar terms have additional explanations so that anyone who wishes to develop "a more refined and elegant speech" can do so through their study. But it is that last book that I find so fascinating: a "recital of seuerall persons, Gods and goddesses, Giants and Deuils, Monsters and Serpents, Birds and Beasts, Riuers, Fishes, Herbs, Stones, Trees, and the like." This is more an encyclopedia than a dictionary, and its impress lay far beyond the "Ladies and Gentlewomen, Clarkes, Merchants, young Schollers, Strangers, [and] Trauellers" for whom it was intended. The third edition of the *OED* draws on nearly sixteen hundred quotations from Cockeram to illustrate the history of English words—many of which appear first, or even only in the *Dictionairre* (he is among the very first to use the words *Atlantic, chameleonize,* and *jargonize*; and, just picking at random, he is the only source for the word *irrumate,* "to suck in," derived from the Latin *irrumare*—a word denoting obscene sexual activity found in Catullus and Martial).

But more than listing terms or giving definitions, Cockeram contributes to an English Renaissance word culture—an obsession with amassing terms, a rhetoric of listing. Just compare Cockeram's list of contents for his *Dictionairre*'s third part with Milton's vision of Hell half a century later: "Rocks, Caves, Lakes, Fens, Bogs, Dens, and shades of death" (*Paradise Lost,* 2.621). Every word in this line is from Old English; every metrical syllable is filled with one whole word. At stake here is not the newness of the words in this line but the new idea of just how to use them. Milton's brilliant catalogue of monosyllables rhetorically resonates with the catalogues of the dictionary makers. This is, then, not so much what Milton's next line dubs "A Universe of death" as it is death's dictionary.

Milton knew what he was doing. Readers have long admired his mastery of English, his voracity of verbs, his knowledge of the noun. In this, he certainly read much (indeed, he may well have read, at some point in his life, everything available to someone of his time). But he had one of the great teachers of the age. In Alexander Gil (1564–1635), headmaster of St. Paul's School, the young Milton would have learned from one of the most linguistically aware and self-conscious pedagogues of early-modern England. Gil's learning shows itself in his most famous publication, the *Logonomia Anglica.* Written in Latin as a guide primarily to proper grammar and pronunciation, the *Logonomia Anglica* appeared in 1619 and was soon reprinted. It has long been valued by historians of English pronunciation for its careful attempts to transcribe the speech sounds of its day:

sounds from the English of the educated, the affected, and the regional. But it is also to be valued for its value judgments. Gil flatly rejects the lexical enhancements and rhetorical amplifications of the time. He looks back to a time when "our forefathers in antiquity" spoke and wrote clearly. No language, he claims, "will be found to be more graceful, elegant, or apt for the expression of every subtle thought than English." But faults have crept in, and he announces (here, in translation) with a vehemence worthy of his most famous student:

> About the year 1400, Geoffrey Chaucer, star of ill-omen, rendered his poetry notorious by the use of Latin and French words. Such is the stupidity of the uneducated masses that they admire most what they least comprehend: from that time on a new scurry appeared in writing and speaking, for since everyone wishes to appear as a smatterer of tongues and to vaunt his proficiency in Latin, French (or any other language), so daily wild beasts of words are tamed, and horrid evil-sounding magpies and owls of unpropitious birth are taught to hazard our words. Thus today we are, for the most part, Englishmen not speaking English and not understood by English ears. Nor are we satisfied with having begotten this illegitimate progeny, nourished this monster, but we have exiled that which was legitimate—our birthright—pleasant in expression, and acknowledged by our forefathers. O cruel country!

Gil begins by rejecting the tradition of Chaucerian linguistic praise. Instead of finding Chaucer the embellisher or polisher of English, that "well of English undefiled" as Edmund Spenser put it, Gil finds him a corruptor of the tongue. Instead of seeing him as something of a lodestar of the language, Gil sees him (in Latin) as *infausto omine*, literally an "unlucky omen." The Latinate and Gallic lexicon that has come into English is a mark, for Gil, not of sophistication but stupidity. And he does not stop there. Such evil evokes a language in chaos, as if the Eden of a pre-Chaucerian language has led to an untamed forest. He writes, in Latin: "ita quotidie fera vocum monstra cicuriat," every day the feral monsters of words are tamed. Society is filled, not with people, but with screeching birds, horrid (the same word in Latin), full of bad luck (again, that word *infausti*, unlucky or unpropitious). English is a bastard tongue, a monster living in the house that should be the home of the legitimate.

I cannot read Gil's words without thinking of Milton's vision half-a-century later. "Horrid," coming from the Latin, *horridus*, meaning bristling, is one of his favorite words in *Paradise Lost*. Right from the poem's start, we see it: Satan's "horrid crew" (1.50); Hell as a "Dungeon horrible" (1.61); the "horrid silence" of the fallen (1.83); Moloch, the "horrid king" (1.392). And in book 2, Satan discovers his own awful progeny. On his voyage from Hell to Earth, he meets Sin and Death: the former, Satan's daughter, the latter, the child of their incestuous coupling. Compare Sin's speech to Satan with Gil's phrasing:

Pensive here I sat
Alone, but long I sat not, till my womb
Pregnant by thee, and now excessive grown
Prodigious motion felt and rueful throes
At last this odious offspring whom thou seest
Thine own begotten, breaking violent way
Tore through my entrails.

(2.776–82)

The horrors of the illegitimate are everywhere in Milton; monstrous figures, exiles, beasts. See Satan entering Eden in book 4 of *Paradise Lost*, shifting his shape to "view his prey": "A Lion now he stalks"; "Then as a Tiger" (4.399; 401; 402). And then, "Squat like a Toad, close at the ear of Eve" (4.800).

Milton's mastery of English in all of its forms owes much, I think, to Gil's tuition. But his is a vast empire of words. Throughout *Paradise Lost*, in particular, new terms appear and old terms enter bristling with their etymologies and histories. Two always strike me as I read: *hubbub* and *lantskip* (Milton's spelling of "landscape"). The first connotes the sound of devilish debate in hell.

At length a universal hubbub wild
Of stunning sounds and voices all confus'd
Born through the hollow dark assaults his ear
With loudest vehemence.

(2.951–54)

Hubbub appears in English of the sixteenth century as an onomatopoetic term. It evoked the incomprehensible babble of the Irish or the Welsh, or the non-European native. The first entry in the *OED* from 1555 brings such imagined savages together. Writing of the Ichthiophagi (that is, the fish-eating people of Africa), a certain W. Watreman notes how "Thei flocke together to go drincke . . . shouting as they go with an yrish whobub." In Spenser's *Faerie Queene* of 1590, *hubbub* is associated with the bagpipe. Early-seventeenth-century explorers heard *hubbub* in the war cries of the Native Americans, and the New England colonists used the word to describe a noisy game played by the Massachusetts Indians. Hell's hubbub, then, is not just noise: it is the sound of savagery, an evocation of a century-old association of the untamed Indian and the Irish.

But if Hell is horrid place, then Eden is, at least at first, a glossy work of artistry. Satan may be the "artificer of fraud" (4.121), but Eden appears as art itself. It is, as Satan enters it, "grottesque and wild," with

> Cedar, and Pine, and Firr, and branching Palm,
> A Silvan Scene, and as the ranks ascend
> Shade above shade, a woodie Theatre
> Of stateliest view.
> . . . .
> And higher than that Wall a circling row
> Of goodliest Trees loaden with fairest Fruit,
> Blossoms and Fruit at once of golden hue
> Appeerd, with gay enameled colors mixt:
> On which the Sun more glad impress'd his beams
> Then in fair Evening Cloud, or humid Bow,
> When God hath showrd the earth, so lovely seemd
> That Lantskip.
>
> (4.136–53)

All of the themes of Renaissance English I have been tracing come together here. Eden is a place of copia, of fruits and blossoms, colors and lights, all bursting at the seams. But it is, too, a place of theater, as if Satan and we see it as a stage set shaped by a divine dramaturge (compare this image of a "woodie Theater" with Shakespeare's enticing image, in the Prologue to *Henry V*, of *his* theater as "this wooden O"). It is *enameled*, a word that, since the Middle Ages, connoted the glossiness of art applied to otherworldly scenes: in the Middle English poem *Sir Orfeo*, the fairy underworld appears with castles colored "Of ich maner diuers aumal" (line 364; in every different kind of enamel). Indeed, in Dante's *Divine Comedy*, there is the "smalto" (enameling) of Limbo and of Purgatory—phrases that evoke a kind of anticipatory Paradise, a place of looking forward to the final union of the hero with God and his beloved. The idiom appears throughout European romance, from the Old French *Roman d'Eneas*, through Ariosto's *Orlando Furioso*. All of these enameled Edens have behind them something of the feel of artifice, as if what we are looking at are not real Paradises but illusory representations of Paradise.

There is, it seems, a double edge to Milton's Eden, then. True, it is not the work of a Satanic artificer of fraud, but there is something about it that looks forward to the fall. It is a place of theater, of rhetoric, of copia, of shiny surfaces. It is "grottesque," not grotesque in the modern sense, but resonant with a certain style of art associated, in the sixteenth and seventeenth centuries, with the Italian grottoes. John Florio, in his translation of Montaigne's *Essays* (1611), writes of the *grotesca* as "anticke or landskip worke of painters."

And that is where Milton's *lantskip* comes in. The word came from the Dutch, *landschap*, a technical term for the genre of painting natural scenery. It shows up, in English, beginning in the early seventeenth century under a variety of spellings (landscape, landtshap, lantshape, landskip, lantskip) all of which evoke the imported, technical quality of the word. It is not, for this century, a word of scenery itself (it does not appear in that sense until the early eighteenth century), but a term of technique. What we see in Eden is a collocation of artistic terms, a language drawn from manuals of painting, lives of painters, descriptions not of the natural but the shaped and painted world.

For this is, in the end, a world of seeming. "Lovely seemed / that Lantskip." And that, it seems to me, lies at the heart of the expanding English lexicon and the character of the Renaissance vernacular. This is a world of seeming: of performances and pictures. Shakespeare's Hamlet has trouble with this world, as he seeks constantly to get behind the costumes and duplicity of public life to hit the core of feeling: "Seems, madam? I know not seems." The new vocabulary comes like a new cloak of language, to be tried on, worn in public, strutted on the streets and in the corridors (another word that first appears in the early seventeenth century), or paraded in private before mirrors of the self. Was this vocabulary something at the heart of English, and of English men and women, or was it instead merely an enameling? In reading speeches, letters, and polemics of the time, are we engaging with a new sense of Englishness, or are we only listening to hubbub? Such were the questions not just of our time but of theirs, and we will see in the work of grammarians and orthoepists an attempt, throughout this early Modern period, to tame the beasts of words, to find right ways of writing and pronouncing, to control the new world English had become.

CHAPTER 11

Visible Speech

The Orthoepists and the Origins of Standard English

AS A YOUNG MAN, Isaac Newton became fascinated by phonetics. In a few pages in a notebook dating from his eighteenth or nineteenth year, Newton came up with a system of presenting English sounds. He arranged the vowels and consonants by means of their articulation; tried to describe the workings of the mouth and throat; and speculated, somewhat obliquely, on whether there could be something like a universal language for humankind. In these sparse jottings, Newton illustrated the features of mid-seventeenth-century English pronunciation. Some of the idiosyncrasies of his transcriptions may be because of his own regional dialect. Some may be caused by his attempts to describe certain sounds in what may seem to us to be odd ways. For example, he described the pronunciation of the *f* sound (what we would call a bilabial continuant) as "caused by shutting the lips and then forcing the breath through them." He comments on sounds produced in the back of the throat as sounding like the Welsh "jarring of the throte as when wee force up flegme" may seem skin-crawlingly clinical. His closing sample letter to a "loving friend," presented in both regular spelling and in the special system of phonetic symbols he devised, seems almost delightfully naïve.

Newton was but the best known of the sixteenth- and seventeenth-century intellectuals who turned their attentions to the study of English pronunciation and spelling. Though his remarks are brief, they bear witness to the profound impact that the study of language had on English scientific culture. For over a century and a half, from John Hart in the 1550s until Jonathan Swift in the 1710s, English scholars, teachers, poets, and public figures weighed in on the pressing language matters of the day. Should there be a standard English, and should its mark be one of region, class, or education? Should spelling reflect history, or should it match the sounds of spoken English? Is there an empirical way of representing speech sounds such that a reader, regardless of his or her dialect, could pronounce those sounds equally well? And finally, behind all of these detailed questions, lay a larger philosophical problem: Was there a universal language for all people, a language of Adam, as it were, from which we have fallen away? Was language, in other words, something that inhered in the human mind, or was it a social convention? Were living languages descended from a common root?

The scholars who investigated such questions have come to be known as the orthoepists. "Orthoepy" was a word coined in the late sixteenth century out of two Greek roots: *ortho*, meaning right, and *epos*, meaning diction. It was the science of correct pronunciation, and the word begins to appear in the early seventeenth century in a clutch of texts concerned with finding ways of representing directly and systematically English pronunciation. In 1668, Bishop John Wilkins, in his *Essay Towards a Real Character and a Philosophical Language*, defined grammar as the subject "concerning the most convenient marks or sounds for the expression of such names or words; whether by writing, Orthography; or by speech, Orthoepy." Orthography and orthoepy, correct writing and correct speaking, provide us with two historical insights into the English language: first, these disciplines enable us to reconstruct the sound of English from about the middle of the sixteenth century on, with levels of detail we cannot really find for Old and Middle English; second, these disciplines participate in the larger, philosophical inquiry into language that motivated much English and European early-modern intellectual life, and they show us questions being asked about speech and writing, word and thing, language and mind, that we still ask today.

Though I have discussed scholars such as Hart and Gil for what they have to say about spelling and word choice, their major contribution to the historical study of the language lies in their attempts to record speech sounds of their times. Hart's goal in his *Orthographie* (1569) was to reform spelling. We should spell as we speak, plain and simple. There should be, he put it, "as many letters in our writing, as we doe voices or breathes in speaking, and no more" (6). In order to bring writing into line with speech, however, Hart needed to come up with a new system of orthography. Figure 11.1 reproduces a page from his book to illustrate how he came up with new spelling conventions and new characters to show those sounds. But just what were those sounds?

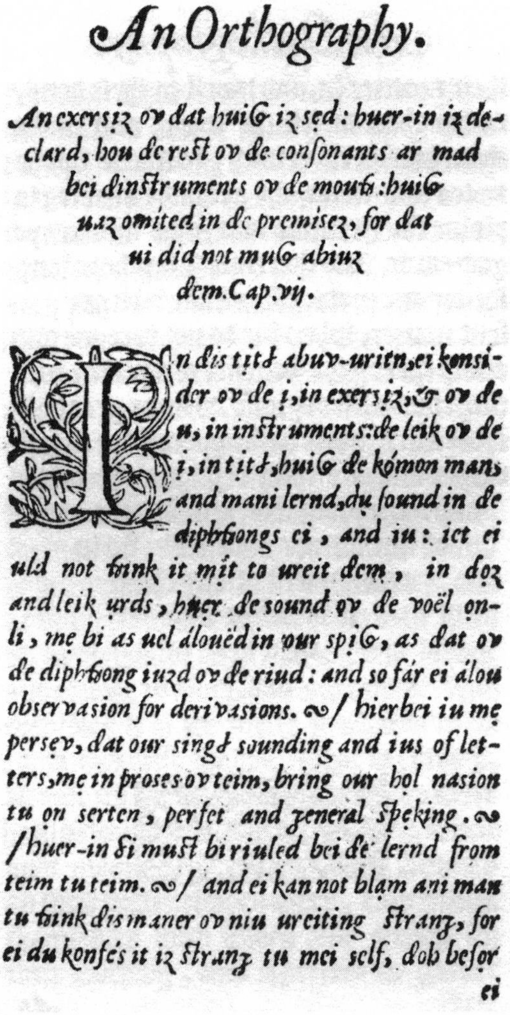

An Orthography.

An exersiz ov dat hui𝔊 iz sed: huer-in iz de-
clard, hou de re𝔰t ov de consonants ar mad
bei din𝔰truments ov de mouth: hui𝔊
uaz omited in de premisez, for dat
ui did not mu𝔊 abiuz
dem. Cap. vij.

n dis titd abuv-uritn, ei konsi-
der ov de i, in exersiz, & ov de
u, in instruments: de leik ov de
i, in titd, hui𝔊 de komon man;
and mani lernd, du found in de
diph𝔰songs ei , and iu: ict ei
uld not think it mit to ureit dem , in doz
and leik urds, huer de sound ov de voël on-
li, me bi as uel áloued in our spi𝔊, as dat ov
de diph𝔰song iuzd ov de riud: and so fár ei álou
observasion for derivasions. ∞/ hierbei iu me
persev, dat our sing𝔰 sounding and ius of let-
ters, me in proses ov teim, bring our hol nasion
tu on serten, perfet and zeneral speking. ∞
/huer-in si must bi riuled bei de lernd from
teim tu teim. ∞/ and ei kan not blam ani man
tu think dis maner ov niu urciting stranz, for
ei du konfes it iz stranz tu mei self, dob befor
ei

FIGURE II.I

An illustration of Hart's system of phonetic transcription.
Source: Hart, *An Orthographie*.

Hart clearly understands the effect of the tongue's height in the mouth on vowels. He describes the five sounds represented by the letters *a, e, i, o,* and *u*, according to the place of the tongue, the rounding of the lips, and the force of the breath. His are some of the first attempts at articulatory phonetics: that is, the description of sounds according to the physical means of their production. But reading through his descriptions is hard, and it is unclear, even to modern, professional phoneticians, just what sounds he is describing. It would appear, for example, that Hart sees the vowels in the words "did" and "teeth" as differing only in quantity, not in quality; similarly, he describes the vowels in the words "but" and "do" as also differing only in quantity; this seems to contradict other evidence that these two sets of words differed in vowel quality—that is, that we have two different vowels in each, not the same vowel held for different periods of time. But there are other sounds that Hart describes that are unambiguous. For example, he describes the pronunciation of the sounds represented by the letters *d* and *t* as the product of putting the tongue "full in the palate of your mouth and touching the hardest of your fore-teeth." This process produces what modern linguists call a dental sound: a sound produced at the teeth. Modern speakers of English, however, tend to produce these sounds by placing the tip of the tongue at the alveolar ridge, just behind the teeth (a pronunciation clearly described by mid- to late-seventeenth-century orthoepists). What Hart is describing, therefore, is an older historical pronunciation.

Scholars have been explicating Hart's work ever since the great Otto Jespersen published a monograph on him in 1907. My concern here is not to parse in detail Hart's phonetic system but, instead, to understand what he based that system on. The best English is that of the "learned": "that speech which euery reasonable English man, will the nearest he can, frame his tongue thereunto; but such as haue no conference by the liuely voice, nor experience of reading, nor in reading no certaintie how euery letter shoulde be sounded, can neuer come to the knowledge and use, of that best and most perfite English" (*Orthographie*, 21r). Hart imagines, then, a community of knowledgeable speakers, literate in the vernacular. He implies, elsewhere, that such speakers will most likely be found in London, in the university towns, and at the court and that such speakers will not be those of such dialect regions as "Newcastell upon Tine" or "Cornewale."

By positing a regional, an educational, and a class level of standard, Hart does more, therefore, than simply record speech sounds. He sets out to provide a model for linguistic performance, and he argues for the unity of social status and linguistic performance. "Some are of the opinion," he writes in the *Orthographie* (in his own, phonetic spelling, which I am translating here), "that it becomes not an emperor, prince, or nobleman to write well and truly. . . . But the more uniformly and stricter any man dost write, no man doubtest but it is the better" (55v). Uniformity and strictness thus become the ideals of both spelling and governance, and there is a sense throughout the *Orthographie* that Hart's is as much a political as it is a linguistic project. For by reforming spelling, he is doing nothing less than reforming society: making it possible for English speakers to write unambiguously, making it possible for those outside of England to understand precisely what is being written. And, so too, for the English to understand their European compeers. At the book's close Hart deploys his phonetic alphabet to record the sounds of Italian, Spanish, and French. His final section is entitled: "Examples how certain other nations do sound their letters, both in Latin, and in their mother tongue, thereby to know the better how to pronounce their speeches, and so to read them as they do" (59r).

Throughout the *Orthographie*, terms such as "reason" and "profit" reappear, and Hart appeals both to the reason behind his phonetic transcriptions and to the profit that his volume offers up its reader (66v). These two terms yoke together the ideas behind Renaissance spelling reform: that there should be a rational motivation for human expression and its forms; that the goal of that expression should be social or economic or political advancement; and that if we profit, intellectually or socially, from forms of learning, such a profit makes ideas into new commodities for the Renaissance world of commerce and exchange.

For all the vigor of his argument, however, Hart's reforms met with opposition. Perhaps the most pointedly articulate of the schoolmasters who opposed new spelling was Richard Mulcaster (1530–1611), the first director of the Merchant Taylor's School in London (and the poet Edmund Spenser's teacher). His *Elementarie* of 1582 was but the first part of a projected (but never completed) guide to English education. Reading and writing, drawing and music were all to form a part of his ideal syllabus, and the *Elementarie* serves as an introduction to the ways of spelling English. But this is more than just a technical manual. Good practice in any discipline, he argues, leads to moral virtue; "profit," here, too, has both a social and a personal goal, grounded both in the possibilities of accomplishment and in the ideals of reason. Mulcaster, much like Hart, yokes these two terms together, notably in the title to his chapter 4: "that this Elementarie and the profitablenese thereof is confirmed by great reason, and most euident proufs" (18). But the relationship of profit and reason leads Mulcaster to a different view of spelling than Hart. "Custom" is Mulcaster's guide, and if the customs of English spelling lead to mockery from abroad, the English may well find the same oddities and inconsistencies in foreign tongues: "If foren peple do maruell at vs, we maie requite them with as much, and return their wonder home, considering theie themselues be subiect to the

verie same difficulties, which theie wonder at in vs, and have no mo letters than we have, and yet both write still, and be vnderstood still" (88).
Languages simply must make do, and English must "rest content with
the number of our letters" (89). The spelling reformers, Mulcaster claims,
"cumber our tung, both with strange caracts, & with nedelesse dipthongs,
enforcing vs from that, which generall rule hath won, and rested content
with" (89).

Mulcaster does not advocate complete reliance on old spellings. Even
a cursory glance at his text shows some idiosyncrasies calibrated to make
words more transparent in their pronunciation. But, in the end, his goal
is not to recast but refine (his own term for what he wants to do is to
"fine" English). He seeks a middle way between phonetic transcription
and historical spelling, and he devotes more than fifty pages to an alpha-
betic table of words designed to get the student both to spell clearly and
to speak well. In the process, he offers information about some historical
pronunciations. For example, Mulcaster introduces words beginning with
the letter *h*: "H, is so gentlie pronounced, or rather so no pronounced in
our tung, as manie words, which begin with it, maie be sought for by their
first vowel, rather then h, onelesse the originall be well known, as honest, humble, honor, hostage, &c. which sound upon the o, not aspirate"
(194). From such a remark, we can see that even among educated speakers,
dropping the initial *h*-sound was commonplace. In the case of the letter *g*,
Mulcaster's note on pronunciation leads him to simplify certain spellings.
"The strong g, before, e, and i, in English is warranted by the like in greke
tung." Thus, in words such as *guilt*, *guise*, *guest*, and the like, the initial
spelling *gu-* is unnecessary. As he put it earlier in the *Elementarie*, "Why do
some vse to put an u, after the strong g, in som places, . . . and not write
them all without the u, and with the g onlie" (120). In cases such as this
one, commonsense pronunciation rather than historical precedent should
guide the spelling (historically, as Mulcaster may or may not have known,
gu- spellings entered Middle English as a French convention indicating the
voiced stop /g/). But this discussion also tells us something about English
pronunciation at the end of the sixteenth century, for Mulcaster would re-
serve the *-gu-* spellings for words such as *language*, *Guichiardine*, *Guin*, and
guerdon. All of these words would have the *-gu-* pronounced as /gw/, and
so what we have here is an attempt to make certain spelling conventions
uniquely correspond to certain sounds (we know from evidence such as
this that the Middle English word *langage*, /langaʒə/ had, by Mulcaster's
time, changed in pronunciation to the modern *language*, /langwidʒ/).

For Alexander Gil, custom and history go further back than Mulcaster would think. Gil looks to the original Germanic settlers in Britain, arguing that their speech had a "purity": that it resisted loan words, save through Chaucer, but that it could accept new words if they could represent new concepts without fundamentally corrupting English. Corruption in spelling, too, came from abroad, with printers such as Wynkyn de Worde (whom Gil incorrectly brands a German) altering the old conventions to conform to newer European models. In short, Gil's goal is to get English spelling to conform to native English sounds: not to use the conventions of other languages to present those sounds (an obvious example here is Gil's retention of the Old English letter ð instead of -th-). Custom, for Gil, evokes the essence of a people, not mere social convention. But when such custom is "manifestly at variance with proper pronunciation," then it should be abandoned in favor of such propriety. But what is "proper pronunciation" [in his Latin, *vera prosodia*]? He answers:

> In morals the agreement of good men, and in language the practice of the learned, is the determining rule. Therefore writing will have to conform not to the pronunciation of plowmen, working-girls, and river-men [*bubulci, muherculae, potiores*], but to that used by learned and refined men [*docti et culte eruditi viri*] in their speech and writing. And just as accomplished artists represent the appearance of the human face so that it resembles the living feature, so it should be proper to transcribe the sounds of the human voice so that we do not misrepresent the true pronunciation in any way.
>
> (Gil, *Logonomia Anglica*, Alston trans., 87)

On the one hand, Gil is acutely conscious of the social registers of speech sound. Learning and refinement contrast with menial labor (Gil's words for the plowmen, working-girls, and river-men are, in fact, terms from a rarified, Ciceronian vocabulary: terms for a lesser class that only display Gil's own learning). Speech marks social class, and social class is a function of education. But spelling, too, has something of an artistic or representational function. It mimes the voice much as a painting mimes the face. And so, his arguments for orthography have not just a rational or customary basis but an aesthetic one.

To these ends Gil, like Hart and many other orthoepists of the time, develops his own phonetic alphabet, and the pronunciations he records are not so much the transcripts of lived speech as they are ideals of accomplishment. But also Gil distinguishes not only lower-class pronunciations or regional dialect forms but affectations. The group he calls the Mopsae (after the figure of Mopsa, an affected, ignorant girl in Sir Philip Sidney's *Arcadia*) represents a level of social aspiration that Gil finds tasteless. He lists many Mopsae pronunciations, some of which seem to conform to the dialect sounds of South Eastern English, and some of which seem, in retrospect, to be advanced sounds, anticipating later changes in pronunciation that would become standard. Here are some of his examples (using his spelling system):

> *len* instead of *laun* (linen)
> *kembrik* instead of *kambric* (cambric)
> *kepn* instead of *kapon* (capon)
> *medz* instead of *maidz* (maids)
> *ple* instead of *play* (play)
> *gi* instead of *giv* (give)

Modern scholars have gone through this evidence in great detail, illustrating how these Mopsae sounds, at times, raise standard English vowels or drop certain sounds altogether. Gil summarizes all this evidence as illustrating how the Mopsae "affect the thinness" of what he calls "the Eastern dialect" (Dobson, *English Pronunciation*, 149). But what strikes me is less his philological rigor than his judgment calls. What we have, really for the first time, is a sustained account of how pronunciation signals "affectation"—indeed, what we have embedded in this claim is a notion of affectation itself. That word, according to the *OED*, begins to appear in English at the close of the sixteenth century and the beginning of the seventeenth to connote false display, nonnatural behavior, a putting on of airs. Shakespeare, of course, was well aware of this social performance. In his *Merry Wives of Windsor* (written at the close of the 1590s and first printed in 1602), a work of staggering wordplay, characters' pronunciations hold themselves up for unsparing mockery. The Welshman Sir Hugh Evans (who speaks in a clearly identifiable Welsh accent) can make fun of rustic Pistol, who in uttering the phrase, "He hears with ears," enjoins the response:

> What phrase is this, "He hears with ears"? Why, it is affectations.
>
> (1.1143)

As Mulcaster would have us know, just about anyone, let alone Pistol, would have probably said something like "Ee eers with ears." But in this passage, Pistol clearly says his *hs*, to distinguish "hear" and "ear" and drive his wordplay home. For Sir Hugh Evans, this is affectation.

And it would have been affectation, too, for Gil and his followers. In the century after the publication of the *Logonomia Anglica*, savants of all stripes looked into the ways in which English pronunciation signaled social status and how spelling should, or should not, be reformed. Their works are legion: literally hundreds of books appeared throughout the seventeenth and eighteenth centuries on these subjects, and to survey them all would demand volumes. Among the most important, and among my favorites, is John Wallis's *Grammatica* of 1663, a brilliant work (written in Latin), that had such a lasting impact that as late as 1819 Walter Scott could rely on its observations to show, in his novel *Ivanhoe*, that (as I noted in an earlier chapter) the names of the animals are Old English, while the names for the meats are French. Wallis is, at one level, no more accurate than any other orthoepist. He describes vowels and consonants according to their physical means of production no better, or no worse, than anyone else. But what sets his work apart is his systematic presentation. The *Grammatica* is full of charts: attempts to place speech sounds in symmetry, to classify them, not just to describe them. His chart of the sounds anticipates the modern phonetician's arrangement according to the place and manner of articulation.

This need to diagram, to locate physically and visually the sounds of speech, also informs *The Vocal Organ*, by Owen Price, of 1665. This volume's opening presents a picture of the human head and mouth and the location of the vowel sounds in it (see figure 11.3). As far as I can tell, this is the first time anyone had sought to represent English pronunciation pictorially. We see the vowels emerging from the throat at different levels. We see the tongue, the lips, and teeth arranged to form the consonants. This man and woman here give us anatomy of speech but also a guide to making such sounds on our own. This guidance governs, too, the chart of sounds in Bishop John Wilkins's *Essay Towards a Real Character and a Philosophical Language* (1668). Sounds, now, are not just abstractions or disembodied vibrations of air. They are embodied, physical phenomena: actions of human heads and mouths. Such pictures are designed not just to illustrate "correct" pronunciation for the native speaker; they are offered, too, as models for non-English men and women who would learn the language (see figure 11.2).

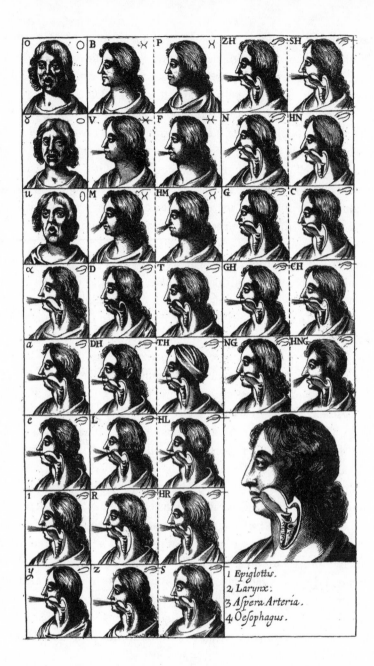

FIGURE II.2

The shapes of the mouth according to the sounds of spoken English.
Source: Wilkins, *Essay Towards a Real Character*, 36.

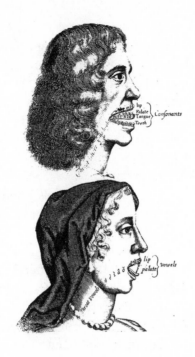

FIGURE 11.3

The location of the sounds of spoken English in the
human mouth and throat.
Source: Price, *The Vocal Organ*.

What can we learn from all this evidence? From among the welter of
their transcripts and descriptions, some key features emerge. First and
foremost, is the evidence that the Great Vowel Shift had not fully run its
course by the end of the seventeenth century. The Middle English high
vowel /iː/ appeared as diphthongs of varying quality: some people seem
to have pronounced it as /əi/, others as /ɛi/, others as /ei/, others as /æi/,
others still as /ai/. Some orthoepists do not even record diphthongization.
Certain other sounds were also in transition. The back vowel /a/ after
/w/ tends, in modern pronunciation, to be rounded and altered in quality:
thus we pronounce words like *can*, *arm*, *hand*, and *scar*, differently from
wan, *warm*, *wand*, and *war*. Evidence from the orthoepists corresponds to
evidence from poetic rhymes that, in fact, this change had not fully happened and that words such as *can* and *wan*, or *arm* and *warm*, could be full
rhymes. (Roger Lass, in his chapter on phonology in the *Cambridge History*

of the English Language, notes that this evidence shows "that the rounding of ME /a/ after /w/ . . . must postdate the reign of Queen Anne," that is, after the second decade of the eighteenth century [67].) This material also explains such rhymes as "one" and "shoon" in Shakespeare or "one" and "soon" in Milton: that is, that the initial glide /w/ had not become standard in the pronunciation of the word "one" and that the vowel was being pronounced as a long /o/ or even a long /u/. And there are many other subtleties of pronunciation that a close study of the orthoepists can reveal: for example, the emerging differences between the sounds in such words as "put" and "cut"; or the instability of vowels before *r* (for example, the pronunciation of words such as *clerk*, *servant*, and *Berkeley* with the /ar/ sound or the /ɪr/ sound).

But what we also learn from orthoepists is a philosophy of language. Scholars such as Wallis, Price, and Wilkins differ from their predecessors such as Hart and Gil in what the modern scholar Murray Cohen calls their "phonetic specificity and visual descriptions." But, Cohen continues, "unlike the phonetic spelling reformers of the late-sixteenth century, the new linguists seek in the physical nature of sound a natural or rational connection between speech and reality." Wallis, Cohen illustrates, suggests that "the physical elements of speech [form] the basis of a complete linguistic description of existence" (*Sensible Words*, 77). It is as if sounds themselves bear the essences of meaning: as if works look back to old originals from which one could recapture sense. In fact, Wallis's fascination with onomatopoeia (a word, by the mid-seventeenth century, still so much a part of the technical, linguistic vocabulary that Wallis spells it out in Greek) comes out of an impression, as he states it, that there are words "which indicate by their actual sound the different characters of the things they signify" (Wallis, *Grammar*, 119). Wilkins takes these impressions further, arguing explicitly that "The Essence of Letters doeth consist in their Power or proper sound, which may be naturally fixed and stated, from the manner of forming them by the instruments of speech; and either is, or should be the same in all Languages" (*Essay*, 357). The precise physical description of sounds, then, is an equally precise description of reality itself. In such works as Price's *Vocal Organ* or Wilkins's *Essay*, the concern with organizing, ordering, and placing sounds is part and parcel of a larger, philosophical concern with showing how the sonic and linguistic order mirrors the natural order. There is, for Wilkins, nothing less than a "Natural Character of the Letters" (*Essay*, 375), a direct association between sound and sense that transcends local languages or social habits.

It is precisely this attachment to an essentialist, or metaphysical, notion of sound and word that the nineteenth-century historical philologists rejected, and the legacy of their tradition remained still alive in the Oxford philology I saw in the mid-1970s. For all its detail, E. J. Dobson's *English Pronunciation, 1500–1700*, a masterpiece of scholarly recovery, pays almost no attention to the philosophical motives of the orthoepists. What he does, strikingly, attend to is the scholarly and social modeling that these sixteenth- and seventeenth-century savants offer the modern academic. Much like his sources, Dobson writes a book of values. He judges his sources. Hart, for example, "commences, as a good phonetician should, with a description of the organs of speech" (73), and he praises "the excellence of his analysis of speech and his understanding of phonetic method" (88). William Bullokar remains "incomparably the inferior" of Hart (117), while Richard Mulcaster, "one of the greatest Elizabethan pedagogues" (117), offers work that "is on the whole disappointing, but it has certain merits which should not be overlooked" (127). Alexander Gil, by contrast, is something of the hero, albeit an almost tragic one, for while his system of spelling reform "was not a perfect phonetic representation of English, . . . it would have served as a more practical basis of a reformed spelling than any of those we have yet discussed. It was thoroughgoing and simple and did not depart too far from the old orthography." Dobson continues: "It may indeed be thought a great pity that it was not adopted, for a reform was at that time still practicable; and though it might have been found later that changes in the system were necessary, it would not have been difficult to make them. Gil's failure involved the failure of the whole movement for reform in his time" (131).

I vividly remember Dobson. Small, slight, and quiet, he was in his early sixties when I attended his Oxford lectures and tutorials—but he seemed much older, freighted by the academic gown he always (and even then somewhat anachronistically) wore. His own pronunciation was so careful and precise, so perfect in its miming of Oxonian donnishness, that I never would have known that he had grown up in Australia. That may have been exactly the point (indeed, many of the Oxford philologists of my time there were not British: Norman Davis was from New Zealand; Bruce Mitchell was from Australia; Eric Stanley was from Germany). For *English Pronunciation* is a book about class and region. Throughout, Dobson calls attention to the provincial origins of his orthoepists and their attitudes toward social class. Bullokar's phonetic transcriptions, for example, reveal that for all of his "adoption" of Standard English, his own speech "nevertheless retained many traces of [his] dialectical or vulgar pronunciation" (116). Gil, though originally from Lincolnshire, was schooled at Oxford and lived in London: "we may assume that his speech was that of the educated classes, the standard speech of his time . . . in fact, he describes the speech of Lincolnshire in a way that makes it clear that he himself did not use it, though he admits that he is a native of that country" (131).

What does it mean to be a native? How does the study of the orthoepists grant us insight into attitudes to class and language? What seems clear from their work is that in the early-modern period, education and standard English came to be associated. The orthoepic manuals presented guides to good behavior: models of performance for a changing world, where speech and writing offer access to profit. Spelling "reform" was both a linguistic and a social goal: a way of re-forming society. But there is, too, throughout the orthoepists, a wonderful eccentricity. These were obsessive men, brilliantly attentive to the smallest details of linguistic life, seeking to rephrase language and experience into their own idiosyncratic spelling systems, looking for the essences of nature in airways of the human throat. In the last note on "Further Reading" in his chapter in the *Cambridge History of the English Language*, Roger Lass passes judgment on Dobson much as one would pass judgment on his sources: *English Pronunciation, 1500–1700* remains "phonetically eccentric and linguistically naïve, and should be read with great care" (186). But in that eccentricity or naïveté lie the most fascinating insights, if not into language, then into the linguists who would re-form themselves, whatever their origin, into authorities and scholars. Read them with care.

CHAPTER 12

A Harmless Drudge

Samuel Johnson and the Making of the Dictionary

WAS SAMUEL JOHNSON MAD? We tend, these days, to pathologize the past, to understand creativity in illness. Robert Schumann's mania, Virginia Woolf's depression, Vincent van Gogh's psychosis, Isaac Newton's Asperger's syndrome—all are invoked to frame imaginative works in ways that we can explain, or explain away. For modern students, Johnson's quirks evoke more than the eccentricities of intellection. His great biographer, James Boswell, records him struggling to get out of a doorway, only to at last hurl himself through (a sign, some think, of an obsessive-compulsive disorder); he tells tales of Johnson muttering and sputtering, hands flailing as he holds court in the coffee house or tavern (a sign, some think, of Tourette's syndrome); and he recounts, as Johnson himself often did, despair at failing to accomplish anything of note or taking on great projects that could never be completed (a sign, some think, too, of depression). For the clinically minded reader, all of the characteristics appear at the beginning of the preface to the *Dictionary* Johnson published in 1755.

It is the fate of those who toil at the lower employments of life, to be rather driven by the fear of evil, than attracted by the prospect of good; to be exposed to censure, without hope of praise; to be disgraced by miscarriage, or punished for neglect, where success would have been without applause, and diligence without reward.

Among these unhappy mortals is the writer of dictionaries; whom mankind have considered, not as the pupil, but the slave of science, the pionier [sic] of literature; doomed only to remove rubbish and clear obstructions from the paths of Learning and Genius, who press forward to conquest and glory, without bestowing a smile on the humble drudge that facilitates their progress. Every other authour may aspire to praise; the lexicographer can only hope to escape reproach, and even this negative recompense has been yet granted to very few.

There is an unmistakable sadness to these lines, a sense that the lexicographer toils lowly, that he cannot be rewarded for his true accomplishments, that all he can aspire to is lack of blame, rather than praise. But there is, at the level of the clause, an almost obsessive rhetorical parallelism. Phrases concatenate on one another here; alliterations ring ("slave of science," "remove rubbish"); assonances chime ("success . . . applause," "humble drudge," "author . . . aspire"). It is as if the rhetoric reveals the man, as if these feints expose his compulsions in their verbs: *toil, driven, attracted, exposed, disgraced, punished.*

From the start, Johnson's *Dictionary* feeds our need to see the person in the work, and generations of his readers (long before anyone would diagnose him medically) have found him at such moments "captivating" and "enticing." As the scholar Ruth Mack puts it, in a recent study of the Johnsonian persona, we find always in the *Dictionary*—in its preface and its commentaries, but also in its definitions and selections of illustrative quotations—"the personal, emotional presence of its author" (61). Though there were dictionary makers before Johnson, and though two centuries of orthoepists had made language study a true discipline, Johnson effectively invented the persona of the lexicographer and, in the process, reinvented himself as the great figure out of literary history we know him to be.

Of course, Johnson's *Dictionary* did more than present a linguistic persona. It created the public idea of the dictionary as the arbiter of language use. It made such a book the kind of object everyone would have and use. More pointedly, it shaped the English of its time and for a century afterward. It regularized spelling and grammatical forms. It codified and sanctioned pronunciations. It broadened the vocabulary of everyday speech, while at the same time seeking to excise slang and colloquial expressions from polite discourse. And, in its use of literary examples to illustrate word uses, forms, and histories, the *Dictionary* affirmed a canon of English literature and critical appreciation: it was both a product of and subsequent teacher of taste. In all these areas, Johnson set the mold for later lexicographers: from Noah Webster and his *Dictionary of the American Language* (first published in 1828), to the founders and the editors of the *Oxford English Dictionary* (published from 1889 to 1928), who, in fact, first called their work the *New English Dictionary*—for the *old* one was Johnson's.

Just what did Johnson do; what were the sources of his work; how does his lexicography write out not just a history of English or a record of its use but an autobiographical account of its maker? Can there really be an *author* of a dictionary, or is such work so necessarily collaborative that individual authority is but a ruse? And, finally, how is this *Dictionary* (or any dictionary, really) not some static object but a work in dialogue with readers and, indeed, itself? For almost as soon as the *Dictionary* first appeared in 1755, Johnson went to work revising it. New quotations, new definitions, and new orderings took shape, such that by the fourth edition of 1773 a very different kind of book appeared: richer with literary texts but following a more articulated arc of politics, philosophy, and poetic imagination.

Johnson's original ideas for a dictionary came out of a constellation of personal ambition and commercial enterprise. Hard-word books proliferated in the seventeenth and early eighteenth centuries to deal with the verbiage of colonial expansion, scientific inquiry, and rhetorical display. Such volumes, for the most part, were but word lists, little concerned with locating their entries either in the history of the language or the speech and writing of their promulgators. By the first decades of the eighteenth century, however, makers of such books perceived a need to order their information systematically. Ephraim Chambers's *Cyclopaedia* of 1728 and Nathan Bailey's various dictionaries (from the *Universal Etymological Dictionary* of 1721, through his *Dictionarium Britannicum* of 1730, to his *Dictionary* of 1736) set out to find ways of arranging verbal information. Central to both was the location of the word in history. The etymologies of words had long been debated. The old traditions of essentialist, or metaphysical, etymology had sought word meanings in some imagined, precise relationship of sound and sense. There still is some of this tradition in the early dictionaries, but what Bailey in particular did was to use etymology as a way of organizing the hierarchy of a word's usages or connotations. He defined etymology as "a Part of Grammar, shewing the Original of words, in order to fix their true Meaning and Signification" (quoted in Reddick, *The Making of Johnson's Dictionary*, 48), and, therefore, the order in which one presents the definitions of a word should follow that original. Take a familiar word like "mother." The hard-word books offered only the technical or new uses of the term. Henry Cockerham (1623) gives only, "A disease in women when the wombe riseth with paine upwards." Elisha Coles (1676) begins with "a painful rising of the womb," while the anonymous *Gazophylacium Anglicanum* of 1689 starts with "The mother of Wine, from the Belg. Moeder, lees, thickning." Bailey begins by attesting all of the Germanic and

Romance cognates for the word and then orders the initial range of definitions from the most obviously oldest or original to the most technical: "method of a child; also the womb itself; also a disease peculiar to that part; also a white substance on stale liquors." Bailey then ranges pages of quotations, sources, and authorities for the idea of the "mother tongue," in essence offering a miniature dissertation on linguistic history.

Johnson was clearly provoked by the rise of these new dictionaries, and he was provoked, too, by the new culture of bookselling in the London of the first third of the eighteenth century. Books were commodities; they made people money (Johnson himself famously averred, "No man but a blockhead ever wrote except for money"). But booksellers often functioned as publishers themselves, often commissioning authors to produce volumes that they then would manufacture and distribute. Some booksellers, like Jacob Tonson, were not only publishers but claimed to be copyright holders—in fact, Tonson claimed to hold the rights to Shakespeare's works, preventing anyone who did not publish with him from producing an edition of the playwright (this move stifled Johnson's attempt to publish a Shakespeare edition with the publisher Edward Cave). Tonson was also alive to the popularity of dictionaries, and he apparently offered the journalist Joseph Addison three thousand pounds "to make an English dictionary and put it out under his name" (Reddick, *The Making of Johnson's Dictionary*, 16).

Johnson knew that he could not produce a work as large as a dictionary without the agreement of the London book trade, and his course of action was to rely both on this new institution and on a very old tradition: aristocratic patronage. His initial ideas, published under the title *The Plan of a Dictionary of the English Language*, were dedicated to Lord Chesterfield. Johnson recognizes that there is a precedent for patronage for such a work. "I had read indeed," he notes, "of times, in which princes and statesmen thought it part of their honour to promote the improvement of their native tongues, and in which great dictionaries were written under the protection of greatness" (2). The *Plan* is a plea for patronage, and much of its rhetoric is designed to subordinate the lexicographer to the lord. "Low" and "lowly" are the terms it uses to define the dictionary maker's job (terms that will reappear, though subtly changed, in the preface to the *Dictionary* itself). And throughout, the *Plan* seeks to align language along patterns of control and hierarchy. Johnson's goal is to "fix" usage; to "adjust" etymology; to explain the "irregularities" of inflections. "Thus, my Lord," Johnson writes, "will our language be laid down, distinct in its minutest subdivisions, and resolved into its elemental principles" (18).

Lexicography becomes a form of social ordering, and the *Plan* offers up not just a program for research but an essay on the politics of language. Much as one might wonder who should be a subject or a citizen, a colonist or one colonized, so Johnson reflects on just what kinds of words to let in to the language. Some words from foreign languages, he notes, "are not equally to be considered as parts of our language, for some of them are naturalized and incorporated, but others still continue aliens, and are rather auxiliaries than subjects" (6). Words are like foreigners, some to be *naturalized* (a word Johnson would define in the *Dictionary* as "to adopt into a community; to invest with the privileges of native subjects"), others to remain *aliens*. The very word *subjects*, here, signals membership in the imperium of England (the *Dictionary*, again: *subject*, "one who lives under the dominion of another"). Johnson returns to this imperial idiom at the *Plan*'s close:

> When I survey the Plan which I have laid before you, I cannot, my Lord, but confess, that I am frighted at its extent, and, like the soldiers of Caesar, look on Britain as a new world, which it is almost madness to invade. But I hope, that though I should not complete the conquest, I shall at least discover the coast, civilize part of the inhabitants, and make it easy for some other adventurer to proceed farther, to reduce them wholly to subjection, and settle them under laws.
>
> (33)

Notice the terms here: *survey*, the action that the English were best known for when they entered a new land; and then *invade, conquest, civilize, subjection*, and *settle*. And if the goals of empire were to control, then so too were the goals of lexicography.

> This, my Lord, is my idea of an English dictionary, a dictionary by which the pronunciation of our language may be fixed, and its attainment facilitated; by which its purity may be preserved, its use ascertained, and its duration lengthened.

Such a task, Johnson notes, is equal to the attempt "to correct the language of nations by books of grammar, and amend their manners by discourses of morality" (32).

The goal of Johnson's *Plan* was to create a dictionary that would fix the English language: that would settle matters of pronunciation, spelling, usage, and etymology; that would be "design'd not merely for critics but for popular use" (7); that would arrange and order definitions ranging from literal and historical to metaphorical and current. But after years of false starts, failures, and impediments—he was unable to complete the task in the three years he set himself; his wife died in the process; his amanuenses found his work almost impossible to follow; he abandoned Chesterfield's patronage—after all this he realized that it is impossible to fix a language. In the preface to the *Dictionary* that finally appeared in 1755, he saw a language not imperial but "sublunary," mutable and transitory. Like Caxton, who saw English living under the "domynacioun of the moon," Johnson found himself incapable of fixing usage. His purpose, now, had become "not to form, but register the language; not to teach men how they should think, but relate how they have hitherto expressed their thoughts."

Why did he change his mind? Scholars have long noted Johnson's despair during the eight years that the *Dictionary* took shape. They have noticed how he came to realize that the ordering of definitions was hardly as straightforward as he imagined in the *Plan*. They have noticed, too, how, as Johnson came to rely more and more upon his store of literary quotations, the *Dictionary* moved progressively away from a complete description of the English language to a personal account of Johnson's own: in Alan Reddick's words, "to a unique and more personal dictionary, one reflecting Johnson's critical brilliance" (50). But it is certainly true that Johnson's rejection of Chesterfield's patronage had much to do with the form and the idiom of the *Dictionary*. Chesterfield, in fact, had little to do with the work. After Johnson's initial dedication of the *Plan*, he seems to have done little to support the lexicographer; only when the *Dictionary* seemed about to appear did the old patron return to try to claim some credit. Johnson threw him off, and that rejection changed, I think, the nature of his lexicography. For if the lexicographer himself was not to be subordinated to the lord, then how could language be subordinated to the rules of lexicography? How could one fix, correct, adjust, or regularize usage when one would, himself, refuse such fixing?

Without a patron, Johnson saw himself at sea. In the great letter that he wrote to Chesterfield (February 7, 1755), he makes this imagery explicit:

Is not a Patron, My Lord, one who looks with unconcern on a Man struggling for Life in the water and when he has reached ground encumbers him with help. The notice which you have been pleased to take of my Labours, had it been early, had been kind; but it has been delayed till I am indifferent and cannot enjoy it, till I am solitary and cannot impart it, till I am known, and do not want it.

How can we not see Johnson's views of lexicography and language not inflected by this turmoil? In the preface to the *Dictionary* he remarks on how words change so often and so quickly that their true "relations . . . can no more be ascertained in a dictionary, than a grove, in the agitation of a storm, can be accurately delineated from its picture in the water." Words, much like Johnson, are in turmoil; what is left is solitary labor.

And so Johnson's *Dictionary*, for all its reliance on amanuenses, is a work of solitude, a product of a life of reading. It develops an authoritative voice all of its own. Its definitions read like maxims. Its illustrative quotations feel (for that is the only way to put it) just right. But for all of the *Dictionary*'s personality, this is a book for the general reader. In the words of the preface, it is designed for the reader who would "aspire to exactness of criticism or elegance of style." Lexicography had become a branch of aesthetics. But language here is not a static thing, some well-wrought urn to be admired. Language is an act; style and criticism are verbal performances, the first a matter of the production, the second a matter of the reception of texts.

In his selection of those texts, as well as in the technicalities of his lexicography, Johnson enacts what many modern critics have seen as a uniquely mid-eighteenth-century critical ideal: to discover what had proven to be the most generally durable or characteristic quality in things, and then to profit by using that quality as a standard working basis (see Wimsatt, *Philosophic Words*). From this perspective, Johnson attempted to find the best in English usage of his day and, by recording it, to sanction and to stabilize it. But, in keeping with his ideals of an English literary and linguistic culture, he rejected the formation of any institution that would legislate the ways of language. One of the great debates among the pedagogues and poets of the generations before Johnson was whether England should form a language academy on the model of the Académie Française or the Accademia della Crusca. Both of these institutions had inaugurated great dictionary projects for their respective vernaculars—dictionaries that were to be collaborations of the savants of the nations. English writers from Dryden to Swift had advocated the establishment of such an academy, and Joseph Addison began work on a dictionary that, though never finished, was advertised as made "according to the Method of the celebrated one of the French Academy" (quoted in Reddick, *The Making of Johnson's Dictionary*, 14).

Johnson would have none of this. Boswell recounts a conversation Johnson had soon after he began work on the *Dictionary* in which he is told that the "French Academy, which consists of forty members, took forty years to compile their Dictionary." Johnson replies, recalling that he claimed he could produce his work in three years, working alone: "Sir, thus it is. This is the proportion. Let me see; forty times forty is sixteen hundred. As three to sixteen hundred, so is the proportion of an Englishman to a Frenchman." And so, the Englishness of Johnson's *Dictionary* was to lie in an ideal of individual accomplishment (again, perhaps this individuality hearkens back to his rejection of Chesterfield's patronage). Philology, to paraphrase a famous maxim, was politics by other means, and in the 1740s and 1750s—with England constantly at odds with France—lexicography became aesthetic *and* political. Even some words from French were not to be admitted (or at the very least, not without qualification). Look up *chaperon* in the *Dictionary* and you find this judgment: "an affected word of very recent introduction."

But there may also be an Englishness to Johnson in the method he pursued. The *Dictionary*'s underlying theories of language owe much to the work of John Locke, in many ways the founder of a distinctively British strain of empiricism and, for the eighteenth century in particular, the most influential thinker about knowledge, language, and social action. Locke seems almost everywhere in Johnson's writings: from his lexicography, to his criticism, to his personal ruminations, Johnson clearly held to Locke's idea that words stood for "the Ideas in the Mind of him that uses them." Sensation was the source of understanding, and words need to be carefully discriminated. Signification was a process of engaging with the world and with the passions of the mind, and both Locke and Johnson saw the business of defining words as sorting out and ordering the meanings from the oldest or the literal, to the newest and the figurative.

Locke permeates the *Dictionary*. His ideas inform the *Plan* and the preface; his quotations fill the illustrations of the words. Hardly a page goes by without a source in Locke (it has been calculated that the first volume of the first edition alone has 1,674 quotations from Locke—close to a fifth of all its philosophical or intellectual illustrative texts; Hedrick, "Locke's Theory of Language," 423–24). One can choose words, almost at random, and find something Lockean about them. *Covetous*, and there, right after Shakespeare, is Locke: "Let never so much probability hang on one side of a covetous man's reasoning, and money on the other, it is easy to foresee which will outweigh." *Flail*, following Milton and Dryden: "the dextrous handling of the flail." *Argue* gets three quotations, including this one: "I do not see how they can argue with any one, without setting down strict boundaries." *Prosecute*: "He prosecuted this purpose with strength of argument and close reasoning, without incoherent sallies."

If Locke provides the underpinnings of the *Dictionary*'s theory of language and many of its intellectual quotations, then it is John Milton who provides it with its sense of poetry. True, Shakespeare stands almost unrivalled in the first edition of 1755, but as Johnson reread and revised for the later editions, Milton takes over. By the fourth edition of 1773, he has displaced Shakespeare as the most frequently quoted, named author. Johnson had grown to admire Milton, far more than he had as a young man (his famous bon mot about *Paradise Lost* was "none wished it longer"). But, as he noted to Boswell in 1773, "I think more highly of him now than I did at twenty" (Reddick, *The Making of Johnson's Dictionary*, 123). And of all his works, it was *Paradise Lost* that formed the core of Johnson's Miltonism. As Reddick puts it, explaining the increase in Miltonic quotations throughout the *Dictionary*'s revisions, "The combination of the lyric power, moral seriousness, scriptural subject, and inherent authority of the Miltonic voice made Milton a powerful rhetorical figure for Johnson's purposes" (122). Indeed, Johnson may well have seen the making of the *Dictionary* itself as an endeavor comparable to Milton's writing of *Paradise Lost*, a thing "unattempted yet in prose or rhyme." As Johnson remarks in the preface, "it must be remembered that I am speaking of that which words are insufficient to explain."

And yet, for all the boasting, there is elegy. Johnson misses things: misses the sureness of the *Plan*, misses stability in language and in life. His evocations in the preface have the flavor of a paradise now lost.

> I saw that one enquiry only gave occasion to another, that book referred to book, that to search was not always to find, and to find was not always to be informed; and that thus to persue perfection, was, like the first inhabitants of Arcadia, to chace the sun, which, when they had reached the hill where he seemed to rest, was still beheld at the same distance from them.

Johnson began much like, perhaps, Milton's own God, who made order out of chaos and brought light with but a word. "When I took the first survey of my undertaking," he writes in the preface, "I found our speech copious without order, and energetick without rules: wherever I turned my view,

there was perplexity to be disentangled, and confusion to be regulated."
Survey is one of the most charged verbs of *Paradise Lost*: a word of knowing vision applied both to God's creation ("God saw, surveying his great
work, that it was good") and to Satan's bad empire ("he then survey'd Hell,
and the gulf between"). From the start, Johnson is a figure out of Milton's
poem: surveying and seeking to control.

From Locke and Milton, too, Johnson derived not just an Englishness
of idiom or ideology, but also an ideal of figurative language. The great
Miltonic similes, with their extended yoking of disparate things into new
figurative forms, gave Johnson something of an inkling not of English's
linguistic past but of its future. They show a move from technical and literal senses to metaphorical connotations. Johnson, in fact, took it almost as
a general principle of linguistic change that technical words become metaphorical ones—a principle that may have motivated Milton's imaginative
diction, but that also motivated Locke's view of signification. "The original
sense of words," Johnson wrote in the preface,

> is often driven out of use by their metaphorical acceptations, yet must
> be inserted for the sake of a regular origination. Thus, I know not
> whether ardour is used for material heat, or whether flagrant in Eng-
> lish ever signifies the same with the burning. Yet such are the primi-
> tive ideas of these words . . .

Look up *ardent* in Bailey's *Dictionary* and you find: "hot as it were burning, very
hot; also vehement, eager, zealous." Bailey makes the psychological meaning
a special instance of a more general definition. Johnson, by contrast, makes
the scientific meaning the primary, natural one, and he relegates the psychological meanings to secondary status through his numbering arrangement.
But if we look at the whole arc of definitions, running from *ardent*, through
ardently, to *ardour*, we can see vividly the move not just from the technical to
the figurative, but from the philosophical and natural to the imaginative and
literary. *Ardent* begins with Newton's *Opticks*, and Newton's "ardent spirits"
are not creatures out of fantasy but volatile liquids. Now, move to definition
2 and see how Dryden illustrates "ardent eyes"—still burning, but somewhat
figuratively. Definition 3 is the most figurative, "passionate," and the illustration comes from Prior's poetry. Then, we see the sequence again in *Ardour*:
from technical and prose, through Dryden once again, to Pope, and finally to
Milton. These really are, now, ardent spirits, and the path to Milton in these
quotations is always, too, a path from darkness to light, a path of observation,

The ineffable happiness of our dear Redeemer must needs bring an increase to ours, commensurate to the *ardency* of our love for him. *Boyle.*

A′RDENT. *adj.* [*ardens*, Lat. burning.]

1. Hot; burning; fiery.

Chymists observe, that vegetables, as lavender, rue, marjoram, &c. distilled before fermentation, yield oils without any burning spirits; but, after fermentation, yield *ardent* spirits without oils; which shews, that their oil is, by fermentation, converted into spirit. *Newton's Opticks.*

2. Fierce; vehement.

A knight of swarthy face,
High on a cole-black steed pursued the chace;
With flashing flames his *ardent* eyes were filled. *Dryd. Fab.*

3. Passionate; affectionate: used generally of desire.

Another nymph with fatal pow'r may rise,
To damp the sinking beams of Cælia's eyes;
With haughty pride may hear her charms confest,
And scorn the *ardent* vows that I have blest. *Prior.*

A′RDENTLY. *adv.* [from *ardent.*] Eagerly; affectionately.

With true zeal may our hearts be most *ardently* inflamed to our religion. *Sprat's Sermons.*

A′RDOUR. *n. f.* [*ardor*, Lat. heat.]

1. Heat.

2. Heat of affection, as love, desire, courage.

Joy, like a ray of the sun, reflects with a greater *ardour* and quickness, when it rebounds upon a man from the breast of his friend. *South.*

The soldiers shout around with gen'rous rage;
He prais'd their *ardour*, inly pleas'd to see
His host. *Dryden's Fables.*

Unmov'd the mind of Ithacus remain'd,
And the vain *ardours* of our love restrain'd. *Pope's Odyssey.*

3. The person ardent or bright. This is only used by *Milton*.

Nor delay'd the winged saint,
After his charge receiv'd; but from among
Thousand celestial *ardours*, where he stood
Veil'd with his gorgeous wings, up-springing light,
Flew thro' the midst of heav'n. *Paradise Lost, b.* v.

ARDU′ITY. *n. f.* [from *arduous.*] Height; difficulty. *Dict.*

A′RDUOUS. *adj.* [*arduus*, Lat.]

1. Lofty; hard to climb.

High on Parnassus' top her sons she show'd,

FIGURE 12.1

Definitions and quotations for *ardent* and *ardour* from Johnson's *Dictionary*.
Source: Johnson, *A Dictionary*.

beaming sun, and feeling. It is as if Johnson moves us from the chemical hell of Newton's burning lake to Milton's "up-springing light" and the vision of the "midst of heav'n."

Generations of the *Dictionary*'s readers have found such embedded narratives: sequences of quotations that give voice and volume to a literary sensibility. Johnson, here and in all his work, was a great canon maker. In *Lives of the Poets*, in *Rambler*, and in his *Idler* essays, as well as in the *Dictionary*, he sought out those "wells of English undefiled," the "pure sources of genuine diction." It is a curious paradox: abandoning the stated goal of fixing language, Johnson still remains a literary prescriber. And in this personal tension lies something of the larger paradox of late-eighteenth-century linguistic thought.

Broadly speaking there were two different approaches to language pedagogy in Johnson's time. The so-called prescriptive grammarians may be epitomized by William Lowth, bishop of London and author of many popular works of English grammar. Lowth claimed that of all the world's languages, even the most ancient, English was the simplest, and that what is at fault in common usage is not the tongue itself but the "practice." Grammar, he wrote in his *Short Introduction to English Grammar*, "is the art of rightly expressing our thoughts by words." And English grammar, in particular, seems the most right to Lowth. Of all the European languages, he claims, English is "much the most simple in its form and construction." Whatever difficulties may exist in communication is the fault of "practice," not of language itself, and what Lowth dubs "propriety and accuracy" are the goals. His pedagogy is prescriptive: "To teach what is right by showing what is both right and wrong."

Joseph Priestley, on the other hand, sought not to prescribe patterns of speech and writing but rather to observe, record, and analyze current practice. From such analysis, he argued, one could induce patterns of acceptable behavior. Priestley embodied the scientific empiricism of the late eighteenth century (he was, by the way, one of the discoverers of oxygen, as well as the founder of Unitarianism), and he embraced Johnson's public stance as but an observer of linguistic usage. Unlike Lowth, he did not favor the use of Latin grammatical names for English parts of speech (he lost out on this one), and he did favor specific grammatical changes, originally advocated by Johnson, as being simpler, clearer, and more naturally "English" than others. In one case, which he explores at length in his *Rudiments of English Grammar*, Priestley argued that we should make a participle different from the preterit of a verb, "as a book is written, not wrote, the ships are taken, not took" (he won on this one).

As in Johnson's *Dictionary*, the debate between prescriptivism and descriptivism goes on at the level of the literary quotation. Lowth draws on writers of the past: Milton, Dryden, Swift, and most frequently the King James Bible. His examples invariably include some weighty platitude or memorable phrase, and much like primer writers from the Middle Ages through the present, he seeks to instruct in good linguistic usage and in moral action. Priestley, by contrast, favors writers of his own day, in particular his fellow Scotsman David Hume. He seeks (again, in the *Rudiments*) "the real character and turn of the language at present," and his word "real" here is no mere intensifier but a specialized term of late-eighteenth-century natural philosophy. The study of language is one of the "real sciences," that is, a study of nature subject to observation and analysis. "Real character" therefore means something like the natural state of language: the way things are. For Priestley, "Language is a method of conveying our ideas to the minds of other persons, and the grammar of any language is a collection of observations on the structure of it, and a system of rules for the proper use of it." At the heart of this statement is an empiricist trajectory from Locke to Hume. Rules can be deduced from experience; they are not (as Lowth would have had it) preexisting forms keyed to a universal structure that must be imposed on lived behavior.

For all these writers, regardless of ideology or influence, *propriety* remains the goal. This word remains one of the key terms of late-eighteenth-century linguistic thought, a lexical window into theory and pedagogy. The word originally entered English with the sense of property or ownership. Johnson defined it in the *Dictionary*, first, as "peculiarity of possession; exclusive right." His secondary definition is "accuracy; justness." In linguistic terms, propriety has less to do with social suitability than with grammatical correctness: a matter of deciding the right grammatical ending, the proper structure of syntax, agreement between noun and verb. When Lowth writes of "the propriety of the [English] language," he means the proper grammatical forms and declensions. When Priestley uses it, he means an accuracy of expression—fitting the proper word to the concept (this sense inheres in his definition of language in the *Rudiments*: "Language is a method of conveying our ideas to the minds of other persons, and the grammar of any language is a collection of observations on the structure of it, and a system of rules for the *proper* use of it"). When Johnson writes in the preface to the *Dictionary* that the illiterate "forget propriety" in their speech or writing, he means that they use English ungrammatically. Throughout these uses, however, propriety emerges as a nascent social category. What is proper grammatically becomes proper socially. Less than thirty years after Johnson published the *Dictionary*, one of the great eighteenth-century arbiters of public taste and decorum, Fanny Burney, could write, in her 1782 novel *Cecilia*: "Such propriety of mind as can only result from the union of good sense with virtue" (vol. 2, chap. 5, xiii).

And yet Samuel Johnson was, in life, perhaps the most improper of literary figures. His tics and ticklishness made for good anecdotes, if bad friendships, and it is as if his *Dictionary* writes out not only a life story of a language but that of a man. Readers have long seen the personal in definitions such as that of lexicographer, "a harmless drudge," or in the reminiscences, throughout the preface, of those "dreams of a poet doomed to wake a lexicographer." But, as I have sought to show here, the heart of Johnson's life lies in his reading: in the authors and quotations ranged as illustrations not just of a word but of a world. *Propriety* has it all: from the opening quotation from Suckling on "propriety in love," to Hammond's lines about peace and the "laws to secure propriety," to Milton on wedded love and human offspring, "sole propriety / Of Paradise," to Dryden on "propriety and peace," to Atterbury on the "propriety of our possessions," and finally to Locke: "Common use, that is the rule of propriety, affords some aid to settle the signification of language." Once again, Milton and Locke stand as the two central authors. Once again, Johnson chooses quotations that juxtapose the personal and the political: love and peace. Johnson knew, and lost, both. His drudgery in dictionary making went beyond self-pity, for if we complete that famous definition it is of a harmless drudge "that busies himself in tracing the original, and detailing the signification of words." Johnson was always tracing out the original, seeking to signify himself, finding the words that matched the thought. His reading sought to match the proper quotations with meanings. If he was mad, or miserable, it may have been out of the recognition that his work, in any form, would always be unfinished. "No dictionary of a living tongue," he wrote at the conclusion to the preface, "can ever be perfect, since while it is hastening to publication, some words are budding, and some falling away." "A whole life," he went on, "cannot be spent on syntax and etymology," for "even a whole life would not be sufficient." Johnson's awakenings, in the end, are less those of a poet doomed to rise a lexicographer than of an eighteenth-century prescriptivist, incapable of fixing words; or of a patronized poet who wakes to find himself a modern author. Like some man trying desperately to get out of a doorway, he realizes that all he can do is hurl himself forward into whatever halls await him.

CHAPTER 13

Horrid, Hooting Stanzas

Lexicography and Literature in American English

THERE ARE NO ENTRIES FOR *America* or *American* in Johnson's *Dictionary*, but the lexicographer had his opinions nonetheless. "To a man of mere animal life," he wrote, "you can urge no argument against going to America. . . . But a man of any intellectual enjoyment will not easily go and immerse himself and his posterity for ages in barbarism." "I am willing," he wrote elsewhere, "to love all mankind, except an American." And, again: "Sir, they are a race of convicts, and ought to be thankful for anything we allow them short of hanging." On the language of the colonists, he was equally dismissive. In a review of Lewis Evans's collection of essays, he considered it "written with such elegance as the subject admits tho' not without some mixture of the American dialect, a tract of corruption to which every language widely diffused must always be exposed" (quoted in Algeo, *The Cambridge History of the English Language*, 6:168).

Johnson was hardly the first to react badly to the American language. Almost a century and a half before his *Dictionary* appeared, Alexander Gil had grudgingly admitted that new words were coming from the New World. Sometimes, he wrote in the *Logonomia Anglica*, the English have been compelled to borrow words for new things, even from *Americanis* for such terms as "maiz" (which he glosses as *triticum Indicum*, "Indian grain") and "Kanoa." Words from the landscape and the peoples of North America were filtering in to Britain throughout the seventeenth and eighteenth centuries, and some made it into Johnson's *Dictionary*: *tobacco*, "from tobacco or Tobago in America"; *chocolate*, "It is a native of America"; *barbecue*, "a term used in the West Indies"; *moose*, "the large American deer"; *squash*, "An Indian kind of pumpion that grows apace."

The early history of American English is thus a history of both idiom and attitude. The colonists not only borrowed words for new things; they adapted old words for new concepts, or developed new locutions that the British saw as peculiar to the colonies. The New World was full of moose and raccoon, moccasins and possums, and, with the advent of the slave trade (a phrase first recorded in 1734), mullatoes and quadroons. But it was also full of words made unfamiliar by new usages. Expressions such as "right away," "admire," and "fix" (meaning to prepare) were some of the earliest examples of (in the words of one visitor in 1839) "how very debased the language has become in such a short period in America." Americans were using grammar differently (the choice of whether to use *shall* or *will* became a focus of debate). Some areas even preserved grammatical phonological forms that were becoming archaic in eighteenth-century Britain: for example, certain strong verb forms (*clum* and *clomb* for the past and participial forms of "climb"; *holp* for "helped"); or certain vowel sounds that, in pockets of pronunciation, made American English seem old fashioned.

Phonology, morphology, and vocabulary combined to make American distinctive. But there was, almost from the beginning of the country, a linguistic imagination: a sense that the nation needed a new language all its own, new ways of spelling, speaking, and conceiving of relationships among the word and the world. Noah Webster announced, in his *Dissertations on the English Language* (1791): "As an independent nation, our honor requires us to have a system of our own, in language as well as government" (quoted in Simpson, *Politics of American English*, 82). "A national language," he continued, "is a band of national union." Two years later, William Thornton could address the nation in his *Cadmus*:

> You have corrected the dangerous doctrines of European powers, correct now the languages you have imported, for the oppressed of various nations knock at your gates, and desire to be received as of your bretheren. As you admit them facilitate your intercourse, and you will mutually enjoy the benefits.—The AMERICAN LANGUAGE will thus be as distinct as the government, free from all the follies of unphilosophical fashion, and resting upon truth as its only regulator.
>
> (Quoted in Simpson, *Politics of American English*, 25)

Language and nationhood had taken on equivalences by the end of the eighteenth century, and by the early nineteenth, Washington Irving could distill that equivalence into a single word: America was "a pure unadulterated LOGOCRACY or government of words" (quoted in Jones, *Strange Talk*, 15).

Linguistic habit and national identity run like a river through the American consciousness. John Witherspoon, the Scottish theologian who emigrated to America in 1769 (and who eventually became the president of Princeton) coined the term "Americanism" in 1781 to express precisely this association.

> I understand a use of phrases or terms, or a construction of sentences, even among people of rank and education, different from the use of the same terms or phrases, or the construction of similar sentences in Great-Britain. It does not follow, from a man's using these, that he is ignorant, or his discourse upon the whole inelegant; nay, it does not follow in every case that the terms or phrases used are worse in themselves, but merely that they are of American and not English growth. The word Americanism, which I have coined for the purpose, is exactly similar in its formation and significance to the word Scotticism.
>
> (Quoted in Algeo, *The Cambridge History of the English Language*, 6:185)

Witherspoon's Americanisms were no worse than anything else; they were just peculiar to the colonies. Of course, Witherspoon was not above correcting his newfound countrymen: every day he heard and read "errors in grammar, improprieties and vulgarisms, which hardly any person of the same class in point of rank and literature would have fallen into in Great-Britain." Still, he does note that "the vulgar in America speak much better than the vulgar in Great-Britain, for a very obvious reason, viz., that being much more unsettled, and moving frequently from place to place, they are not so liable to local peculiarities either in accent or phraseology."

Witherspoon identifies the three major features of American English that would dominate discussions for the next two centuries. H. L. Mencken's *American Language* (first published in 1919, revised continuously until 1948, and still in print) distilled them as "The Hallmarks of American":

> The characters chiefly noted in American English are, first, its general uniformity throughout the country; second, its impatient disregard for grammatical, syntactical and phonological rule and precedent; and third, its large capacity (distinctly greater than that of the English

or present-day England) for taking in new words and phrases from outside sources, and for manufacturing them of its own materials.

(98)

Such features of the language demanded new forms of teaching and new dictionaries, and by the first decade of the nineteenth century, Noah Webster was preparing lexicons and primers for the nation. By 1828, his work had taken its defining shape in the *American Dictionary*, which announced in its preface:

> Language is the expression of ideas; and if the people of our country cannot preserve an identity of ideas, they cannot retain an identity of language. . . . No person in this country will be satisfied with the English definitions of the words *congress, senate,* and *assembly, court,* &c. for although these are words used in England, yet they are applied in this country to express ideas which they do not express in that country.

There is, of course, an obvious political position behind such remarks, reaching back to Webster's writings of the 1780s and 1790s. But there is, too, a profound debt to Samuel Johnson and his philosophical inspiration, John Locke. Words, to recall Locke's phrasing in the *Essay on Human Understanding*, "stand for nothing but the Ideas in the mind," and this notion stands behind Johnson's own avowal, in one of his *Idler* essays, that "Difference of thoughts will produce difference of language" (Hedrick, "Locke's Theory of Language," 423). For Locke and Johnson, sensation remains the source of ideas; the mind, at birth, is a blank slate on which experiences script out our knowledge.

There is a homespun reality to Webster's Lockean world: a world in which instruction in the arts of language takes place on the slates of schoolroom children, a world in which looking out a window reveals just how varied is the landscape of the nation and the nation's minds. Johnson had taken such an attitude in the preface to his *Dictionary*, where he noted how human passions, senses, and opinions constantly mutate the language that we use. Words come in, change their meanings and their sounds, and to attempt to fix a language is as futile a gesture as trying to distinguish "a grove [which] in the agitation of a storm" cannot "be accurately delineated from its picture in the water." "To enchain a syllable," he continued, "and to lash the wind, are equally the undertakings of pride." Things *flow* in

Johnson's preface (a favorite word), as if the language were a river. So, too, for Webster. Americans, he writes,

> had not only a right to adopt new words, but were obliged to modify the language to suit the novelty of the circumstances, geographical and political in which they were placed. . . . It is quite impossible to stop the progress of language—it is like the course of the Mississippi, the motion of which, at times is scarcely perceptible; yet even then it possesses a momentum quite irresistible. Words and expressions will be forced into use in spite of all the exertions of all the writers of the world.

Webster's impact was immense. At one level, he sought to reform spelling and pronunciation to reflect a distinctive American economy of life. Thus, he pares down the *-our-* spellings of England to the *-or-* spellings of America (*color*, for *colour; honor* for *honour*). He eliminates the final *k* in words such as *music, logic, physic*, and the like. He respells British *-re* endings into *-er* endings to reflect pronunciation (*center* for *centre*), and similarly replaces the British *c* in *defence, offence*, with an *s* (*defense, offense*). Webster also recorded (and thus codified) the American habit of uniformly pronouncing the unaccented syllables of words. We still say "necessary," "secretary," and "literature," while in Britain they say "necessry," "secretry," and "litrature."

But at another level, Webster's impact lay in the American imagination. "This country," he wrote in *A Grammatical Institute of the English Language* (1783), "must in some future time, be as distinguished by the superiority of her literary improvements, as she is already by the liberality of her civil and ecclesiastical constitutions" (14). For generations, American literary writers turned to Webster for their inspiration. Frederick Douglass turned to him when, as a slave boy, he surreptitiously learned to read and write. Seeking to improve his handwriting, he copied out the italics in Webster's *Spelling Book*, "until I could make them all without looking on the book." And in his master Tommy's copybooks, "in the ample spaces between the lines I wrote other lines as nearly like his as possible."

Is American literature written between Webster's lines? For Douglass, the emergence into literacy comes after much trial: first, hearing his mistress read the Bible and learning to spell out a few words from the book; then, watching the carpenters in the Baltimore shipyard, marking the initials on the timbers for their placement in a ship. Douglass learns to copy, and soon, "With playmates for my teachers, fences and pavements for my copybooks, and chalk for my pen and ink, I learned to write."

The power of this passage lies not only in its heartfelt reminiscence of a slave who would become a free man. Knowledge, as Douglass learns, "unfits a child to be a slave," and he takes his master's dismissive comment as a goad to freedom: "If you teach him how to read, he'll want to know how to write, and this accomplished, he'll be running away with himself." But the power of this passage lies, too, in its profound understanding of Webster's own philosophical groundwork. All the world is a slate; sensation and impression come into the mind much as the letters of the carpenters are etched into the logs.

There is as much Locke as liberty in these lines. For as the carpenters erect their ships, they take their lettered lumber and build boats of the imagination. Locke thought of sense impressions as the furniture of the mind and of the mind itself as something built out of the raw materials of sense impression (his favorite image is a cabinet of thought). Throughout his writings, there is a material experience to learning. But as Locke recognized as well, the best learning comes through play. Toys, games, and playthings were the objects that taught children how to read and write (Locke has a delightful moment in his *Treatise on Education* where he argues that children should learn their letters by writing them on spinning tops or dice). "A child," wrote Locke in *Human Understanding*, "knows his Nurse and his Cradle, and by degrees the Play-things of a little more advanced age." This is the very quotation that Webster used to illustrate the word *plaything* in his *American Dictionary* (and the same one, by the way, that Johnson used in his *Dictionary*). And, in many ways, Webster's own *Spelling-Book* is an essay on the role of play in learning. Again and again, he stresses how the good boy keeps to his book, plays well with his fellows, and knows the boundaries between learning and disorder.

"Mind your book." This admonition lies at the heart of Webster's speller, and for Douglass—or, for any of the countless other young Americans who used it—what he finds are moral lessons of American life. The lists of polysyllables that Webster offers are (like those of any primer) chosen to reflect the moral virtues. They offer up a lexicon of ethics, and for any reader of the *Spelling-Book*, a knowledge of italics is essential. Italic is the display type for chapter headings and instructions. What Douglass realizes is that the American language is not only made of sounds but of signs: that there is a look to the letter, that words are not just the expression of ideas but objects in themselves. Webster defined *italics* in his dictionary as letters "used to distinguish words for emphasis, importance, antithesis, &c.," and in his definition of the word *adjunct* he notes the following: "In *grammar*, words added to illustrate or amplify the force of other words; as, the History of the *American revolution*. The words in Italics are the adjuncts of *History*." The words in italics are the adjuncts of history. By attending to the italics in the *Spelling-Book*, Douglass sees what the most important adjuncts are: the titles, display types, and centerpieces of instruction. These are the letters of his history, the marks of his own American revolution, the timbers of his alphabet ship-wrought into speech.

And for Emily Dickinson, "There is no Frigate like a book." Dickinson, as scholars have known for decades, spent days with Webster's *Dictionary* (in the 1844 edition), checking meanings, finding collocations, teasing out the connotations of vocabulary. As she wrote to her friend Thomas Higginson, her "Lexicon" was often her only companion. Webster—his books, his name, his heirs—was everywhere in mid-nineteenth-century Amherst, and Dickinson's poetry bristles with his words. Much like the young Frederick Douglass, her own letters may be written in between the lines of Webster.

Scholars have discerned a "lexical cohesion" in Webster and Dickinson. In Webster's definitions, words may come together, and many of Dickinson's collocations mime those of the dictionary. One little poem, for example, reveals word associations from that lexicon.

> Perhaps you think me stooping
> I'm not ashamed of that
> Christ—stooped until He touched the Grave—
> Do those at Sacrament
> Commemorate Dishonor
> Or love annealed of love
> Until it bend as low as Death
> Redignified, above?

> (833)

Webster defines *stooping* as "Bending the body forward," generating the association between stoop and bend in Dickinson's poem. Looking up the words *commemorate, dishonor, low, dignify,* and *above* in Webster generate a set of verbal associations that would have provoked Dickinson to collocate them in her poem. The words *commemorate, death, love,* and *Christ* all appear in Webster's definition for *sacrament.* And Webster's etymology of *anneal* as coming from "to anoint with oil" (an etymology we now know to be bogus) may have led to a string of associations leading to Christ (Webster defines *Christ* as "the anointed").

I have taken this example from the ongoing work of the Emily Dickinson Lexicon project, based at Brigham Young University. There is something undeniably fascinating about the idea of juxtaposing Dickinson and Webster. But Dickinson's verse is more than the sum of Webster's words. It gives voice to a markedly American view of language: a way of reading both the lexicons and literature of English and transforming them into imagined landscapes. As Webster said, "It is quite impossible to stop the progress of language." It is as unceasing as the Mississippi River, "the motion of which, at times is scarcely perceptible; yet even then it possesses a momentum quite irresistible. Words and expressions will be forced into use in spite of all the exertions of all the writers of the world."

Dickinson never saw the Mississippi, but she had seen something Webster could not have imagined: the railroad. By the 1840s, it was already known as the "iron horse," a locution that the *Oxford English Dictionary* locates in America. Here is their quotation from 1846: "The iron horse . . . with the wings of the wind, . . . vomiting fire and smoke" (s.v., *iron*, adj., def. 4.c.; quotation from *The Congressional Globe*). Dickinson sees the train as such a horse, and in one of her poems we can see not just the onset of technology but what Webster would have called the progress of language: impossible to stop, with a momentum quite irresistible.

I like to see it lap the Miles—
And lick the Valleys up—
And stop to feed itself at Tanks—
And then—prodigious step

Around a Pile of Mountains—
And supercilious peer
In Shanties—by the sides of Roads—
And then a Quarry pare

To fit its Ribs
And crawl between
Complaining all the while
In horrid—hooting stanza—
Then chase itself down Hill—

And neigh like Boanerges—
Then—punctual as a Star
Stop—docile and omnipotent
At its own stable door.

Look up *lap* in Webster: "to take into the mouth with the tongue; to lick up; as a cat laps milk. Shaks." (Johnson, too, quotes "cat laps milk" from Shakespeare). *Lap* and *lick* are already together here, though the benignity of feline feeding disappears as soon as we come to *prodigious*. Webster quotes Thomas Browne to illustrate his definition: "It is prodigious to have thunder in a clear sky" (again, so does Johnson). There is the noise, now, of the thundering train—a noise that anticipates the final stanza's Boanerges (from Mark 3:17, the name given to the apostles James and John and meaning "sons of thunder"). The image of that sky, of something greater than mere machinery, embeds itself in *supercilious*: "lofty with pride." Now, we are riding not along the iron rails but along lines of verse. That horrid, hooting stanza calls up the canon of British poetry. *Horrid* is, for Webster, a distinctively Miltonic word: "horrid sympathy," he quotes, but also Dryden ("Horrid with fern and intricate with thorn"; again, Johnson's quotation too). *Hoot* has its illustrative quotations from Dryden, Shakespeare, and Swift. *Punctual* means, first and foremost, "consisting in a point, as in this punctual spot"—the last words of this clause are Milton's (and the same in Johnson).

The language of America is like this train, lapping up miles of meter, feeding on poetry and prose. But we can see the American lexicon lapping up Johnson, too. That lexicon draws on many sources, and finding echoes of Johnson in Webster is much like finding echoes of Webster in Dickinson— to see evidence of the voracity of reading. One might as well try to enchain a syllable or lash the wind as hold this horse of language. *Enchain, lash*: these are Johnson's words from the preface to his *Dictionary*, but they are, too, the words of slavery. One cannot enslave language, much as one cannot enslave the language-loving child. Douglass knew this. Recall the words of his master: if you teach the slave to read and write, "he'll be running away with himself." And so the locomotive runs away; so runs away the writer. Douglass and Dickinson, like Witherspoon and Webster, pare the quarry of English to fit their ribs, and if their language comes out, in the end, like horrid, hooting stanzas—well, that is what it's like to speak with wings of wind.

And the American, as H. L. Mencken knew, was horrid in the root sense of that word. "Bristling" is what it means for Milton, Johnson, and Webster, and bristling is what the American does.

The American, from the beginning, has been the most ardent of recorded rhetoricians. His politics bristles with pungent epithets; his whole history has been bedizened with tall talk; his fundamental institutions rest far more upon brilliant phrases than logical ideas.

Mencken may seem, at moments such as this one, sublimely American— miming the very brazenness of rhetoric in his own choice of words. But at this moment, he is really at his most lexicographical, most engaged with the line from Johnson to Webster. His words drip with Johnson's phrasings. *Ardent*, as we have seen, remains one of his favorite terms, illustrative of both the change in language and the ways in which that change could be illuminated through quotations ranging from Newton to Milton. Webster, too, indulges in Johnson's affection for this word (as well as for *ardor*, where he repeats, almost verbatim, Johnson's Miltonic commentary). *Bristle* and *pungent* go together for the lexicographer, for both signal the feel of the poking spike or the sharp edge. *Bedizened* is a word that Mencken must have found in Johnson: "to dress out; a low word" (Webster, too, calls it "a low word"). Mencken, much like Dickinson, stands as an etymologist of the imagination, and the pungent, bristling alliterations of his brilliant phrases hoot like a train.

→>-→>-◄-◄-◄-◄

Some Early Differences in British and American English Pronunciation

Early Modern English short /a/ became /æ/ in American pronunciation, as in the words *cat, hat*, etc. But it remained short /a/ in *father*. In British English, /a/ becomes a long vowel and is extremely retracted (that is, pronounced farther back in the mouth). This difference was noticed as early as Webster's *Dissertations on the English Language* (1789). In American pronunciation, words from Early Modern English /æ/ such as *fast, calf*, and *bath* kept the /æ/ sound; in British English, the vowel was retracted.

Other vowel sounds were variable in eighteenth-century English, and their pronunciation settled out differently in Britain and America. There is evidence that, in the colonies, the sounds in *pen* and *pin* (/ε/ and /ɪ/ respectively) were not distinguished. The short /o/ in words such as *not, hop*, and *hot* remained as a rounded /o/ in British English, but was often unrounded to /a/ in American pronunciation. In early-eighteenth-century British pronunciation, the vowel in such words as *join* was often pronounced as /aɪ/. The poet Alexander Pope could rhyme "line" and "join." This pronunciation is recorded in early America, though now it is thought to survive only in certain regional dialects or "folk speech."

The pronunciation of /r/ was complex. In Early Modern English, it was probably more pronounced in its final position, as in *father*. In later British pronunciation, it is often reduced to an undifferentiated or unaccented schwa sound. In American English, the /r/ is more pronounced in medial positions. The word *lord* in American has a discernable /r/, but in British English it rhymes with "laud." In certain dialects (e.g., New England), the medial /r/ has disappeared ("Hahvahd yahd"), but it occasionally shows up in final positions as a kind of hypercorrection (for example, John F. Kennedy's famous pronunciation of Cuba as if it were "Cuber").

Early Modern English speakers tended to pronounce all the syllables in polysyllabic words, with relatively equal weight. Webster calls attention to the need to pronounce all such syllables, contrasting American with British pronunciations that had begun to shorten such words (e.g., "necessary" vs. "necessry"; "literature" vs. "litrature"; "secretary" vs. "secretry").

CHAPTER 14

Antses in the Sugar

Dialect and Regionalism in American Literature

"THERE IS," WROTE THE REVEREND JONATHAN BOUCHER in 1832, "no dialect in America." For the first centuries of settlement, the language of the colonies, and of the new republic, seemed to be distinguished by its lack of regional variation (at least when compared to Britain). The mobility of settlers and pioneers, the fluidity of class and economic strata, and the urban mixing of a populace from different parts of Britain and Europe all were believed to contribute to the uniformity of American English. And yet, differences were there almost from the beginning. Patterns of settlement created nodes of different speech. Eastern New England, western New England, New York City, the mid-Atlantic area, the mountains of the inland Atlantic coast, the deeper South—all were original points of ingress for the colonists and all developed, by the early nineteenth century, distinctive habits of pronunciation (see figure 14.1). Even Reverend Boucher recognized these differences, for his commentary continues, "unless some scanty remains of the croaking, guttural idioms of the Dutch, still observable in New York; the Scotch-Irish, as it used to be called, in some of the back settlers of the Middle States; and the whining, canting drawl brought by some republican, Oliverian and Puritan emigrants from the West of England, and still kept up by their unregenerated descendants of New England—may be called dialects" (quoted in Mencken, *The American Language,* 449).

Boucher grudgingly admitted that Americans did differ in their regional speech; but he also raised a question central to the study of those differences. What *is* an American dialect? Is it a pattern of pronunciation or a class of idioms? Is it a habit that emerges or the legacy of immigration: scanty remains kept up by the unregenerated? Are dialects the eddies and

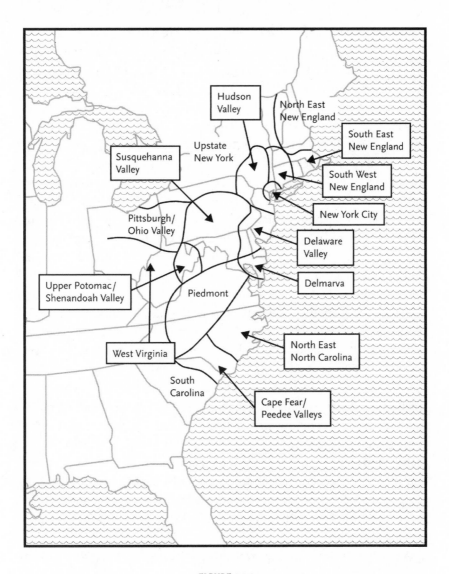

FIGURE 14.1

Dialect boundaries and points of entry for American dialects.

backwaters of what Noah Webster saw as the "progress of language"—is it like the course of the Mississippi? We still tend to see regional variation as a mark of unregeneration. Sometimes we may mock it, other times we may celebrate it. My own Brooklyn language—fostered in the 1950s but bled out of me by my mother, who was a professional speech therapist—has long been seen as a test case for these attitudes. Conflicting evidence abounds. A *New York Times* story from September 21, 1998, "Tawking the Tawk," argues that my old speech—the confusion of the "oi" and "er" sounds, the large rounded "aw" in names like Paul, standing "on line" instead of "in line," the peppery Yiddishisms—are evaporating. New Yorkers, the article concludes, "are sounding more like everybody else." And yet, for William Labov, the linguist whom the *New Yorker* magazine (in a story from November 14, 2005) called the Lewis and Clark of American dialectology, the city's language remains. True, certain caricature sounds have disappeared (what the *New Yorker* called "the adenoidal 'oi' sound"), but the *New Yorker* still titled its story "Talking the Tawk," and they rely on Labov's authority for the assertion that "Brooklynese has remained unchanged for the past fifty years." The story quotes Labov: "The dialect spoken by all those firemen on TV after September 11 was pure, unmodified New York speech from the nineteen-fifties."

The study of American dialects remains the study not just of our selves (past or present) but of the suppositions we bring to our national identity. Such study differentiates our dialect awareness from that of Great Britain. Scholarship on Middle English dialects centered on the conviction that scribes wrote mostly as they spoke and that their writings constituted trustworthy evidence for the phonology, morphology, and lexis of medieval Britain. Dialect difference keyed itself to regional identity, still today very much a part of British social consciousness, and each dialect had a history that could be traced back to the patterns of Germanic settlement and Anglo-Saxon culture. Behind the study of such dialects, and behind, too, literary representations such as Chaucer's "Reeve's Tale" and the *Second Shepherd's Play*, lay the opportunities for humor, social satire, and political response.

American dialectology has something of that edge, but with a difference. Dialect may be something less than "standard." But it may, too, become something more. It is the place of the proverbial, the wisdom of the folk, the unadulterated voice of felt experience. American dialectology took on the same nationalistic flavor as American lexicography had done. The essence of nation was to be found in its folk wisdom: as if tellers of tall tales or homespun Homers could be counted on to give us the truth of experience. After the Civil War, preoccupations with linguistic variation became particularly acute. Scholars grew fascinated by the sources of cultural difference. Linguistic usage came to be associated with political or economic or even moral development. Some in late-nineteenth-century America saw regional pronunciation as a sign of "moral obliquity" (Jones, *Strange Talk*, 20). Others (notably the great American philologist William Dwight Whitney) saw "standard English" as really nothing less than the accepted form of a particular dialect. The ideals of democracy, of immigration, of cross-country pioneering could be seen as demanding the acceptance of all American dialects—what Whitney called the "mixture and intimate intercourse of all ranks and of all regions" (quoted in Jones, 22). The study of American dialects became, in part, a celebration of American identity and the fuel for a distinctively American philology. "The natural, careless, unconscious, colloquial speech," wrote E. S. Sheldon in 1902, "furnishes the philologist with his best illustrative and explanatory material" (quoted in Jones, 17).

The American Dialect Society was founded in 1889 with the goal of collecting that material. Over a hundred years later, the *Dictionary of American Regional English* began with a quotation from one of the society's early leaders, William E. Mead, as a gesture of affiliation with these earlier projects.

> The most ardent admirer of the achievements of the Society must admit that all the investigation that has been done, however thorough for certain districts, is fragmentary in the extreme. . . . To one who has reviewed the whole situation it seems clear that the time has come when we should definitely abandon the drifting policy which we have followed and set out on a systematic investigation. If our chief aim is to publish detached studies of a district here or there as chance may offer them, we shall doubtless accomplish something of value . . . but if we cherish the hope that by such means we shall, within a reasonable time, succeed in preparing an adequate dialect map of our vast country and in bringing together a sufficient amount of trustworthy material for an *American Dialect Dictionary* worthy to stand beside the *English Dialect Dictionary*, we are optimistic indeed.
>
> (xi)

Ardent—a word that has shown up repeatedly in writings about language to define the nature of linguistic change itself (recall Johnson's illustration of that word) and the emotions of its users. "The American remains the most ardent of recorded rhetoricians," wrote Mencken in *The American Language*. And there are other users. Adams Sherman Hill, the Boylston Professor of Rhetoric and Oratory at Harvard, could mock the nativist tradition of linguistic study at the end of the nineteenth century by writing, "The words of some of the most ardent champions of the Anglo-Saxon abound in words from the Latin" (quoted in Lerer, *Error and the Academic Self*, 193). Basil Lanneau Gildersleeve, perhaps the most brilliant classicist of nineteenth-century America and the first professor appointed at Johns Hopkins University, could recall his childhood in pre–Civil War South Carolina as "an ardent lover of literature," and, in his 1878 address as the president of the American Philological Association, defined academic scholarship as "the ardent quest of truth" (quoted in Lerer, *Error and the Academic Self*, 205). Philology burned in America.

But the emotions of the scholar needed to be tempered by empirical research. Mead's address makes clear that enthusiasm needs a system. The goals of his project are to map the language of the nation; to seek out trustworthy informants; and to offer up an American volume equal to a British one. The study of American dialects is therefore about more than cataloguing vowel sounds or folk idioms or whether people say "bucket" or "pail." It is about a social and political attitude; it is about defining the nation as the sum of its linguistic parts; it is about trust. This fixation on regional vernacular went hand-in-hand with a literary movement to present the speech of local people in as realistic a manner as possible. The rise of dialect literature and the rise of professional dialectology in America both contributed to "popular debates about the national significance of the nonstandard voice" (Jones, *Strange Talk*, 62). Mark Twain is but the best known of American writers who engaged with dialect vernaculars. His version of Missouri speech of the mid-nineteenth century (in novels such as *Huckleberry Finn*), together with his essayistic reflections on language use, variety, and sound make up one of the most sustained of American encounters with the English language—and, as such, deserve a chapter all their own. In addition to Twain, writers such as Herman Melville, Henry James, and Stephen Crane engaged with the variants of English. But there were other, less well known but perhaps philologically more compelling cases: Sarah Orne Jewett's version of the "down east" speech of Maine; Jesse Stuart's presentation of Kentucky speech; Marjorie Kinnan Rawling's versions of the "cracker" talk of northern Florida; and, perhaps most notoriously for modern readers, Joel Chandler Harris's evocation of African American discourse. Such writers, much like Chaucer and the playwright of the *Second Shepherd's Play* half a millennium before, often rely less on phonetic transcription than on "eye dialect." They may conflate sounds from adjoining regions.

They may synthesize the speech of several generations into one character. But, much like Chaucer and his medieval compeers, these writers have been used by modern scholars and teachers to illustrate regional variation. At stake, for me, is not just what these writers did, therefore; it is how they may function in the classroom.

When I began to teach the history of the English language in the early 1980s, one of the most helpful workbooks was John Algeo's *Problems in the Origin and Development of the English Language*. A manual of exercises designed to supplement another textbook, Thomas Pyles's *Origins and Development of the English Language*, Algeo's *Problems* set the student texts for study and analysis. He chose a range of texts to illustrate American dialects, and his choice was not just a linguistic but also a literary one.

LITERARY REPRESENTATIONS OF AMERICAN DIALECTS

1. New England (Sarah Orne Jewett, "Andrew's Fortune")

"We was dreadful concerned to hear o' cousin Stephen's death," said the poor man. "He went very sudden, didn't he? Gre't loss he is."

"Yes," said Betsey, "he was very much looked up to;" and it was some time before the heir plucked up courage to speak again.

"Wife and me was lotting on getting over to the funeral; but it's a gre't ways for her to ride, and it was a perishin' day that day. She's be'n troubled more than common with her phthisic since cold weather come. I was all crippled up with the rheumatism; we wa'n't neither of us fit to be out" (plaintively). "'T was all I could do to get out to the barn to feed the stock while Jonas and Tim was gone. My boys was over, I s'pose ye know? I don' know's they come to speak with ye; they're backward with strangers, but they're good stiddy fellows."

"Them was the louts that was hanging round the barn, I guess," said Betsey to herself. "They're the main-stay now; they're ahead of poor me a'ready. Jonas, he's got risin' a hundred dollars laid up, and I believe Tim's got something too,—he's younger, ye know?"

2. New York City (Damon Runyon, "Pick the Winner")

Well, anyway, when Hot Horse Herbie and his everloving fiancee come into Mindy's, he gives me a large hello, and so does Miss Cutie Singleton, so I hello them right back, and Hot Horse Herbie speaks to me as follows:

"Well," Herbie says, "we have some wonderful news for you. We are going to Miami," he says, "and soon we will be among the waving palms, and reveling in the warm waters of the Gulf Stream."

Now of course this is a lie, because while Hot Horse Herbie is in Miami many times, he never revels in the warm waters of the Gulf Stream, because he never has time for such a thing, what with hustling around the race tracks in the daytime, and around the dog tracks and the gambling joints at night, and in fact I will lay plenty of six to five Hot Horse Herbie cannot even point in the direction of the Gulf Stream when he is in Miami, and I will give him three points, at that.

3. Midwest (Ring Lardner, "Gullible's Travels")

I promised the Wife that if anybody ast me what kind of a time did I have at Palm Beach I'd say I had a swell time. And if they ast me who did we meet I'd tell 'em everybody that was worth meetin'. And if they ast me didn't the trip cost a lot I'd say Yes; but it was worth the money. I promised her I wouldn't spill none o' the real details. But if you can't break a promise you made to your own wife what kind of a promise can you break? Answer me that, Edgar.

I'm not one o' these kind o' people that'd keep a joke to themself just because the joke was on them. But they's plenty of our friends that I wouldn't have 'em hear about it for the world. I wouldn't tell you, only I know you're not the village gossip and won't crack it to anybody. Not even to your own Missus, see? I don't trust no women.

4. Missouri (Samuel L. Clemens, *The Adventures of Huckleberry Finn*)

So Tom says: "I know how to fix it. We got to have a rock for the coat of arms and mournful inscriptions, and we can kill two birds with that same rock. There's a gaudy big grindstone down at the mill, and we'll smouch it, and carve the thing on it, and file out the pens and the saw on it, too."

It warn't no slouch of an idea; and it warn't no slouch of a grindstone nuther; but we allowed we'd tackle it. It warn't quite midnight, yet, so we cleared out for the mill, leaving Jim at work. We smouched the grindstone, and set out to roll her home, but it was a most nation tough job. Sometimes, do what we could, we couldn't keep her from falling over, and she come mighty near mashing us, every time. Tom said she was going to get one of us, sure, before we got through. We got her half way; and then we was plumb played out, and most drownded with sweat. We see it warn't no use, we got to go and fetch Jim. So he raised up his bed and slid the chain off of the bed-leg, and wrapt it round and round his neck, and we crawled out through our hole and down there, and Jim and me laid into that grindstone and walked her along like nothing; and Tom superintended. He could out-superintend any boy I ever see. He knowed how to do everything.

5. Kentucky (Jesse Stuart, *Taps for Private Tussie*)

Watt Tussie was one man that I didn't get around. He didn't look right outten his eyes and I was afraid of him. I think Uncle George was afraid of him too. He didn't belong to either clan of Tussies. He just heard about the big house where all the Tussies were a-couiin, so he brought his family to jine the rest in peace, rest and comfortable livin. Grandpa figured for hours to find out if he was any kin to Watt Tussie and he finally figured he was a son of his second cousin, Trueman Tussie. Watt Tussie wore brogan shoes laced with ground-hog-hide strings.

6. Georgia (Joel Chandler Harris, "A Run of Luck")

"Well, suh," he said, after a while, "I come mighty nigh gwine off wid my young marster. I'speck I'd'a' gone of he'd'a' had any chillun, but he ain't had a blessed one. En it look like ter me, such, dat of de Lord gwine ter stan' by a man, He gwine ter gi' 'im chillun. But dat ain't all, suh. I done been out dar ter Massysip wid my young marster, en dat one time wuz too much fer me. Fust dar wuz de rippit on de steam-boat, en den dar wuz de burnin' er de boat, en den come de swamps, en de canebrakes; en I tell you right now, suh, I dunner which wuz de wuss—de rippit on de boat, er de fier, er de swamps, er de canebrakes. Dat ain't no country like our'n, suh. Dey's nuff water in de State er Mas-sysip fer ter float Noah's ark. Hit's in de ve'y lan' what dey plant der cot-ton in, suh. De groun' is mushy. En black! You may n't b'lieve me, suh, but dey wuz times when I wuz out dar, dat I'd 'a' paid a sev'mpunce fer ter git a whiff er dish yer red dus' up my nose. When you come to farmin', suh, gi' me de red lan' er de gray. Hit may not make ez much cotton in one season, but it las's longer, en hit's lots mo' wholesome."

7. Florida (Marjorie Kinnan Rawlings, "My Friend Moe")

As he worked, he noticed a row of glass jars of huckleberries that I had canned. His grave face brightened.

"Now that's the way to live," he said. "All the good things we got here in Florida, blueberries and blackberries and beans and cow-peas, all them things had ought to be canned and put up on a clean cupboard shelf with white paper on it. That's the way my Ma did. She lived fine, not the way you live, but just as good when it come to cannin' things and keepin' things clean."

His face darkened. "I've tried and I've done tried to get my wife to do that-a-way but it just ain't no use. One time I bought two dozen glass jars and I went out by myself and I picked about a bushel o' blackberries and I went to the store and bought a twenty-five pound sack o' sugar and I takened it home, and I said, 'Wife, here's a bait o' blackberries to put up for us for jam and jelly for the winter.'" He hesitated, his loyalty pricking him.

"She probably didn't have time to do it," I suggested.

"She had time. She let the blackberries spoil, and the antses got in the sugar, and I found the jars throwed out in the back yard."

Take the example used to illustrate "New England," from Sarah Orne Jewett's "Andrew's Fortune." Now, anyone who has lived in New England knows immediately that the sounds and idioms evoked here are specific to the "down east" speech of Maine. Spellings such as *gre't, be'n, wa'n't, spose, stiddy,* and *a'ready* attempt to reproduce the long aesch sound /æ:/ charac-teristic of Maine speech, and in the case of *stiddy* in particular (for "sturdy") Jewett's spelling indicates the loss of the *r* sound after a vowel and the fronting of the back vowel. In terms of grammar or morphology, Jewett's example illustrates the confusion of nominative and objective cases for pronouns ("wife and me," "them was"), and the use of "was" as the first- and third-person plural ("we was," "boys was"). The adjectival ending -ly appears gone ("dreadful concerned," "very sudden"), and certain syntactic patterns and idioms have a distinctively regional feel to them: "very much looked up to"; "all crippled up"; "fit to be out." The vocabulary is distinc-tive, too: for example, *lotting* (meaning counting on or looking forward to), obviously comes from the practice of drawing lots, and was recognized as a New Englandism as early as the 1820s.

It is an easy task to catalogue these features. But if we read through the passage as a whole, we see more than just a list of quirks. This is a dialogue about the dead, about old age, about illness and bad behavior. Its rural speakers talk in ways that mime the very subject of their plaints—a dialect "all crippled up" with sounds and slangs. The passage evokes an imagined habit of mind: a regional aloneness in which it remains a great way to ride to a funeral, in which boys are backward with strangers.

But if there is one word that emblematizes region, dialect, and distance in this passage it is *phthisic*. The *Oxford English Dictionary* charts its appearance as a term of pulmonary illness (consumption or asthma) from the fourteenth century. Originally from a Greek term, *phthisis*, meaning consumption, it came into the English language spelled phonetically ("tisik"), before being respelled in the eighteenth century in its learned form. By the mid-nineteenth century in England, the word seems to have evaporated, but in regional America, it flourished. The *Dictionary of American Regional English* offers up a veritable essay on identity, beginning with the word's emergence in Webster and then running through all kinds of learned texts, folk stories, answers to questionnaires, and popular histories of American speech. There's nothing particularly New England about it, but there is a telling entry that the *DARE* quotes from Gould's *Modern English Lingo* of 1975:

> *Tizzic*—Included here because somebody who didn't know how to spell it suggested it was a "good Maine word." *Phthisic* is in any good dictionary. Its peculiar orthography made it a favorite in old-time spelling bees, and until spelling bees went out of style almost all Mainers could spell *phthisic*.
>
> (Cassidy, ed., *DARE*, 4:111)

This commentary may hint at its use in the Maine of Sarah Orne Jewett, but it says more about how the modern academic linguist could display it. It is a word with a peculiar spelling, something that leaps out of the page, so that even the most sluggish student of the history of the language would attend an eye in this assignment. The word becomes a test case, too, not just for regional expression but for lexicography: its appearance is evidence of a "good dictionary" (I note here that it's obviously missing from my computer's vast spell checker). And it survived as part of a social practice of the spelling bee—that ritual of school performance that, it was believed, shaped a distinctively competitive spirit among the young (look up *bee* in the *DARE* for a history of what one entry from 1909 calls "a neighborhood gathering for special work").

Phthisic is a touchstone both for regional linguistic use and academic pedagogy. It leaps off the page of both the literary fiction and the lexicon. It is a word of such tongue-twisting challenge that its saying makes us palpably aware of speech as physical activity—and, as a consequence, of dialect itself as something laborious for the uninitiated to pronounce.

I could find comparable examples in all of Algeo's passages. "Plenty of six to five" arrests the reader of the Runyon selection—a phrase that evokes the world of horseracing, that enables us to see the urban landscape through a bookie's eyes. Ring Lardner's speaker "wouldn't spill none o' the real details"—but, of course, he does, for what is the literary presentation of a dialect about other than spilling the real details? Twain's boys set out to *smouch* a "gaudy big grindstone," as something of a tablet for their simple script. And yet, this is tough thing to do, for in the process of their theft, the object rolls away, falls down, tires them out, and practically kills them before Jim comes in to take over. Getting the language down is much like trying to move that grindstone: it is a process ill-beset with dangers. "It was a most nation tough job"—not just, of course, a [dam]nation tough job, but a tough job for the nation. "A nation's language," wrote Twain elsewhere, "is a very large matter"—as large as that intractable grindstone that might hone us into shining edges or collapse before our feet.

Wat Tussie, in the passage from Jesse Stuart, wears "brogan shoes laced with ground-hog hide strings." Is regional American English like good shoes laced up with hog hide? Is the dialect of northern Florida like "antses in the sugar," infesting the sweetness of accepted speech? Is the language of the African American South like the marshy swamps of the Joel Chandler Harris excerpt? As my student readers navigated through the spellings, sounds, and symbols of this passage, how could they not see themselves as mired on a Mississippi shoreline? Recall Noah Webster on the motion of that river, and in turn of language: "at times [it] is scarcely perceptible; yet even then it possesses a momentum quite irresistible."

Can we resist the momentum of Joel Chandler Harris? There is an almost biblical prowess to this narration, a flavor of the pulpit orator. "Dey's nuff water in de State er Massysip fer ter float Noah's ark." And in this miniature flood, the verbal repetitions put the reader in a landscape as unlikely and untamed as any we have seen before: Wulfstan's account of the Danish incursions; the *Peterborough Chronicler*'s lament over the anarchy under King Stephen; the wilderness of rape for the plaintiff in fifteenth-century Chancery; Milton's hell; the quarry pared apart by horrid, hooting stanzas. "Dat ain't no country like our'n."

And in such a country, there are words for things we may see nowhere else. *Canebrakes*—thickets of vegetation—grew along the stream banks in the southern states. As early as 1770 (according to the *DARE*), the landscape of South Carolina was defined in its terms: "There is a large Neck, or Island, of Swamp or Cane-Brake land." An entry for 1883 uses the word to define an entire region of Alabama: "The chief crops in the Canebrake." This is the Canebrake country.

"De groun' is mushy." The ground is always mushy when it comes to studying American dialects. For it is impossible to see the variation in our speech as simply a matter of geography. Social stratification, as William Labov and others revealed in the 1960s, often shapes speech as much as region, and within a given region individuals may evidence a wide range of sounds and idioms. I love, in particular, Labov's observation that the floor-walkers at Saks' Fifth Avenue pronounced the *rs* in "fourth floor" more than those at Macy's, and the least amount of *r* was heard at S. Klein's (the bargain basement, as it were, of haberdashery, and the store my family most often frequented). Far more sophisticated than this kind of anecdotal evidence is Labov's recent, massive *Atlas of North American English*, the Web site for which can give even the most casual browser an awareness of the nuances of regional pronunciations. What Labov's *Atlas* shows is how potentially misleading earlier dialectology has been that focused on lexical variation—that is, whether people said "pail" or "bucket," whether they "waited for" or "waited on" someone, or whether they used a distinc-tive regional vocabulary for certain items, actions, or experiences. Labov's *Atlas* establishes its dialect boundaries according to "the systematic study of phonological relations in the vowel system" (116). Sometimes, he and his coauthors note, there may be "a high degree of convergence" between maps "based on regional vocabulary" and those based on sound. Some-times, there will be differences.

All studies of lived speech rely on informants, but it is one thing to ask someone to pronounce a word and something very different to ask some-one to come up with a word for a concept, a thing, or an experience. The questionnaire technique of the *DARE* keys itself to lexical variation, and while this remains a brilliant and long-lasting social and linguistic achieve-ment, the ground is mushy in some of its interpretations. To the question, "What other names do you have around here for the dragonfly," the *DARE* fieldworkers got two terms: "mosquito-hawk," and "skeeter-hawk." Plotted on to a map of the United States, we see uses cluster on the East Coast and the South. Plotted, however, on to the *DARE* map (a map with the states distorted into shapes keyed to their population density), we can see the weight of regionalism (see figure 14.2). And, in *DARE*'s own explana-tion we can see, too, the weight of nearly two centuries of speculation on American dialect.

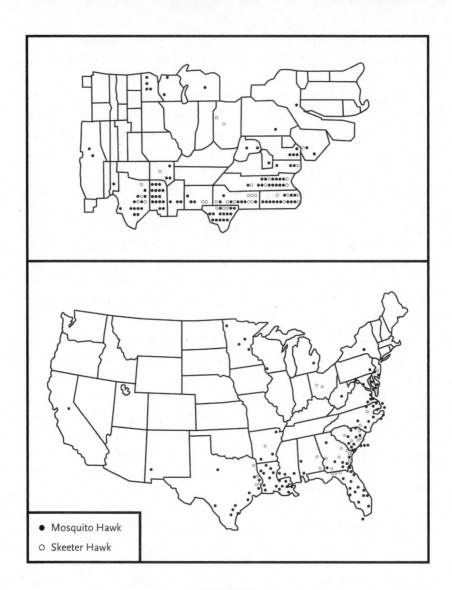

FIGURE 14.2

DARE map of the distribution of *mosquito-hawk* and *skeeter-hawk*.
Source: Cassidy, ed., *The Dictionary of American Regional English*, xxviii. Reproduced by permission of Harvard University Press.

The *DARE* map gives a concise visual statement of the overall clustering of responses. For example, it is just as easy, if not easier, to see on the *DARE* map as on the conventional map that the variant *skeeter hawk* is especially concentrated in the South Atlantic states from North Carolina to northern Florida. The *DARE* map is essentially a scatter diagram that economically illustrates degrees of clustering—that is, degrees of regionality.

(xxvii)

I'm fascinated by this notion of degrees of regionality—as if the axis of variation was not horizontal but vertical. Surely what *DARE* implies here is that such degrees of regionality are really degrees of separation from a modern norm. The passage into geographic depth—moving into the canebrake country of the language, if you will—is a passage back in time, a passage into unregeneration (Labov makes this point precisely: "Words are selected for study on the basis of their regional heterogeneity and their possible connection with settlement history" [116]). But if we read on in the *DARE* we see more: "The clustering of *mosquito hawk* is a notably tight one, but even here the map reveals some stray responses deep in Yankee territory." Is mosquito hawk like some Confederate, infiltrating into the Yankee territory? Is the divide left by the Civil War still unhealed in the annals of the linguist? "As the user of this Dictionary will soon realize, language refuses to stay within strict geographical boundaries and almost always ignores political or state boundaries." Again, language is like that Mississippi, ignoring the artificial boundaries of human politics. In the phrasing of Craig Carver's *American Regional Dialects* (1987):

A map of language variation is merely a static representation of a phenomenon whose most salient characteristic is its fluidity. It is an almost seamless fabric covering the land. . . . What follows, then, is not the definitive description of regional dialects of America, because such a description is impossible. It is merely one attempt to seize the linguistic river as it flowed through.

(19)

Language is a social habit, the behavior of individuals. Yet we grant it personality and power. Metaphors abound, whether they be organic or political. For, in the end, our dialects, whatever their origins in region or in class, ethnicity or background, are here to stay. They may buzz past like some mosquito hawk, only to be swatted away by the floorwalkers of our language. But when they alight, we see them for the dragonflies they are: rare, beautiful, and iridescent in the shifting light of culture or the classroom.

CHAPTER 15

Hello, Dude

Mark Twain and the Making of the American Idiom

"A NATION'S LANGUAGE," WROTE MARK TWAIN, "is a very large matter"—
and he should have known. His concern with the relationships of speech and
nationhood place him on a distinctively American philological trajectory running from Noah Webster to H. L. Mencken. His writings constantly reflect on
the nature of regional dialect, on differences between languages, and on the
discipline of linguistic study itself. He counted among his correspondents the
Yale professor William Dwight Whitney (known in the late nineteenth century as the greatest living scholar of languages) and Sir James A. H. Murray
(the patriarchal editor of the *Oxford English Dictionary*). In fact, when Twain
went to visit Murray at Oxford in 1900, he did so (in the words of Murray's
granddaughter and biographer) "with the excuse that as a last resort he was
thinking of making a dictionary, and wanted to see how it was done."

Most of us think of Twain as a dialectician. The brilliance of his *Huckleberry Finn*, for example, lies for many readers in Twain's gift for capturing
the flavor of his characters' speech. As he wrote, in an explanatory preface
to the novel,

> In this book a number of dialects are used, to wit: the Missouri negro
> dialect; the extremest form of the backwoods South-Western dialect;
> the ordinary "Pike-County" dialect; and four modified varieties of this
> last. The shadings have not been done in a hap-hazard fashion or by
> guess-work; but pains-takingly, and with the trustworthy guidance and
> support of personal familiarity with these several forms of speech.

But Twain was no mere antiquarian of local language. His fictions and
his polemics participated in a larger cultural debate on dialect in late-

nineteenth-century America. The contacts between North and South and East and West following the Civil War sparked fears of progressive loss of American linguistic and social identity. William Chauncey Fowler wrote, in his *English Grammar* of 1868: "As our countrymen are spreading westward across the continent and are brought into contact with other races, and adopt new modes of thought, there is some danger that, in the use of their liberty, they may break loose from the laws of the English language." Dialects were dangerous things, symbolizing for the arbiters of culture a kind of anarchy of speech. But with that fear of anarchy came, for others, the hope for freedom. The West held out the promise of individual accomplishment. There was more than gold in the hills, as Maximilian Schele de Vere wrote in his *Americanisms: The English of the New World* in 1872:

> The student of English finds in the West a rich harvest of new words, of old words made to answer new purposes, often in the most surprising way, and of phrases full of poetical feeling, such as could only arise amid scenes of great beauty, matchless energy, and sublime danger.

Twain knew that to express the shape of Western selves he would have to record new forms, new words, new sounds. Even in the little preface to *Huckleberry Finn*, he make words crackle with surprise: a word like "painstakingly," hyphenated to reveal its etymology, is recorded first only from the 1860s, while a much older word like "hap-hazard," again hyphenated by Twain, takes on a new and perhaps poetical feeling, when paired with the term "shadings."

Twain also knew that new words come into the language not just from regional travel or imaginary evocation but also from science and technology. The last half of the nineteenth century saw the American lexicon absorb new coinages from warfare, transportation, electricity, the telephone, and (by its end) the motor car. Two such words in particular have come to stand as nodal points in the American idiom: words that reveal both the late nineteenth century's and our own concern with social change, technological innovation, personal relationships, and gender roles. These two words are *hello* and *dude*. Mark Twain uses them for the first time in any work of literature in his *Connecticut Yankee in King Arthur's Court* (published in 1889). They represent the kinds of idiomatic shifts in American English to which Twain was particularly sensitive. But, as representatives of such shifts, they also epitomize the problems faced by historians of language. Their origins defy conventional lexicography. Their social status provoked reflections that say as much about American popular culture of the late nineteenth century as they do about specific shifts in language. In the "hello-girls" and "iron dudes" of *Connecticut Yankee*, we see modern American English in the making.

A Connecticut Yankee in King Arthur's Court offers up a theater of Arthurian legend, where scenes of magic and technological progress appear as dramatic shows. Hank Morgan (the novel's hero) can beat the sorcerer Merlin at his own game—not so much because of his knowledge but because of his stagecraft. Hank is always, in Twain's words, making a "spectacle" of things, and no spectacle is greater than his attempts to electrify the medieval court into which he has found himself transported. Hank strings cable, sets up telephone exchanges, and generates energy in ways that would have resonated with a contemporary reader's knowledge of that great, living wizard—not Merlin, but Thomas Edison, the Wizard of Menlo Park (a title given Edison as early as a newspaper report of 1878).

Enabling immediate communication by distant interlocutors, the telephone not only revolutionized the passage of information, it changed irrevocably social relationships in late-nineteenth-century America. The magazine *Scientific American*, in 1880, imagined the consequences of this invention as "nothing less than a new organization of society—a state of things in which every individual, however secluded, will have at call every other individual in the community." By 1889, such telephonic assemblies seemed almost magical. As if in resonance with Hank Morgan's electric spectacles, the *Reading Herald* wrote of a long-distance call from New York to Boston: "It beat all to smash all the old incantations of Merlin and the magi[c] of Munchhousen [*sic*], Jules Verne, or Haggard."

But the problem for the early telephone was how to address someone you could not see. Forms of address are invariably linked to social class and gender. When you meet someone, you gauge his or her social class by dress or bearing or by his or her speech to you. The conundrum for the telephone was what to say first to a speaker whose class or gender you could not know. And so a neutral word was needed. Phone greetings, culturally, are arbitrary. German *bitte*, Italian *pronto*, Spanish *bueno*—each culture confronts the problem differently, in these cases by adopting other words of politesse to telephonic social interaction. American English, by contrast, adopted the interjection *hello*—etymologically, from *hallo* or *halloa*, a term of address among sailors between ships. This maritime metaphorics inflected more directly Alexander Graham Bell's own usage, and until the end of his life (in 1922) Bell is said to have answered the phone with a loud, "Ahoy," while Edison favored "hello."

In the words of the *Reading Herald*, "hello" was "plain United States," a distinctively American idiom that soon covered the country: "That Hello! took advantage of its opportunities and traveled." It was the essence of America, much as Edison himself came to be seen, by the early 1880s, as the quintessential American inventor. Take, for example, this version of the story as it appeared in the 1931 biography, *Thomas A. Edison: Benefactor of Mankind*:

> It was Edison who originated the salutation "HELLO!" over the telephone. This historic fact was verified by Frederick P. Fish, late President of what is now the American Telephone and Telegraph Company: 'Years ago,' said Mr. Fish, 'when the first telephones came into use, people were accustomed to ring a bell on the box and then say, ponderously: "Are you there?" "Are you ready to talk?" Mr. Edison did away with that awkward, un-American way of doing things. He caught up the receiver one day and yelled into the transmitter one word—a most satisfactory, capable, soul-satisfying word—"HELLO!" It has gone around the world.'

This anecdote encapsulates an ideal of American directness and invention that had been embraced for half a century. It signals a kind of linguistic manifest destiny, a hello gone round the world.

The word *hello* became so current that the operators at the phone exchanges (often, young women with mellifluous voices) came to be known as *hello-girls*. The earliest appearance of this phrase in literature is at that moment in *Connecticut Yankee* when Hank seeks to teach Sandy, his beloved at Arthur's court, a lesson about female behavior.

> The women here do certainly act like all possessed. Yes, and I mean your best, too, society's very choicest brands. The humblest hello-girl along ten thousand miles of wire could teach gentleness, patience, modesty, manners, to the highest duchess in Arthur's land.

"Hello-girl?" Sandy queries. To which Hank responds:

> Yes, but don't you ask me to explain; it's a new kind of girl; they don't have them here; one often speaks sharply to them when they

are not the least in fault, and he can't get over feeling sorry for it and ashamed of himself in thirteen hundred years, it's such shabby mean conduct and so unprovoked; fact is, no gentleman ever does it—though I—well, I myself, if I've got to confess— . . . Never mind her, never mind her; I tell you I couldn't ever explain her so you would understand.

Just what is it that Hank cannot explain? Hello-girls were not simply operators in a new technology. They stood at the nexus of desire and decorum in the 1880s. The hello-girl eroticized feminine vocality, and Hank's stuttering allusion cracks a fissure in the fabric of accepted social life.

"The telephone girls may fairly boast of being connected with the best people of the city—by wire," noted the *Boston Transcript* in 1888. Carolyn Marvin, in her book *When Old Technologies Were New*, comments on this passage and reflects on the social impact of the telephone in late-nineteenth-century America: "It was necessary to present her as a socially competent performer, a smooth and knowledgeable broker of social relations between middle-class households, and to make clear at the same time that she was only a servant, not truly a member of the class to whose secrets she had access." And what secrets! Such women were, Marvin goes on, "often objects of fantasy," and by 1905 the magazine *Telephony* noted that they offered "little glimpses of life at other seasons forbidden." Or, even earlier, from the *Electrical Review* of 1891 (in an article titled, "Said She Liked It"): "One of the young ladies at the Central office has a singularly pleasing voice, and it is just possible that her features match it." Men of a certain social class were quick to use such hello-girls as private alarm clocks, leaving instructions for wake-up calls with central.

> 'Hello, girlie,' he gurgles to the sweet voiced operator at the other end. 'I want to get up at 6:30 to-morrow morning. Will you be so good as you sound and ring me up then? If so, there will be something in your stocking about Christmas time. Ever go to the theater?
>
> That's the way it begins. The telephone girls are an accommodating lot, but even if they were not there would be trouble if they failed to awake several thousand Bostonians every morning of the summer, for here it is a rule of the company that they accommodate patrons.

But what happened when the wife answered the phone? This article from *Telephony* goes on to record such an encounter.

The next morning the telephone rings. Horrified hubby sits up in bed in dazed surprise, while Mrs. Jones goes to the 'phone.

'Hello,' says Mrs. Jones.

'Hello, pet,' comes back in a woman's voice. 'Hurry up and get up. I've been ringing for you long enough.'

Has someone been ringing for Hank Morgan long enough? Has Sandy interrupted something of a sad remembrance—tinged with desire—that Hank's awkward explanation offers?

Years later, when Hank and Sandy marry, they have a little girl who is named . . . Hello-Central. What? In this bizarre turn on parenting and popular culture, we learn that Sandy would hear Hank call out "hello-central" in his sleep. But she imagines "it to be the name of some lost darling," and so, in honor of her husband, she names their daughter after it. The hello-girl of late-nineteenth-century fantasy becomes the Hello-Central of domestic bliss. Just look at the illustration for the original edition of *Connecticut Yankee* to see how the wizardry of Hank's electric spectacles has morphed into the melodrama of the family (see figure 15.1). Roles of seduction have become roles of devotion. And even Sandy's hair, once long and flowing, is now put up in the bun of domesticity.

Against this trajectory of sentimentalism, *Connecticut Yankee* poses another version of the public life of gender. During the last quarter of the nineteenth century, manhood found its challenges not just from the temptations of the telephone, but from the allure of aestheticism. The word *dude* was picked up in the early 1880s to define the new dandy of that movement. But it had appeared earlier, in the late 1870s, to describe the fastidious man of the city. The artist Frederic Remington wrote to a friend, in 1877, "Don't send me any more [drawings of] women or any more dudes. Send me Indians, cowboys, villans [*sic*] or toughs." The dude finds his associations with the weak, the feminine, the soft. But he is also, from his first appearance, a creature of the stage: a foolish character of costume and performance. In the 1878 book, *Fighting Indians*, by a man who joined the cavalry after Custer's massacre, the foppish soldiers of Fort Snelling, Minnesota, are dudes. "Company C, 20th Infantry, was at the time composed of dude soldiers, pets of dress parade officers." These men had become objects of mockery at the base. The commanding officer's wife asked them to parade by their porch because it made her baby laugh, and the author of this account comments: "We lonely and homesick recruits laughed in our sleeves when

"HELLO-CENTRAL!"

FIGURE 15.1

Source: Mark Twain, *A Connecticut Yankee in King Arthur's Court*.

we overheard expressions of indignation among the 'baby entertainers'
over the incident."

By the early 1880s the word was everywhere. New York newspapers
made sport of it. Provincial papers noted its spread. Even Ulysses S. Grant
deployed it (conscious of its recent coinage) in his *Memoirs*: "Before the car
I was in had started, a dapper little fellow—he would be called a dude at

FIGURE 15.2

Source: Mark Twain, *A Connecticut Yankee in King Arthur's Court.*

this day—stepped in." For Twain, the knights of Arthur's kingdom are the "iron dudes": creatures of posturing and dress-up (see figure 15.2). Hank imagines their condemnation of his need to wipe the sweat away from under his helmet. "Of course, these iron dudes of the Round Table would think it was scandalous, and maybe raise Sheol about it, but as for me, give me comfort first, and style afterwards."

If the affectations of the dude posed a challenge to American ideals of public life, the origins of the word itself posed challenges to British and American dictionaries. With its unrecoverable etymology (did it come from the word *dud*, or *duds*, meaning clothing, or from the Dutch word for

Dude (diūd). *U.S.* [A factitious slang term which came into vogue in New York about the beginning of 1883, in connexion with the ' æsthetic' craze of that day. Actual origin not recorded.]

A name given in ridicule to a man affecting an exaggerated fastidiousness in dress, speech, and deportment, and very particular about what is æsthetically 'good form'; hence, extended to an exquisite, a dandy, 'a swell'.

1883 *Graphic* 31 Mar. 319/1 The 'Dude' sounds like the name of a bird. It is, on the contrary, American slang for a new kind of American young man..The one object for which the dude exists is to tone down the eccentricities of fashion .. The silent, subfusc, subdued 'dude' hands down the traditions of good form. **1883** *North Adams* (Mass.) *Transcript* 24 June, The new coined word 'dude' .. has travelled over the country with a great deal of rapidity since but two months ago it grew into general use in New York. **1883** *American* VII. 151 The social 'dude' who affects English dress and the English drawl. **1883** *Harper's Mag.* LXVII. 632 The elderly club dude. **1884** in Bryce *Amer. Commw.* (1888) II. App. 642 Dudes and roughs, civil service reformers and office-holding bosses..join in midnight conferences. **1886** A. Lang in *Longm. Mag.* Mar. 553 Our novels establish a false ideal in the American imagination, and the result is that mysterious being 'The Dude'.

Hence **Du·dedom, Du·deness, Du·dery, Du·dism** (*nonce-wds.*), the state, style, character or manners of a dude; **Dudine** (-ī·n), a female dude; **Du·dish** *a.*, characteristic of a dude; foppish.

1883 *Philad. Times* No. 2892. 2 Not..to encourage the development of the dude or the dudine in his dominion. **1885** *Boston* (Mass.) *Jrnl.* 15 June 2/3 The intense dudeness of Lord Beaconsfield in his early days is illustrated by a letter written in 1830. **1889** *Bookworm* 237 Any dudish Anglomaniac or Fifth Avenue 'bud'. **1889** *Voice* (N. Y.) 2 May, The Pharisaical dudery which presumes to deny her [woman] a place in the world..equal with man. **1890** *Teacher* (N.Y.) Sept. 101 Are we traveling the way of the Greeks?.. Is dudism becoming more contagious among us than philanthropy? **1891** A. Welcker *Woolly West* 69 Joe then went east, and .. married a young dudine out there. **1894** Dickson *Life Edison* 230 A dudish applicant, with an overweening sense of his own self-importance. **1894** *Forum* (U. S.) May 345 [It] would relegate its champion to the realms of dudedom.

FIGURE 15.3

Definition and quotations for *dude*.

Source: Murray, ed., *A New English Dictionary on Historical Principles*, vol. 3.

a fool?), the word's origin had to be placed in the realm of some indefinable Other, some landscape far away and foreign. When the *Oxford English Dictionary* volume for the letter D appeared in 1897 (under the title, as all the original volumes appeared, of the *New English Dictionary*), dude was defined as: "A factious slang term which came into vogue in New York about the beginning of 1883, in connection with the 'aesthetic' craze of that day. Actual origin not recorded." The lexicography practically drips with condescension here, and the citations in this first edition of the *Dictionary* are recorded in such detail that they bear reproducing in full, as a document to the remarkable hold that this word had on the contemporary populace (see figure 15.3).

In this entry lies a social history of gender and its idioms in the last two decades of the nineteenth century. The dude connotes excess, eccentricity, affectation. But at the heart of dudedom is not simply affectation but imagination. The dude is fiction brought to life, a literary creature plopped down on the streets of the quotidian. And, yet, the dude is also something of a threat to power: a self-imagined ruler of a landscape given up to foppery and fools. Look at the range of quotations that the *NED* assembles to illustrate the nonce words of *dudedom* and the like. Phrases such as "the dude or dudine in his dominion"; "the intense dudeness of Lord Beaconsfield"; "the Pharisiacal dudery"; "A dudish applicant, with an overweening sense of his own self-importance"; and, again, "the realms of dudedom." There is a politics to dudery, a sense that somehow this affected or imaginary persona poses a threat to the established order—that what replaces power politics or social class or the familiar hierarchies of control is something strange. Are we, the *NED*'s concatenation of quotations seems to ask, living not in a kingdom but in a dudedom? Is the American experiment (for many of these quotations come from American sources) posing a threat to British habits, lives, or even novels?

But what did *American* scholars think of *dude?* William Dwight Whitney's *Century Dictionary* appeared in 1889 just as the *New English Dictionary* was being published. Its volume D has this definition of the word:

[A slang term said to have originated in London, England. It first became known in general colloquial and newspaper use at the time of the so-called 'esthetic' movement in dress and manners, in 1882–83. The term has no antecedent record, and is prob. merely one of the spontaneous products of popular slang. There is no known way, even in slang etymology, of 'deriving' the term, in the sense used, from duds (formerly sometimes spelled dudes), clothes, in the sense of 'fine clothes'; and the connection, though apparently natural, is highly improbable.] A fop or exquisite, characterized by affected refinement of dress, speech, manners, and gait, and a serious mien; hence, by an easy extension, and with less of contempt, a man given to excessive refinement of fashion in dress.

Unlike the *NED*, the *Century Dictionary* locates the word's origin in England, rather than America, and that is precisely the point. For the dude is some indefinable other. The lexicographer, whether British or American, refuses to claim ownership or origin. The creature arises, in this entry, as some social equivalent of the "spontaneous" generation—the product of the colloquial, the popular, the slang, the improbable. In these entries, both the *Century* and the *NED* offer social criticism through philology. Their extended definitions center on the theater of dudedom: the logic of costume and affectation.

Whitney had elsewhere reflected on the process by which words such as *dude* enter language. In his popular volume of 1875, *Life and Growth of Language*, he notes that words may enter languages through many venues, but they invariably gain acceptance through the authority of their users and through the consent of the general populace. Great writers may, by their authority, condone a new word; so, too, may the authorities of etymologists and pedagogues. "Downright additions . . . to the vocabulary of a spoken tongue" come, he claims, from "human agency." And "no man in his sober senses" would believe that "language itself *spontaneously* extrudes a word for its designation!" (emphasis mine). But notice Whitney's phrasing here. The word *dude*, in his *Century Dictionary*, was "merely one of the spontaneous products of popular slang." There are no great authorities who sanction it, no great authors (at least none cited by his *Dictionary*) who approve it. And this is where Twain comes in. His dudes and dudesses remain self-conscious additions to the language: words that he will sanction through his status as an author. As a product of the popular press or the dime novel, the dude stands at the intersection of ephemeral print and public performance.

Hello and *dude* tell us much about the language of technology, the idioms of performance, and the ways in which new words had entered English in the 1880s. But they are not alone. Twain's writings both shaped and recorded the new shaping of the language in his day. According to the evidence collected for the *OED*, he is responsible for the first literary appearances of the verb *call* (meaning to make a telephone call); *central* (denoting a telephone exchange); *random* (used as a verb); *slim-jim*; and *up-anchor* (used as a verb). *Ironclad* first appeared in 1852, but Twain uses it in fiction for the first time. Other words that emerged from the Civil War and the years immediately around it, and for which Twain is the earliest literary usage, include *gripsack*, *boss-ship* (Twain clearly loved the word *boss*), *give-away*, *home plate*, the interjection *rah*, *unreasoning*, and *way-back*. Even words that were in common usage in the late nineteenth century were given added currency by Twain's appropriation of them—and the current edition of the *OED* relies on Twain for over 1,700 examples. He is, in fact, one of the six most quoted modern authors in the entire *Dictionary*.

Part of Twain's authority clearly lies in his ability to coin or use in a distinctly memorable way recent words and phrases. Such idioms as "pass the buck," "land-office business," "shenanigan," "high-muck-a-muck," "bite the dust," and "as easy as rolling off a log" were probably current by the mid-nineteenth century, but Twain used them in his speeches, letters, and his literary fictions in ways that made them uniquely his own. Twain also brought words in from North American Spanish, such as *cherimoya* and *machete*, and he took some old and out-of-date usages, such as *scrouge* (meaning "to crowd or shove") and *dust* (meaning "to whip or thrash") and gave them new currency.

The point about Mark Twain, therefore, is not whether he really did personally increase the vocabulary of American English (as Shakespeare really did for British English), but that he presented himself as a linguistic innovator. Throughout his writings, there remains the feel of English being used in a creative and new way. He calls attention, as in *Huckleberry Finn*, to his attentiveness to dialect. Whether or not Twain really was an accurate transcriber of the dialects he claims to record, he was a brilliant evoker of those dialects. What linguists call "eye-spellings" fill his writings to create the illusion of phonetic transcription. This device has long been a feature of the literary representation of regional speech (as we have seen, Chaucer used it at the end of the fourteenth century to evoke the Northern Middle English in his "Reeve's Tale," and Shakespeare used it, among other places, to flavor the inflection of his French Princess Katherine in *Henry V*). What is significant about Twain's use of eye-spelling is both the range of its deployment and its comic effect. Take, for example, the passage from *Huckleberry Finn* cited in John Algeo's *Problems in the Origin and Development of the English Language*:

> So Tom says: "I know how to fix it. We got to have a rock for the coat of arms and mournful inscriptions, and we can kill two birds with that same rock. There's a gaudy big grindstone down at the mill, and we'll smouch it, and carve the thing on it, and file out the pens and the saw on it, too."
>
> It warn't no slouch of an idea; and it warn't no slouch of a grindstone nuther; but we allowed we'd tackle it.

Spellings such as "warn't" and "nuther" create, in the reader's mind, not just the sound of those particular words, but the overall impression of dialect speech. A word like *smouch*, meaning "steal," contributes to the overall effect of two rural Missourians of the 1840s in conversation (the word seems to appear in 1820s America, as a corruption of the word *smouse*, a derogatory term for a Jew or itinerant trader). "Gaudy big" has an archaic feel to it, as if an ancient English phrase were fossilized in local speech—which, to some extent, it was (*gaudy*, meaning luxurious or showy, goes back to the sixteenth century). The boys really are killing two birds with one stone here—an expression that as far as I can tell, is proverbial as early as the mid-seventeenth century.

This passage revels in the linguistic old and new; but few passages in Twain rival, for sheer verbal brilliance, the scene in *Huckleberry Finn* when the Duke and the Dauphin show up to do Shakespeare. The Duke, taking control, announces that they'll put on a show. "We want a little something to answer encores with, anyway." The Dauphin asks: "What's onkores?" Here, the eye-spelling tells us nothing about pronunciation. The word "encores" really is pronounced "onkores." Yet, by spelling it in this way, Twain signals the Dauphin's ignorance. It is as if he's never heard the word before, as if he needs to get his mouth around its awkward sounds, as if he sees it in his mind's eye as "onkores." Through the device of eye-spelling, Twain calls attention to a word not so much new to English but new to the language of his characters; a word radically out of place in the idiom of the novel's everyday.

Twain's gift, in short, was to evoke the sound of spoken American English on the printed page. While other writers tried their hands at dialect, none did so with the sustained brilliance of Twain. And while other writers of his day were certainly alert to changes in the sound and lexicon of English, Twain managed—through the memorable power of his prose—to give currency to words and phrases that otherwise would have sunk in the eddies of American expression. Late in his life, Twain was asked what his contribution to the language was, and he replied that he had "coined no words that had achieved the distinction of incorporation into the English language." Whether or not that modest claim is true, the fact remains that Twain captured the new idiom of American English: the rhythm of its speech, the weave of its figurative phrasings, the crackle of its expanding vocabulary. He knew that a nation's language is a very large matter. And much like Hank Morgan or Huck Finn, philologists like us are always lighting out for the territory.

CHAPTER 16

Ready for the Funk

African American English and Its Impact

MIDWAY THROUGH THE FIRST PART OF Frederick Douglass's *Life and Times*, he recalls plans to run away. Together with his friends, the young slave hatches a plot to escape from the masters, make it north, and seek a new life. Troubles beset them.

> The reader can have little idea of the phantoms which would flit, in such circumstances, before the uneducated mind of the slave. Upon either side we saw grim death, assuming a variety of horrid shapes. Now it was starvation, causing us, in a strange and friendless land, to eat our own flesh. Now we were contending with the waves and were drowned. Now we were hunted by dogs and overtaken, and torn to pieces by their merciless fangs. We were stung by scorpions, chased by wild beasts, bitten by snakes, and, worst of all, after having succeeded in swimming rivers, encountering wild beasts, sleeping in the woods, and suffering hunger, cold, heat, and nakedness, were overtaken by hired kidnappers, who, in the name of law and for the thrice-cursed reward, would, perchance, fire upon us, kill some, wound others, and capture all. This dark picture, drawn by ignorance and fear, at times greatly shook our determination, and not unfrequently caused us to
> Rather bear the ills we had,
> Than flee to others which we knew not of.

The eloquence of this passage is the eloquence of Douglass's old age. No slave, however reared on Webster's *Spelling Book*, could have imagined such a phrasing in the 1830s. This is a passage that recalls not just experience but a whole life of reading: from the Miltonic evocations of the "horrid shapes" to the capstone couplet from Hamlet's famed soliloquy. Douglass indulges in all the rhetorical devices at work throughout the history of English: the anaphora of dramatic narration (Now it was starvation . . . now we were contending . . . now we were hunted); the lists of hellish torment; the biblical flavor of pulpit oratory. We have seen this all before, from Wulfstan's laments under Danish oppression, through the *Peterborough Chronicle*'s account of the anarchy of 1137, through the Chancery petition's story of abduction, through Shakespeare, Milton, Johnson, and even Emily Dickinson (those "horrid, hooting stanzas" still come back). Douglass gives us a litany of all the archetypes of terror and, in the process, reveals his deep understanding of the knells and nuances of English.

But Douglass shows us, too, an equally profound appreciation of the slave's voice itself—a voice more likely tuned to the pipes of popular lyric than the meters of Shakespeare or Milton. Just a few pages before this great passage, Douglass recalls poetry equally powerful in its expression of the deprivations of slave life. At times, he writes, the slaves would spend their holidays in celebration, "fiddling, dancing, and 'jubilee beating.'" The performer, he notes,

> improvised as he beat the instrument, marking the words as he sang so as to have them fall pat with the movement of his hands. Once in a while among a mass of nonsense and wild frolic, a sharp hit was given to the meanness of slaveholders. Take the following for example:

We raise de wheat,
Dey gib us de corn;
We bake de bread,
Dey gib us de crust;
We sif de meal,
Dey gib us de huss;
We peel de meat,
Dey gib us de skin;
And dat's de way
Dey take us in;
We skim de pot,
De gib us de liquor,
And say dat's good enough for nigger.
Walk over! walk over!

Your butter and de fat;
Poor nigger, you can't get over dat!
   Walk over—

For all the realism of this passage, and for all of Douglass's efforts to make it sound authentic, it remains as much an archetype as any other moment in the book. The scene comes off as something like a story of black bardistry, as if this episode of feasting and performance generates (at least to my overlearned eye) a kind of slave Caedmon. Sing to me of creation, and that's precisely what Douglass's juba beater does. But it is the creation of an already fallen world. The slave labors only for the dross of land and livestock, and if there is any divine presence in this poem, it is the godlike voice of the slave master who pronounces things not simply good but "good enough for nigger."

These two passages from Douglass's *Life and Times*—the one learned and literary, the other rich with dialect and folk life—form the two poles of the African American verbal experience. They juxtapose rhetoric and realism, standard and dialectal speech. And yet, both do so with a profound biblical resonance: two versions of the hell of slavery. Throughout the nineteenth and the twentieth centuries, African American expression moves between these poles. We can trace a history of dialect poetry, folk tales, and local stories—from the ventriloquisms of Joel Chandler Harris's Uncle Remus fables, through the verse of Daniel Webster Davis, the lyrics of jazz and the blues, the dozens and the jive and rap. But we can also trace a history of impassioned public oratory and passionate prose and verse—speeches running from Booker T. Washington to Martin Luther King Jr.; scholarly prose running from W. E. B. Dubois to Henry Louis Gates; vibrant fiction running from Zora Neale Hurston through Richard Wright, Ralph Ellison, James Baldwin, Alice Walker, and Toni Morrison; and lyric poetry running from Langston Hughes through Gwendolyn Brooks, Amiri Baraka, and Yousef Komunyakaa.

There is no single strain of African American English. Though a good deal of recent scholarship has set out to define the distinctive phonology, morphology, and lexis of the African American community, such features are not fully shared by every speaker of African ancestry. Some are urban, some are rural; some Southern, some not. Indeed, some of the central tensions in the history of African American English lie precisely on these axes of location and migration. Even Douglass gives us, in his passage-work, a story of displacement (the child raised in Baltimore imagines the songs of the rural fieldworker). "African American English" remains not simply a moniker for dialect but a source of influence on American, and indeed, world English, in the large. Its study must go beyond philological description to embrace social life, literary genre, public rhetoric, and private dreams.

But first, philology. Perhaps the most prolific and influential scholar of African American English (as well of American speech generally) has been William Labov. From a series of his articles and books, there emerge four features of the language:

> 1. The Black English Vernacular is a subsystem of English with a distinct set of phonological and syntactic rules that are now aligned in many ways with rules of other dialects.
>
> 2. It incorporates many features of Southern phonology, morphology, and syntax; blacks in turn have exerted influence on the dialects of the South where they have lived.
>
> 3. It shows evidence of derivation from an earlier Creole that was closer to the present-day Creoles of the Caribbean.
>
> 4. It has a highly developed aspect system, quite different from other dialects of English, which shows a continuing development of its semantic structure.
>
> (Labov, quoted in Mufwene, "African-American English," 315)

Let us take each of these positions in order. What is the sound structure and syntax of African American English? Among the most distinctive features of pronunciation is the displacement of *th*- sounds (what linguists call an interdental continuant or fricative) with other sounds, depending on their position in the word. Thus, words that begin with *th*- (*think, them, those*) may be pronounced with an initial /t/ or /d/ (that is, by stops rather than continuants). In the medial or final position, the *th*- may be pronounced as /f/ or /v/ (a labio-dental continuant). Thus, a word such as *mouth* may sound like "mouf," or *with* may sound like "wiv." In addition to these characteristics, African American English often appears to lose the *r*-sound in certain positions. Words like *floor* and *four* may sound like "flow" and "foe." Final stops may also be dropped in certain words: *guest, desk,* and *wasp* may sound like "guess," "dess," and "wass." Some scholars have also argued that expressions such as "She jump over the table" or "brown-eye beauty," are instances where certain sounds are elided in particular phonemic environments. The difference, therefore, between "she jump" and "she jumps," or between "brown-eye" and "brown-eyed" may be matters of phonology, rather than of morphology.

Because the historical black population in the United States came through the Southern states, and because subsequent patterns of migration brought Southern inhabitants north and west, there is much about African American English that may seem inseparable from Southern speech generally. For example, the merging of the vowels in words such as *pen* and *pin* or *ten* and *tin*, or the pronunciation of *get* as "git," is often shared by white and black speakers in the South. Certain diphthongs in words such as *cry* and *toy* come out as monophthongs in many Southern speakers regardless of race (thus, pronunciations that sound like "crah," "taw"). By contrast, certain words such as *bad* and *hand* have their vowels turned into diphthongs (in phonemic transcription, /bæəd/ and /hæənd/). Word stress, too, brings African American English into line with Southern speech: *police*, *Detroit*, and *umbrella* often have their stress on the first syllable (see Mufwene, "African-American English," 297).

The historical origin of the African American population may also place African American English in the ambit of the early Atlantic creoles. Creole languages are complicated, and the term, while evoking a range of cultural and social idioms today, means something quite specific to linguists. A creole is a language that develops over several generations to enable originally different language groups to communicate with one another. Often, creoles develop when the language of a colonizing or an economically dominant group is imposed upon a subordinate or colonized group. Creoles may preserve a basic grammar of the colonized while incorporating the vocabulary of the colonizing. Creoles, however, differ from pidgins. A pidgin (the word comes, in fact, from the mispronunciation of the word "business" by nineteenth-century Chinese traders) is a form of communication that develops in a single generation for two mutually unintelligible groups of speakers to communicate. Pidgins are ad hoc forms of communication, and they are perceived as artificial by both groups of speakers. Creoles, however, are perceived as "native languages" by their speakers. The creole languages of the Atlantic slave trade brought together French, Spanish, English, and Portuguese, along with such West African languages as Wolof, Mandingo, Housa, and Western Bantu. The language known as Gullah emerged as a creole of English and West African languages, and it arose in the eighteenth century in the coastal settlements of South Carolina, the Carolina islands, and, later on, inland throughout the Carolinas, Georgia, and Alabama.

Many scholars find in Gullah the linguistic origins of African American English, and many features of the sound, grammar, and idiom of modern black vernaculars may be traced back to creole origins. Some of the phonology of African American English is traceable to Gullah: for example, the dropping of the *r-* sound or the occasional pronunciation of *v* as something like a *b* (more precisely, what linguists would identify as the phoneme /ß/, bilabial continuant). Grammatical features in common include the lack of a possessive marker: phrases such as "Jane book" (instead of "Jane's book") or "my sister name" (instead of "my sister's name"), or the loss of the plural in "two dog" are features that linguists have identified as characteristic of Gullah.

Among the most distinctive of these creole features is the verbal system, and "aspect," rather than "tense," is the term linguists use to characterize it. A tense language is one that defines relationships in time according to when events happened. Yesterday it rained; tomorrow it will rain. Tense does not tell us when the actions began and ended; we do not know whether the phrase "yesterday it rained" means that it had been raining before yesterday, or that the rain stopped (or did not) after yesterday. Aspect languages, however, define temporal relationships according to duration. Aspects can indicate, say, actions that were begun in the past and completed in the past; or begun in the past and completed in the present; or begun in the past and continuing in the future. In African American English (as well as in some of the Atlantic creoles), such forms of duration are clearly marked. Thus, expression such as "she sick" or "she go" denote actions at a point in time. What matters is not whether the action is present or past, but that the action happened and is not ongoing. Expressions using the verb "to be," such as "she be sick" or "she be going" express duration: that is, the action began at one point and continues on. Sometimes, too, the verb "to be" can be used to signal habitual aspect. An expression such as "I be tired after work" means that I am usually tired after work; an expression such as "She be crying after I leave," means that she usually cries after I go. Forms of the verb "to do" also participate in these expressions. "He be done gone every time I come" means that he usually has left when I arrive. But forms of the verb "to do" can also signal aspects of completion. "She done eat" means that she has completed the act of eating in the past. "He been done gone" means that he left at a moment in the past. There is a sense, too, that the word *done* can signal emphasis. "I talk done," or "I done talking" means not just that I am finished talking but that I am finished and have really nothing more to say. In an expression such as, "He done his homework," done means not simply that he did it, but that he has begun and completed an action in the past: he has finished it.

We can see many features of African American English in the poem Frederick Douglass offered. The characteristic change of *th-* sounds to *d-* sounds is clear, as is the pronunciation of the final *v* in *give* as the voiced bilabial continuant /ß/ (spelled "gib"). The loss of final stops appears in *sif* (for "sift") and *huss* (for "husk"—though Douglass does not indicate the likely pronunciation of *crust* as "cruss"). And while the poem is not written consistently in eye dialect, it does seem clear that the words "liquor" and "nigger" rhyme (one may also assume that, to be consistent about it, the words *your* and *poor* would have been pronounced something like "yo" and "poe").

As with most dialect literature, this poem is an evocation of a sound rather than a transcription of someone's speech. More sustained in its dialect transliteration, and fuller in its presentation of African American syntax and morphology, is the poetry of Daniel Webster Davis (1862–1913). Davis made a career of writing dialect verse that, to modern readers, comes off as uncomfortably sentimental or stereotypical. His lyrics in the voice of indolent or hedonistic speakers may contribute to a legacy of bias:

> O, de birds ar' sweetly singin',
> Wey down Souf,
> An' de bajer is a-ringin',
> Wey down Souf.

But there is much in Davis that is literary and that responds to traditions of American regionalism in the late nineteenth and early twentieth centuries.

Take, for example, the poem "Hog Meat," probably written in the first decade of the twentieth century and published in James Weldon Johnson's *Book of American Negro Poetry* of 1922.

> Deze eatin' folks may tell me ub de gloriz ub spring lam',
> An' de toofsumnis ub tuckey et wid cel'ry an' wid jam;
> Ub beef-st'ak fried wid unyuns, an' sezoned up so fine—
> But you' jes' kin gimme hog-meat, an' I'm happy all de time.
>
> When de fros' is on de pun'kin an' de sno'-flakes in de ar',
> I den begin rejoicin'—hog-killin' time is near;
> An' de vizhuns ub de fucher den fill my nightly dreams,
> Fur de time is fas' a-comin' fur de 'lishus pork an' beans.

We folks dat's frum de kuntry may be behin' de sun—
We don't like city eatin's, wid beefsteaks dat ain' done—
'Dough mutton chops is splendid, an' dem veal cutlits fine,
To me 'tain't like a sphar-rib, or gret big chunk ub chine.

Jes' talk to me 'bout hog-meat, ef yo' want to see me pleased,
Fur biled wid beans tiz gor'jus, or made in hog-head cheese;
An' I could jes' be happy, 'dout money, cloze or house,
Wid plenty yurz an' pig feet made in ol'-fashun "souse."

I 'fess I'm only humun, I hab my joys an' cares—
Sum days de clouds hang hebby, sum days de skies ar' fair;
But I forgib my in'miz, my heart is free frum hate,
When my bread is filled wid cracklins an' dar's chidlins on my plate.

'Dough 'possum meat is glo'yus wid 'taters in de pan,
But put 'longside pork sassage it takes a backward stan';
Ub all yer fancy eatin's, jes gib to me fur mine
Sum souse or pork or chidlins, sum sphar-rib, or de chine.

This poem has long been appreciated (or decried) as an example of the black vernacular. It seems, on the surface, to give voice to simple pleasures of the appetite: a rejection of the fancy cuisine of the city in favor of the basics of the country. And yet, there is much more. The lines move across a litany of pleasures, but by stanza five the poignancy emerges. The poem's speaker must confess to his humanity, and the line, "Sum days de clouds hang hebby, sum days de skies ar' fair," has the flavor of a blues song or even an Ellingtonian lament. But it has the flavor, too, of church. Forgive your enemies; free your heart from hatred. With cracklings and chitlins on the plate, the verse aspires to a kind of down home Eucharist: a sacrament of foods that fill the soul.

But "Hog Meat," too, is a poem on the cusp. It straddles rural and urban— or, more precisely, it presents an essentially rural aesthetic for the delectation of a literate, urban audience. In this way, it responds to a tradition of American regionalism generally, a fascination that the late nineteenth century had with the "authentic" language of American place and personality. More specifically, the poem clearly plays off of the idioms of the Midwestern versifier James Whitcomb Riley (1853–1916), whose "Hoosier" poetry gave voice to a similar blend of the colloquial, the spiritual, and the digestive.

When the frost is on the punkin and the fodder's in the shock,
And you hear the kyouck and gobble of the struttin' turkey-cock . . .

Davis's second stanza must recall these lines, and his poem's ending, too, must recall Riley's spiritual aspirations and the end of his:

I don't know how to tell it—but ef such a thing could be
As the angels wantin' boardin', and they'd call around on me—
I'd want to 'commodate 'em—all the whole-indurin' flock—
When the frost is on the punkin and the fodder's in the shock.

Read against Riley's verses, and the broader tradition of "white" literature they stimulated, Davis's "Hog Meat" may be appreciated not as the unmediated transcriptions of an authentic (or even parodic) black voice, but as a literary realization that the black voice speaks as well: that pumpkins have their frost for everyone, and that the black man, too, is only human. If you prick us, do we not bleed?

But on the other hand, when Southern blacks came north to the great cities, many of them wished to put their taste for hog meat (and, in turn, the language of the rural South) behind them. This collocation of food and identity, feasting and literary inspiration, returns brilliantly in Ralph Ellison's novel, *Invisible Man* (1952). The book's young hero, fresh to New York City, comes across a Harlem street vendor. From his wagon, comes the "odor of baking yams slowly to me, bringing a stab of swift nostalgia." He stops, dead in his tracks. The smell returns him to the South, and to the language of his past. "Get yo' hot, baked Car'lina yam," the vendor calls, and the young man buys one for a dime, takes a bite, and finds himself "overcome with such a surge of homesickness that I turned away to keep my control." But then, he turns angry. "What a group of people we were, I thought. Why, you could cause us the greatest humiliation simply by confronting us with something we liked." And he goes on, imagining a rant against his old college mentor:

Bledsoe, you're a shameless chitterling eater! I accuse you of relishing hog bowels! Ha! And not only do you eat them, you sneak and eat them in *private* when you think you're unobserved! You're a sneaking chitterling lover. . . .

And after paragraphs of this performance, he concludes, "to hell with being ashamed of what you liked. . . . I am what I am!" And again, with another two more buttered yams on the way, "They're my birthmark . . . I yam what I am!"

We all are what we are. The smells and savors of our childhood come back constantly, and in this passage—as much a response to "Hog Meat" as to Proust's madeleine—we all see ourselves as subjects to our tongue. Tongue is the instrument of taste, but it is also the organ of voice. A tongue is a language. And a tongue is song. African American English is a language of song, from Douglass's slave lyrics to jazz, the blues, and gospel. Cab Calloway knew this, and he replaces Webster's *Spelling Book* with what he calls the "Jive Talk Dictionary."

> What's a hepcat? A hepcat is a guy
> Who knows all the answers, and I'm telling you why . . .
> He's a high-falutin' student
> Of the Calloway vocab.
>
> What's the twister to the slammer?
> The twister is the key
> That opens up the slammer
> To my chicken fricassee.
>
> If you want to learn the lingo:
> Jive from ABC to Zee,
> Get hip with
> Mister Hepster's Dictionary.

Once again, language is inseparable from food, and food is often just another way of talking about sex. "My chicken fricassee," much like the hog meat of Davis's poem, is only a thinly coded phrase for pleasure—just recall, too, the words to Bessie Smith's "My Kitchen Man":

> I'm wild about his turnip tops.
> Likes the way he warms my chops!
> I can't do without my kitchen man.
> Now when I eat his donut
> All I leave is just the hole.
> And if he really needs it,
> He can use my sugar bowl.

But, as Frederick Douglass showed, there is another strain to African American expression—not the language of the slave or of the hepster's dictionary, but the arc of Shakespeare, Milton, and the Bible. Black pulpit oratory rang for decades. Ellison gives a brilliant example early on in *Invisible Man*, as we hear the cadences of Homer Barbee, the blind Homer of black aspiration, in the southern college chapel:

> This barren land after Emancipation, this land of darkness and sorrow, of ignorance and degradation, where the hand of brother had been turned against brother, father against son, and son against father; where master had turned against slave and slave against master; where all was strife and darkness, an aching land.

For page after page, the novel's narrator hears Reverend Barbee preach and reminisce about the founding of their college. "Picture it, my young friends: The clouds of darkness all over the land, black folk and white folk full of fear and hate, wanting to go forward, but each fearful of the other." And when the Reverend turns to talk about the college founder, he intones:

> You have heard his name from your parents, for it was he who led them to the path, guiding them like a great captain; like that great pilot of ancient times who led his people safe and unharmed across the bottom of the blood-red sea. And your parents followed this remarkable man across the black sea of prejudice . . . shouting, LET MY PEOPLE GO.

On and on Barbee rings, in language not just biblical in tenor but evoking all who used creation, wilderness, and redemption as their themes. There is the majesty of Milton here; the echoes, too, of Herman Melville's episode in *Moby-Dick* when Father Mapple gives his own great sermon at the outset of the novel; the resonances with the fears of Douglass's escaped slaves. Ellison evokes a tradition of black pulpit oratory and American religious rhetoric. That tradition informs what may well be the best known and, to this day, one of the most vital public addresses in American history: Martin Luther King Jr.'s, "I have a dream," delivered at the March on Washington on August 28, 1963.

King's words are so familiar and so much a part of the texture of American linguistic life, that we may need to pause to see their power and their history again. Like Lincoln's "Gettysburg Address," they create a rhetorical America.

Like a great Southern sermon, they conjure up a congregation. Alliteration, rhythm, cadence are all there, and on the page we miss what anyone who lived through its experience or sees and hears it in recordings knows: the calls and affirmations of the audience; the tone of King's voice and the magic of his body movements. "Five score years ago," he begins, in invocation of Lincoln's "Address" and of the dead president's presence and power. And it concludes, with repetitions, clauses, lists, quotations, and allusions to everything from Handel's *Messiah*, to "My Country 'Tis of Thee," to the old spirituals:

> I have a dream that one day every valley shall be exalted, every hill and mountain shall be made low, the rough places will be made plain, and the crooked places will be made straight, and the glory of the Lord shall be revealed, and all flesh shall see it together. This is our hope. This is the faith with which I return to the South. . . . With this faith we will be able to work together, to pray together, to struggle together, to go to jail together, to stand up for freedom together, knowing that we will be free one day.
>
> This will be the day when all of God's children will be able to sing with a new meaning, "My country, 'tis of thee, sweet land of liberty, of thee I sing. Land where my fathers died, land of the pilgrim's pride, from every mountainside, let freedom ring." And if America is to be a great nation, this must become true. So let freedom ring from the prodigious hilltops of New Hampshire. Let freedom ring from the mighty mountains of New York. Let freedom ring from the heightening Alleghenies of Pennsylvania! Let freedom ring from the snow-capped Rockies of Colorado! Let freedom ring from the curvaceous peaks of California! But not only that; let freedom ring from Stone Mountain of Georgia! Let freedom ring from Lookout Mountain of Tennessee! Let freedom ring from every hill and every molehill of Mississippi. From every mountainside, let freedom ring.
>
> When we let freedom ring, when we let it ring from every village and every hamlet, from every state and every city, we will be able to speed up that day when all of God's children, black men and white men, Jews and Gentiles, Protestants and Catholics, will be able to join hands and sing in the words of the old Negro spiritual, "Free at last! free at last! thank God Almighty, we are free at last!"

How could I forget this speech: an eight-year-old in Brooklyn, watching on a little black-and-white television, as the cadences came down? I felt the sway of the repetitions (the word "together" will never be the same for me). In schoolroom chorals, "My Country 'Tis of Thee" would be irrevocably changed; how could we sing "let freedom ring" without hearing King's voice behind our own? It was from this speech that I learned the word "hamlet," that I learned "prodigious" (was King thinking of Emily Dickinson's phrasing, "and then prodigious step"?). And it was in this speech that I first heard the word "Jews" from the mouth of a black man.

How could I forget five years later, having moved from Brooklyn to the Boston suburbs, my mother coming into my bedroom to tell me he was dead? I remember everything that changed since then: the riots and the anger and the Panthers and the raised fists at the 1968 Olympics. I sat in pristine, suburban schoolrooms while H. Rap Brown was announcing in his autobiography, *Die, Nigger, Die!* (1969), "I learned to talk in the street, not from reading about Dick and Jane going to the zoo and all that simple shit" (quoted in Gates, *The Signifying Monkey*, 72).

Rap got his name from his ability to rap, to play the dozens and to signify, and his way of using language reaches back to the traditions of slave poetry, dialect lyric, and jive talk to infuse African American vernaculars with distinctive political edge. The dozens, as the critic Henry Louis Gates Jr., has explained it, was a kind of virtuoso performance: a way of dexterously manipulating slang terms, parodies of formal speech, and popular rhythms to put down another and raise up the speaker. "Rap is my name and love is my game," and Gates quotes Rap Brown's poetry:

Man, you must don't know who I am.
I'm sweet peeter jeeter the womb beater
The baby maker the cradle shaker
The deerslayer the buckbinder the women finder.

(72)

Such forms of speech, too, offer up what Brown called (and what Gates develops) "signifyin'." Signifyin' also reached back to earlier traditions, but at its heart was not so much the theater of dissing as the theory of denoting. To signify was to appropriate the master's language as a form of comic subversion. It was a way of revising, rewriting, or retelling in a language charged with metaphor. It enabled, in Gates's terms, "the black person to move freely between two discursive universes"—"standard" and African American English. Signifyin' was, as well, a system of indirection, a way of using irony, parody, allusion, or shifts in spoken emphasis. In the words of the linguist Claudia Mitchell-Kernan, it "incorporates essentially a folk notion that dictionary entries for words are not always sufficient for interpreting meanings or messages" (quoted in Rickford and Rickford, *Spoken Soul*, 82). And in the definitions of the linguist Roger D. Abrahams, it is "the language of trickery, that set of words achieving Hamlet's 'direction through indirection'" (quoted in Gates, *The Signifying Monkey*, 75).

And so, we are back to Hamlet. Did Frederick Douglass signify? Are Shakespeare's words transformed simply in the slave's mouth? And what of more modern African American verbal performance? Rap, hip-hop, game, and gangsta—such forms of expression look back to the dialects of Daniel Webster Davis or the "Hi-De-Ho" of Cab Calloway to give us soliloquies as rich as "to be or not to be."

I bet you got it twisted you don't know who to trust
So many playa hating niggaz tryin to sound like us
Say they ready for the funk, but I don't think they knowin
Straight to the depths of hell is where those cowards goin
Well are you still down nigga? Holla when you see me
And let these devils be sorry for the day they finally freed me.

(Tupac Shakur, "All Eyez on Me")

Straight to the depths of hell—rap offers up as much of a phantasmagoria as Frederick Douglass's description of slaves on the run.

The impact of African American vernaculars on English worldwide lies, therefore, on much more than mere vocabulary. It lies in an attitude to language use: a sense of the figurative possibilities behind the sentence; a sense of the flow and flavor of rhyme, meter, assonance, and alliteration. But so much, too, has changed. The lyrics of late-twentieth- and early-twenty-first-century rap often offend. They shock listeners out of their complacencies. Many teachers, parents, critics, public figures, and private listeners find music of this kind simply offensive. And some find, in particular, white popular culture's appropriation of the black vernacular threatening. The singer Marshall Mathers (Eminem) sets out precisely to threaten. His horrid, hooting stanzas seem to advocate violence against women, minorities, gays, and lesbians. "My words," he sings in one song, "are like a dagger with a jagged edge." And in his alter ego, Slim Shady, Eminem appropriates the black personifications of the rapper, trickster, and Signifyin' Monkey who would use the master's verbal tools to undermine the master's house.

I'm like a head trip to listen to, cause I'm only givin you
things that you joke about with your friends inside your living room
the only difference is I got the balls to say it
in front of y'all and I don't gotta be false or sugarcoated at all.

(Eminem, "The Real Slim Shady")

Such lyrics seem, to me, not new at all. They recall H. Rap Brown's persona of the man of sex and violence (Brown: "I'm . . . the gunslinger the baby bringer"). They recall, too, the twisty, signifyin' sexuality of Cab Calloway. But what contemporary writers, singers, and performers all show, too, is language not just as a tool, but as a weapon. The assonance of Eminem's words, "dagger / jagged" cuts our ears. The words *rap* and *funk* have, in their slapping monosyllables and final stops, the very sound of physical contact. If African American English has had an impact, it may well be because it is not just a language of cool or hip or soul, but of defiance. As the poet Amiri Baraka put it:

> 'Rap' is as old as the African beating on a log like the one in which sailors keep their records, as old as the dictum that denied slaves drums because they were 'rapping' to each other after hours, drumming up rhythmic resistance. When the rappers say 'word,' it is old. Our speech carries our whole existence.
>
> (quoted in Campbell, *"Gettin' our Groove On,"* vii)

And in that speech, we may trace a history of enslavement, emigration, travel, and resettlement. Some linguists find in words things older than America itself: in *hep*, or *hip*, a legacy of Wolof, *hepi*, *hipi*, "to open one's eyes, to be aware of what is going on"; in *cat* an echo of the Wolof *-kat*, the suffix denoting a person; in *cool*, a translation of the Mandingo *suma*; in *dig*, an association with the Wolof *deg*, "to understand or appreciate" (see Sidnell, "African American Vernacular English"). These English words may well bear multiple etymologies. They may have once evolved as familiar-sounding terms with unfamiliar meanings—ways of signifyin', terms that have meaning in both black and white worlds. And behind Douglass's allusions, or Homer Barbee's biblicisms, or the cadences of King, we may hear the rap of unfamiliar phonemes, or the funk of ancient etymologies, or the echoes of an audience. *Amen.*

CHAPTER 17

Pioneers Through an Untrodden Forest

The Oxford English Dictionary *and Its Readers*

AMIRI BARAKA WAS NOT THE ONLY READER to hold that "our speech carries our whole existence" or to imagine histories of language in the rap of ancient drumbeats. Nearly a hundred years before Baraka made his claims, Sir James A. H. Murray addressed the Philological Society in London. Reporting on the progress of the recently inaugurated *New English Dictionary* (what would become the famous *OED*), Murray called himself and his assistants "simply pioneers, pushing our way experimentally through an untrodden forest, where no white man's axe has been before us." Speaking to his society in 1884, Murray's words had to recall the explorations of a dark Africa: the world of John Speke and Richard Burton, of Dr. Livingstone and Henry Stanley. The making of this *Dictionary*, much like the making of so many previous English lexicons, shares in the opening and colonizing of another world. From Edward Phillips's *New World of Words* through Johnson's *Dictionary* and to Webster's, the lexicographer stood on the shores of undiscovered lands and brought his verbal treasures back.

The *Oxford English Dictionary* remains the most influential and collaborative project for the history of the English language. With its archives now open to researchers, we know a great deal about just who provided slips of paper for its definitions; how its books and quotations were chosen; how the editors conceived of the linguistics, politics, and aesthetics of their mission; and how the canons of Victorian literary and social behavior shaped its selections, publishing, and presentation. This philological enterprise had a great effect on the culture of its time, and while the history of the *OED* has often been retold, I want to focus on the ways in which it grew not simply from the minds of lexicographers but from the habits of everyday readers. The *OED* was built out of Victorian practices of speaking, reading, and writing. It is a record of the ways in which the scope of English prose and poetry was understood. And in its publication—a series of fascicles, or booklets, issued from 1889 until 1928—it rivaled any great Victorian novel ever published. Indeed, the novelist and critic Arnold Bennett called it "the longest sensational serial ever written." Its heroes are not just the words themselves, but the readers and editors who assembled them.

What would become the *OED* originated in the minds of mid-nineteenth-century English philologists as a *New English Dictionary* (it did not become the *Oxford English Dictionary* until the entire set of volumes reappeared in 1933). Men such as the bibliophile Henry Bradley, the linguist and ecclesiast Richard Chenevix Trench, the polymath Frederick Furnivall, the enthusiastic dilettante Herbert Coleridge, and many other university teachers, journalists, and language hobbyists—all realized that Johnson's *Dictionary* had begun to lose its traction on the changing forms of speech and writing. Comparative philology was flourishing in German universities, and soon to flourish in Oxford and Cambridge, and the discoveries of Indo-European roots and shared word histories among languages running from Celtic to Sanskrit made the etymologies of Johnson's day obsolete. By 1879, the schoolmaster and amateur philologist James Murray had been appointed the supervising editor, and a contract with Oxford University Press was signed for a four-volume work, to be published in ten years. But Murray soon found the resources of the Philological Society (its collections of early books and manuscripts, its scholarly and amateur members) inadequate. And so, only a few months after signing on with Oxford, Murray published in the popular press an "Appeal to the English-Speaking and English-Reading Public to Read Books and Make Extracts for the Philological Society's New Dictionary." In the magazine *The Academy* of May 10, 1879, the call read:

> This is work in which anyone can join. Even the most indolent novel-reader will find it little trouble to put a pencil-mark against any word or phrase that strikes him, and he can afterwards copy out the context at his leisure. In this way many words and references can be registered that may prove of the highest value.

This is precisely what went on, and for the next half century, readers from all over the world contributed their slips and scraps to what became known as the Scriptorium—Murray's word factory and the center of the *Dictionary*'s operations. From the assembly of these bits of information, Murray and his assistants (and, after his death in 1915, his successors) put together histories of words and stories of their use. Like Johnson, they arranged their definitions in order of historical development. Like Johnson, too, they used quotations drawn from literary, intellectual, historical, and documentary texts to illustrate word meanings. But, unlike Johnson, their philology held to the tenets of the new historical comparativists. For behind each word was a history. The German classicist Franz Passow announced, in the preface to his *Handwörterbuch der griechischen Sprache* (4th edition, 1831), that "the dictionary should offer up the life history of every individual word in precise and ordered overview [*Das Wörterbuch soll . . . die Lebensgeschichte jedes einzelnen Wortes in bequem geordneter Ueberschaulichkeit entwerfen*]" (quoted in Aarsleff, *The Study of Language in England*, 255). Herbert Coleridge, in seeking to explain the project of the *New English Dictionary* in 1860, relied precisely on this idea: as Passow put it, he announced, "every word should be made to tell its own story."

What are the stories of this *Dictionary*'s words? Take, for example, Murray's own word, *pioneer*, in the original edition of the *NED* (vol. 7, part 2, *Ph to Py*, originally published in 1909). The word comes from the Old French, *paonier*, originally from *peon* (hence, our modern word "pawn"), meaning a group of foot soldiers who marched in advance of a regiment, digging trenches and clearing the way for the army. In this old sense, the word appears first in the early sixteenth century in English. But, soon, a figurative connotation began: the word could suggest anyone who went ahead, who prepared the way, or originated an action, a plan, or a settlement. Here is the complete set of entries for this figurative definition (def. 3):

1605 BACON *Adv. Learn.* II. vii. §1 To make two professions or occupations of Naturall Philosophers, some to bee Pionners, and some Smythes. **1627** HAKEWILL *Apol.* 22 The other pioner,..which by secret undermining makes way for this opinion of the Worlds decay, is an excessive admiration of Antiquitie. **1700** BLACKMORE *Paraphr. Isa.* xl. 33 Ye Pioneers of Heav'n, prepare a Road. **1768–74** TUCKER *Lt. Nat.* (1834) I. 541 Come then,...Philology, pioneer of the abstruser sciences, to prepare the way for their passage. **1836** W. IRVING *Astoria* III. 262 As one wave of emigration after another rolls into the vast regions of the west,..the eager eyes of our pioneers will pry beyond. **1856** KANE *Arct. Expl.* I. xxiii. 300 The great pioneer of Arctic travel, Sir Edward Parry. **1866** DUKE OF ARGYLL *Reign Law* ii. (ed. 4) 111 The great pioneers in new paths of discovery. **1890** 'R. BOLDREWOOD' *Col. Reformer* (1891) 147 He made the acquaintance of more than one silver-haired pioneer.

Pioneer stands at the crossroads of the intellectual and the imperial. To read these quotations in sequence is to find a narrative of late-nineteenth-century inquiry pressed into the service of political control. And at the center of this definition is philology itself, "pioneer of the abstruser sciences." For Murray to present his project as an act of pioneering, and to see himself and his assistants with their white-man's axe, plays out the etymology and ideology behind the word: men cutting through the forest for an army of advancement, preparing a passage for everything, from natural philosophy to science, to the ends of the earth. Indeed, how could Murray himself—famous with his long grey locks and flowing beard—not imagine his own readers as making "the acquaintance of more than one silver-haired pioneer"?

The *NED*'s self-references abound. Take another example from this same volume: *pigeon-hole*. For any student of the *Dictionary*'s origins, the pigeon-hole is central. Murray's granddaughter, K. M. Elisabeth Murray, in her biography of her forbear, reports that Herbert Coleridge (the *Dictionary*'s first editor, who died young in 1861) had "a set of fifty-four pigeon-holes made which would hold 100,000 slips," and she notes that these holes are still preserved by the Oxford University Press. When Murray himself took over, he adapted Coleridge's model and, in the words of his 1879 address to the Philological Society, "commenced the erection of an iron building" fitted with pigeon-holes. And when the journalist and sometime contributor to the *Dictionary*, Jennet Humphries, visited Murray's office for an 1882 article in *Fraser's Magazine*, she described the walls of the Scriptorium.

> It is pigeon-hole, at any rate, along this wall and along that (barring, only, that intermission across there of a square yard, about, of flat, bare side-window). It is pigeon-hole higher than the arm can reach; going down so low there is need to stoop. It is pigeon-hole, all up and down, and anglewise, of this plain deal screen that shuts off the door, that keeps the inner side—where all is pigeon-hole again—snug and weather-tight for settled sitting.

And Murray himself, in Humphries's report, takes up the repetitions of this word so that it chimes across the hallways.

> 'The pigeon-holes,' he begins—since he sees these are getting lively noting—'I saw at once that we must furnish ourselves with them; that, in fact, they were indispensable. They number more than 1,100 now, though we shall want to add to them even yet, as the work goes

on; and they hold the quotations, or the slips, as our word is, for them. These are all—see—on uniform sheets of paper, of note-paper size, and they are all now being reduced to a uniform plan. . . . The original method differed little from mine, in the position of the catch-words, book-titles, and other details; and now the time has come when differences must no longer be.

These are amazing passages. Their rhetoric, their repetitions, and their flow appear to mime the very state of Murray's office: papers everywhere, a need to organize and to control, an attempt to find uniformity in differ-ence. It is as if Murray had come to find an order in the leavings of his predecessors. As he put it in his 1879 address to the Philological Society, some sections of the *Dictionary* were "in primitive chaos." And three years later, when Humphries shows up, she sees an ordered office. Had there not been such uniformity, she says, "there would be chaos, manifestly."

The *Dictionary* sought an order out of chaos, and when we go to its entries for *pigeon-hole*, we see the world at work. Definition 7 is the one that matters here: "One of a series of compartments or cells, in a cabinet, writing-table, or range of shelves, open in front, and used for the keeping (with ready accessibility) of documents or papers of any kind, also of wares in a shop." In the original *NED*, the quotations read:

> **1789** *Trans. Soc. Arts* (ed. 2) II. 156, I put the papers..into a pigeon hole in a cabinet. **1796** BURKE *Let. to Noble Ld.* Wks. VIII. 58 Abbé Sieyes has whole nests of pigeon-holes full of constitutions ready made, ticketed, sorted, and numbered. **1862** SALA *Ship-Chandler* iii. 48 Pigeon-holes full of samples of sugar, of rice, tobacco, coffee, and the like. **1879** J. A. H. MURRAY *Addr. Philol. Soc.* 8 This has been fit-ted with blocks of pigeon-holes, 1029 in number, for the reception of the alphabetically arranged slips.

Murray's own words cap this definition here—a bit of brilliant self-refer-ence. But as we read on in the definitions, we see more quotations illus-trating finer points. The verb *pigeon-hole* reaches into figurative space (the organizing of the mind, the structuring of thought), and at the very end of that entry, we find this quotation from the novelist George Meredith (dated 1904): "Most women have a special talent for pigeon-holing."

Did they? Murray had his female helpers (Jennet Humphries writes of "two ladies, at their simpler work," in the Scriptorium), and many of the earliest contributors to the *NED* were, in fact, women. According to the list of the first contributors, published in the *Transactions of Philological Society* for 1884, Miss M. Balgarnie was responsible for quotations from George Eliot's *Daniel Deronda*; Miss Florence Balgarnie for the same author's *Theophrastus Such*; Miss B. E. McAllum for *Middlemarch*. Many of the quotations from English novels generally were provided by women. But there were others. The sisters Miss J. E. A. Brown and Miss E. Brown provided over 7,500 quotations from historical and scientific writings; Miss E. F. Burton offered 11,000 quotations from works of natural history. Miss A. Byington (of Massachusetts) sent in Poe. Miss Jennet Humphries herself is recorded as providing 15,200 quotations from everything from Hume, to Hester Lynch Piozzi, to Joseph Priestley, to *The Philosophical Transactions of the Royal Society*.

Who were these people, and the hundreds others (men and women) who provided the quotations? Some names leap out, others remain unknown. This list, which I found in a badly bound copy of the *Transactions*, buried in the back rooms of the Stanford Library, this list which (as far as I know) has never systematically been studied, even by the *Dictionary*'s most assiduous scholars (Linda Mugglestone, John Willinsky, Simon Winchester)—this list is a gold mine for the study of a work that many have come to see not just as a benchmark of lexicography but as a kind of Key to All Mythologies, an explanation of the life of English and its peoples.

That phrase, "A Key to All Mythologies," recalls, of course, the novel of the nineteenth century that, much like the *NED*, sought to explore the nature of linguistic understanding and expression and the ways in which philology and history, science and understanding, come together to locate us in the world. That novel is George Eliot's *Middlemarch*, published in 1870 and 1871, just as the Philological Society was planning out its dictionary and English scholars were attending to the history of language and the techniques of its study. According to the list of readers for the *Dictionary*, it was Miss B. E. McAllum of Newcastle-on-Tyne who read *Middlemarch*. She provided 250 quotations from the novel, of which about 200 or so of them (by my count) eventually made it into the *NED*. Many of these quotations illustrate familiar words, as it should be expected. Murray himself recognized that the challenge for a *Dictionary* reader would be to locate those common words used in representative ways (the "Directions to Readers" sent to those who answered the "Appeal" notes that in addition to "extraordinary words," there must be also "as many good, apt, pithy quotations from ordinary words"). Thus, we find *Middlemarch* illustrating such words as *bald, branch, chill, elbow, marry, without, word*. But *Middlemarch* is also a mine of technical, unusual, and even new words. As might be expected from a novel one of whose main characters is the physician Dr. Lydgate, words from medicine appear: *chyle, diastole, doctor, hypochondriacal, physic, physician, refluent, surgeon, systole*. As might be expected, too, from a novel concerned with religious debate, the big words are there: *evangelicalism, nullifidian*. So, too, are terms from sciences, both natural and human: *geognosis* (a word Eliot apparently has coined, as *Middlemarch* is the only illustrative example in the *Dictionary*), *kleptomania* (for which *Middlemarch* is the last citation in the entry), *theoretic*. There are also technical linguistic terms (*aspirate, vocative*), for this is a novel very much about the scholarly study of language.

But there are also quotations that illustrate what Miss McAllum and the *Dictionary*'s editors clearly found suggestive. The word *slang* is illustrated with this quotation: "Correct English is the slang of prigs who write history and essays. And the strongest slang of all is the slang of poets." One can imagine this quotation fulfilling the "Directions to Readers": "quotations for common words in their common sense and construction need only be made when they are *good*, that is when the reader can say, 'This is a capital quotation.'"

There are also a few words for which *Middlemarch* is the first, or only citation, implying Eliot's coinage ("Take special note," enjoined the "Directions," "of passages which show or imply that a word is . . . new and tentative"): in addition to *geognosis*, there are *pilulous* and *unvoluptuous*. There are words that fulfill the request in the "Directions" for "rare, obsolete, old-fashioned, new peculiar, or used in a peculiar way": *bashaw, glutinous, looby, oary*. And there are other oddities: a word like *miscellaneousness* clearly lives only in the history of lexicography (it is previously attested only in the dictionaries of Bailey and Johnson); *mawworm* refers to a character in an eighteenth-century play. Even when the *Dictionary* was complete, its editors returned to *Middlemarch* for further words. *Alter ego* makes it into the *Supplement* of 1933; the second edition of 1989 offers such phrases as *experto crede, mater dolorosa*, and *parrot-house* (this word listed as first appearing in the novel).

In addition to these entries illustrative of the history of the language, there are also entries that articulate the novel's themes. Any reader would recognize the following as central to its characterizations: *bigwig, bric-a-brac, charlatan, dissimulate, dunder-headed, hyperbolical, interlacement, node, nodus, patchwork, pleasureless, self-admiration*. Clusters of related terms point to an implicit reading of the novel. Illustrative quotations from *Middlemarch* appear in the entries for *comfort* (v), *comfort* (n), *comfortable* (a and n), *comfortably*, and *comforting*. Here is the spine of an interpretation: a reading keyed to presentations of social or intellectual familiarity, one that attends to tensions between lives of comfort (be it personal, or economic) and those of unease. For *comfortably*, adv., definition 5b ("In a way expressing comfort or complacency; with placid self-satisfaction"), the *NED* offered only this quotation from *Middlemarch*: "'That is nice,' said Celia, comfortably," a quotation that epitomizes both the connotation of the word and the character of the speaker. There is, too, a full set of *un-* words: *unapplausive, unbecomingness, uncommuted, unfathomable, ungauged, uninfringed, unnoticeable, unreformed, unsanitary, unstreaked, unvoluptuous*. Taken in tandem, they present a chronicle of negations, a window into *Middlemarch*'s idiom of refusals, oppositions, resistances, disappointments. What better summary of the pedantic Mr. Casaubon's condition than the phrase selected for the *Dictionary*: "the cold, shadowy, unapplausive audience of his life"? And, as if this were not enough, four entries for *worse* and one for *worst* show up, as if whoever was compiling this assembly—putting "a pencil-mark" against a striking word—recognized the judgmentalism of the novel's characters, and the patina of the pessimistic that its earliest reviewers noted, too. "No very good news, but then it might be worse," reads one quotation for the word (*s.v. worse*, def. 2a), a statement that could well stand as an epigraph for *Middlemarch* itself.

If the *NED* becomes a history of language, it also writes a history of reading—a collection of texts selected, and hence canonized, for their ability to represent that language. Murray himself sought a *"literary* interest of being a readable collection of pithy sentences or elegant extracts," a phrasing that recalls the idioms of book reviewing and anthology extraction that grew out of Victorian attitudes to reading and ideals of literary structure.

But what remains distinctive about *Middlemarch*'s place in the *NED* is just how it stands as a novel of philology itself, a novel preoccupied with words and meanings, with the history of language and society, and with the figurations of a great scholarly project. Mr. Casaubon's search for a "Key to All Mythologies" is very much a philological project. It searches for root meanings, for the histories of culture through the histories of words. Of course, it is a failure, not just because Casaubon himself is an inept pedant, but because (as Will Ladislaw notes in the novel), the Germans had already figured it all out. Set in 1828 and 1829, *Middlemarch* centers its intellectual world precisely at the moment when German comparative philology was growing in importance, displacing the old metaphysical or figurative word histories of the seventeenth and eighteenth centuries. George Eliot herself was well versed in the German philological tradition, and her notebooks show a deep awareness of such nineteenth-century linguistic discoveries as Grimm's Law and the place of Sanskrit in the Indo-European language family. For us to read *Middlemarch* and the *NED* together is to see how, in the last third of the nineteenth century, the search for a key to all mythologies became, really, a search for national identity, for individual relationships to language, and for locating the word within the world.

And to read *Middlemarch* and the *NED*, too, is to read Mr. Casaubon against James Murray—not just to compare them as the motivators of vast projects but to see their visions of the reading self. Recall the "Appeal to Readers" Murray published in the *Academy* and compare it to Casaubon's instructions to his new wife, Dorothea, for her help in sifting through and selecting material for his research.

> "You will oblige me my dear," he said, seating himself, "if instead of other reading this evening, you will go through this aloud, pencil in hand, and at each point where I say 'mark,' will make a cross with your pencil. This is the first step in a sifting process which I have long had in view, and as we go on I shall be able to indicate to you certain principles of selection whereby you will, I trust, have an intelligent participation in my purpose."

Such were the ways of reading in the nineteenth century, and such were the ways in which both Casaubon and Murray imagined the processes of literary choice. "Most women," as George Meredith had put it, "have a special talent for pigeon-holing." Whether they did or not, the women of the nineteenth century—whether they be the fictive Dorothea or the real, if elusive, Miss B. E. McAllum—found in their pencil markings and their siftings certain "principles of selection" that would contribute to a key to life.

My extended engagement with *Middlemarch* is but a small way of exploring the deep literary, social, and linguistic resonances of the *NED*. For what the *Dictionary* did was to ensconce an idea of literature, as well as language, in the English national awareness. There were the proper books, and there were, too, the proper words. The men behind its editing may have sought to pigeon-hole each word into its place, but some flitted elusively, without clear etymologies or origins. In my research and teaching, I have pencil-marked some entries out of my own fascination with the *Dictionary*.

Look at *quiz*. In the *NED*, the noun carries with it this remark: "Of obscure origin: possibly a fanciful coinage, but it is doubtful whether any reliance can be placed on the anecdote of its invention by Daly, a Dublin theater-manager." What follows are a list of definitions for an odd or eccentric person; an odd thing; a practical joke. Not quite what we would think of by the word. Only in the second, noun entry, do we find it as "an act of quizzing or questioning; spec. an oral examination of a student or class by a teacher." The *Dictionary* notes this usage as specifically "U.S.," as it notes the verb form of this word ("dial. and U.S."). It seems clear that the early editors do not know what to do with the word. As with the word *dude*, the editors locate *quiz* on the outskirts of the English language (Ireland, America) and demarcate its institutions as the outré (the theater) or the esoteric (school).

By including the word, and yet by demarcating it as odd or marginal, the *NED* performs what Linda Mugglestone has called the "cultural censorship [through] which the real inventiveness of nineteenth-century . . . lexis was habitually dismissed" (*Lost for Words*, 118). During the very decades of the *NED*'s making, the English language was changing. New words from science, technology, popular culture, and diplomacy were coming in. Most people wrote and spoke using an idiom and a vocabulary far more idiosyncratic than the *Dictionary* itself could record. And when it came to words like *dude* or *quiz*—words that were coming into circulation, maybe not from literature or learning—the editors seem to throw up their collective hands.

Another term that clearly provoked such collective exasperation was *protocol*. It comes from the Greek, meaning the first leaf of a volume or a fly-leaf glued into a manuscript to note its contents. It clearly is a word of Renaissance learning, later applied to law, diplomacy, and social justice. But you can almost hear the fingers of the *NED*'s editors trying to brush it away.

> The history of the sense-development of this word belongs to medieval Latin and the Romanic languages, esp. French; in the latter it has received very considerable extensions of meaning. . . . The word does not appear to have at any time formed part of the English legal or general vocabulary; in Sc. [i.e., science] from the 16th c. probably under French influence; otherwise used only in reference to foreign countries and their institutions, and as a recognized term of international diplomacy.

The word exists, but it remains, here, alien to English. Throughout the many headings and subentries, the editors iterate the otherness of the term. "In parts of the United States acquired from Mexico, the name is used for the original record of a grant, transfer, etc. of land." And then, later on, "In France, the formulary of the etiquette to be observed by the Head of State in official ceremonies." The uses of the term cluster in the last decades of the nineteenth century. It clearly was emerging, at the time of the *NED*'s compilation, as an important term in international relations. And yet, its very internationalism makes it suspect. Is it now "part of the English legal or general vocabulary"? Or does it always stand, like French or American political habit, something indigestibly non-English? Perhaps this quotation from the *Westminster Gazette* of 1899 sums up the tone of things: "This will be a change indeed, for M. Faure's time the contrary was the rule, thanks largely to the Protocol, to whose flummery the deceased President too weakly surrendered himself."

And so, the *NED*'s compilers, white men with axes in the jungle of their words, will never weakly surrender themselves to flummery (defined as "nonsense, humbug, empty trifling"). To read through these early volumes is to be struck by value judgments, averrals of national identity, quotations, etymologies, and definitions that contribute to the story of an England and an English language. Every word should tell its own story. But every word, too, tells the story of the men and women who defined it, marked their books and handed in their slips. The *NED* and its successor volumes of the *OED* hover between the two realms of the pigeon-hole and the pioneer: the former, the enclosed space of the study and its organized compartments; the latter, the vast arena of discovery and conquest. Read it—in libraries, in the home, or now online—not simply for the meanings of our words but for the life histories of its makers and the stories of our selves. This is, as Murray said, work in which anyone can join.

CHAPTER 18

Listening to Private Ryan

War and Language

THE FIRST CASUALTY OF WAR, said the Greek tragedian Aeschylus, is truth. In 2002, Terry Jones (scholar, writer, filmmaker, and Monty Python alumnus) wrote that grammar is the first casualty of war. "Words," he wrote, "have become devalued, some have changed their meaning, and the philologists can only shake their heads." But the philologists have been shaking their heads at war almost since its beginnings. War always changes language. It brings in new words, changes attitudes, shifts dialects, and contributes to a larger, public sense of the evaluation of linguistic meaning. Its effects have always been debated. Mark Twain noted that the only good word to come out of the Civil War was *gripsack*—a deliberately absurd assertion for a conflict that not only bequeathed a rich soldier's argot to America but inspired some of the most vivid poetry and prose of the late nineteenth century (Walt Whitman, Herman Melville, Stephen Crane). The British poet David Jones, writing about the trench warfare experience of World War I in his "In Parenthesis," showed how shared "jargon" was one of the "few things that united us," and he looks back, in the preface to that poem, to how writers from Malory and Shakespeare wrought the language of war: for the former, armed landscapes "spoke 'with a grimly voice'"; for the latter, it was "the pibble pabble in Pompey's camp" (*Henry V*, 4.1). "Every man's speech," writes Jones, "and habit of mind were a perpetual showing." World War II, it was long lamented, yielded up no poetry as rich as that of World War I, yet it gave narrative in novels, journalism, and political commentary that opened up the fissures between power and expression.

In his famous essay "Politics and the English Language," George Orwell considered the linguistic debasements wrought by decades of twentieth-century armed conflict.

Things like the continuance of British rule in India, the Russian purges and deportations, the dropping of the atom bombs on Japan, can indeed be defended, but only by arguments which are too brutal for most people to face, and which do not square with the professed aims of political parties. Thus political language has to consist largely of euphemism, question-begging, and sheer cloudy vagueness. Defenceless villages are bombarded from the air, the inhabitants driven out into the countryside, the cattle machine-gunned, the huts set on fire with incendiary bullets: this is called pacification. . . . Such phraseology is needed if one wants to name things without calling up mental pictures of them.

Though writing in 1946, Orwell (for readers of my generation) could not but appear to be predicting the collapse of both political and linguistic legitimacy in the American war in Southeast Asia. The Vietnam of Michael Herr's *Dispatches* (1971) or the daily television broadcasts we remember created a place of euphemism and evasion. *Pacification, Vietnamization,* and the "Five o'clock Follies" (the term used for the daily press briefings in Saigon) seemed to evacuate official words of any meaning, while a whole subculture of allusion—*fragging, greasing, getting some, sack*—gave us a new lexicon of death.

The history of the English language, particularly in America, is a history of war, and much of our colloquial and popular expressiveness has come out of the words of wartime. Look up in the library books on the subject, and you find mostly dictionaries. A. Marjorie Taylor's *The Language of World War II* (1948); Eric Partridge's *Dictionary of Forces' Slang, 1939–1945* (1948); Paul Dickson's *War Slang: American Fighting Words and Phrases Since the Civil War* (2004)—all these, and many other books, offer alphabetically arranged entries, illustrating colorful locutions, explicating acronyms, giving a bit of history to famous names and places. Some of this material is fascinating, some merely curious. But, taken in the large, these books suggest that war simply gave us words.

But war did more than simply augment the vocabulary. War changed the way we *used* words: new idioms and patterns of syntax; new patterns for the arc and ebb of sentences; new visions for what the vernacular could do. I will not neglect here the new words that came in, but what I want to stress is how our sense of language changed and how, in particular, the texture of modern American speech owes much to World War II and Vietnam. And in the deserts of the Middle East, that texture still is changing, as I write this chapter at a time when the official cloudy vagueness of a "homeland" leadership jars markedly against the cries at "Gitmo" and the "oorah" of the grunt.

But, first, let's go back. Wartime language had long been classed as but another species of cant or argot—themselves words that originally connoted the secret talk of thieves or the coded terms of guildsmanship. It was as if the soldier were another kind of specialist. And though wars had always spawned their special terms, it really was with the American Civil War that the cultural idea of military language and of soldier speak took hold in the popular consciousness. Soon after the War's end, R. W. McAlpine offered up "A Word About Slang" in the June 1865 issue of the *United States Service Magazine*. After a lengthy reflection on slang as a "gross perversion of a usage of society," a "corruption of language," and a "shame and sorrow of our race," McAlpine notes that "it is not a matter of surprise that, in the Army, where men are debarred the privileges, the comforts, the luxuries of home, and cut off from all those associations which tend to humanize the roughest, so little attention is paid to the use of that pure speech which distinguishes the gentleman from the rowdy." He then goes on to chronicle just what the Civil War did to English, for six pages of densely packed invective, wit, dismissal, and display of erudition.

> It may be that to the illiterate man slang is a dialect more readily mastered and more easily handled than the *lingua pura*; but by what process does he assimilate his tent-mate to a "skee-sicks" or a "stick-in-the-mud?" It has been remarked that the abecedarian must needs be a natural mnemonician to fix in his mind the letters of the alphabet, apparently so unconnected with any of his material associations; but consider the mental labor of a soldier who likens a pair of boots to "mud-hooks" or "gunboats," and makes "skedaddle" a synonym for retreat!

McAlpine plays on the verbal chasms that open up between his learned rhetoric and the soldier's slang. He catalogues the words: *contraband, Reb, Copperhead, Grayback, dog-robber, Dead Beat, Dead-head, confiscate,* and then the new words for money, *currency, greenback, spondulicks.* Some of these words originated in the Civil War; some were around before, but took on special meaning. *Spondulicks*, for example, brings out the wildest in McAlpine's etymological imagination: "It recalls the wampum of the poor Indian, the cowrie of the Ethiopian, and resuscitates the ancient blackmail man, who, as his kinsman, the dun, does to-day, called upon his victim to 'shell out.' For 'Spondulix' is conchological." I find this simply bizarre. Look up the word in the *OED* and all you get for etymology is "Of fanciful formation," and a word history that predates the Civil War by a decade. Or take McAlpine's etymology for *skedaddle*, a word in use from the 1850s onward but explicitly denoting, in the Civil War, an army's retreat or a soldier's desertion: "*Skedaddle* comes of good Hellenic stock, and in its primitive form may be found in Homer and Hesiod. The original *skedannumi* means to run in a crowd, and it doubles as the parent of our vulgar *skeet* and *scoot*."

McAlpine's essay says less, in the end, about the language of the soldier or the changing shape of English than it does about the philological head shaking of a class and culture. His goal is less to catalogue new words than to argue that the Civil War debased the English language. "Let the soldier drop the disgusting obscenities, the useless by-words, the irrational slang, which army life makes so familiar. . . . Language, like water, is a common necessity. Impure, it causes disease." But McAlpine, too, attributes to that war a level of linguistic impact far beyond what his philology can sustain. For, much as some might wish to see great authors as the agents of verbal innovation (Chaucer, Shakespeare, Milton, Twain), McAlpine imagines the war as the cause of debasement.

It is important, then, to separate the verbal impact of armed conflict from the popular imagination. Did the Civil War change English? No more or less than any other war, for as in all of them, the soldier returned not simply with new words but with a heightened sense of just what language could and could not do. The violence of warfare translates into violent metaphors. The sexuality of young men on the battlefield morphs in sexualized images. A Civil War term for a prostitute, for example, was "The Wolf's Dream," a phrase evocative of everything from lupine masculinity to fairy tale predation. Guns and ammo, too, were always sexualized. The Minié ball (a kind of bullet named after the French soldier who invented it in 1849) came to be pronounced as "Minnie," an utterance that had to have a certain sexualizing quality to it. No accident that, by the World Wars of the twentieth century, "moaning Minnie" came to describe mortar shells. And in those wars, the guns were feminine. From World War I, "Big Bertha" was the German gun that shelled Paris; "hissing Jenny" the large shell; "black Maria" the explosive. From World War II, the woman who would shatter male defenses was a "bombshell," while the "short arm" was the soldier's penis (in contrast to the "light arms" which were hand weapons). Everyone was dressed to kill, and as the twentieth century's conflicts progressed—Korea, Vietnam, the Gulf—war became more sexualized and sex became more militarized.

Everybody knows this. H. L. Mencken, in the final revision of his *American Language* prepared just after the end of World War II, recognized that particular war's gift to the "ancient stock of profanity and obscenity" (755). "All the more observant and intelligent veterans that I have consulted tell me that a few four-letter words were put to excessively heavy service. One of them, beginning with *f*, became an almost universal verb, and with *-ing* added, a universal suffix; another, beginning with *s*, ran a close second to it." The *f-* and *s-* words are the axes of the soldier's life. Obscenity serves to desensitize him from atrocity but also to express the breakdown of conventional expression.

Mencken makes much of the implicit humor in the *f-* and *s-* vocabulary (he has a field day with all the euphemistic translations of SNAFU), but he realizes, as well, that war talk shaped itself not just through soldier's slang but also through the journalism.

> What differentiated World War II from all others in history, aside from the curious fact that it produced no popular hero and no song, was the enormous number of newspaper correspondents who followed its operations, and the even greater number of press agents who served its brass. Many of these literati were aspirants to the ermine of Walter Winchell, and as a result they adorned the daily history of the war with multitudinous bright inventions.
>
> (Mencken, *American Language*, 755)

The impact of war on language is a matter of reportage as well as experience. Mencken's mockery notwithstanding, everybody of my parents' generation can call up the touchstones of war journalism: Edward R. Murrow speaking to his radio audience "from atop a city in flames"; William L. Shirer's *Berlin Diary*; and the daily newspaper reporting from the *Times*, the *Tribune*, and the *Sun*. What they all share is a new, heightened sense of the first person—the way in which events are no longer things that simply happen but are shaped by the observer.

Shirer's *Berlin Diary* brilliantly exemplifies this trend. "I got my first glimpse of Hitler" (September 4, 1934); "This morning, I noticed something very interesting" (September 22, 1938); "Through my glasses I saw the Fuehrer stop" (June 21, 1940). Everything comes through the lens of Shirer's eye; everything is seen. The job of journalism is to picture things through words (*See It Now* was one of the great television programs of my childhood; *Look* magazine, the decorative text in every doctor's office—as if they could make us see anew, to exercise, in some sense, an ophthalmology of the historical imagination). Much like Mencken, too (himself always a brilliant reporter), Shirer conjures rhetorical magic out of juxtaposing learned language with quotidian argot.

> The Hitler we saw in the Reichstag tonight was the conqueror, and conscious of it, and yet so wonderful an actor, so magnificent a handler of the German mind that he mixed superbly the full confidence of the conqueror with the humbleness which always goes down so well with the masses when they know a man is on top.
>
> (*Berlin Diary*, June 27, 1940)

Again, the journalist reports the vision of his eyes. History is a stage play, and Hitler the supreme actor. Shirer, like so many others, gets the theatricality of fascism, its production values, its mass marketing, its histrionics. And yet, notice how he shifts from the allusive polysyllables and alliterations ("the full confidence of the conqueror with the humbleness") to everyday idioms: "always goes down so well," "a man is on top." In such sentences, Shirer offers up a drama of rhetorical deflation: Hitler on top goes down well.

The journalist of war is an observer, but he is also a great reader. Shirer's first-person visions turn the actors and the actions of the 1930s into signs to be interpreted or texts to be read. Hitler, too, is always reading—from his speeches, from his maps, from his treaties. So, too, are the figures out of Michael Herr's *Dispatches*. For while this book captures the essence of Vietnam, it also echoes a half century of journalistic eyewitness account: "It was late '67 now, even the most detailed maps didn't reveal much any more; reading them was like trying to read the faces of the Vietnamese, and that was like trying to read the wind" (3). Herr's narrator is always trying to interpret. For all its tales of actions, this is a memoir of books. "It was about this time that copies of the little red British paperback edition of Jules Roy's *The Battle of Dienbienphu* began appearing wherever members of the Vietnam press corps gathered" (99). Life becomes a series of recognizable documents, of pages out of memoranda or snapshots to be sent home.

It was at this point that I began to recognize almost every casualty, remember conversations we'd had days or even hours earlier, and that's when I left, riding a medevac with a lieutenant who was covered with blood-soaked bandages. He'd been hit in both legs, both arms, the chest and head, his ears and eyes were full of caked blood, and he asked a photographer in the chopper to get a picture of him like this to send to his wife.

(82–83)

And on the book's last page, we're still with such visions: "I saw a picture of a North Vietnamese soldier sitting in the same spot on the Danang River where the press center had been" (260).

In reading through these passages, words make us see, and this, it seems to me—more than new acronyms or creative vulgarities—is what the legacy of war is to the English language. Look at the dazzling trajectory of feeling, sight, and language in this passage from Anthony Swofford's *Jarhead* (2003):

After my stool solidified, I spent three days on a work crew. My single duty was changing the marquee at the base theater. I don't recall the titles of the movies I advertised, though I'm sure they were either hyperpyrotechnic combat stories or sorry love stories. Morale builders. On the third and final day of my duty, I spelled FUCK IT, SHOWING ALL DAY. An officer's wife noticed the marquee as she left the base beauty parlor or a wives' meeting, and she called the theater manager, a grungy first sergeant, and complained.

(47)

Soldier time clocks itself, now, not in casualties but stools. To read Herr is to watch the recognition of war's hell solidify in his mind. To read Swofford is to recognize that his war is not hell but shit and fuck (see table 18.1). And what truly solidifies in this passage is his own realization that war remains a theater, and that the responsibility of every soldier, every officer, and every politician is to set up a marquee to title up the fight. No beauty parlor can disguise the truth. Fuck it, showing all day.

These diaries and memoirs are the literature of war, but there were also poems, plays, and novels. Edward Thomas, killed on the Western Front in 1917, could capture the soldier's idiom and hold it in the net of his iambic pentameter:

Only two teams work on the farm this year.
One of my mates is dead. The second day
In France they killed him. It was back in March,
The very night of the blizzard, too. Now if
He had stayed here we should have moved the tree.

("As the Team's Head Brass," lines 24–28)

"I too, saw God through mud," wrote Wilfred Owen in one of his greatest lyrics, and again we find the first person as seer (in all senses of that word). The transformation of experience into mere lists—parts, duty rosters, catalogues of things lost, men dead—brilliantly emerges in Henry Reed's poem of World War II, "Naming of Parts."

Today we have naming of parts. Yesterday,
We had daily cleaning. And tomorrow morning,
We shall have what to do after firing. But today,
Today we have naming of parts. Japonica
Glistens like coral in all of the neighbouring gardens,
    And today we have naming of parts.

(lines 1–6)

Elegies become mere epitaphs in war verse, as in Randell Jarrell's "Death of the Ball Turret Gunner," which reads, in its entirety:

> From my mother's sleep I fell into the State,
> And I hunched in its belly till my wet fur froze.
> Six miles from earth, loosed from its dream of life,
> I woke to black flak and the nightmare fighters.
> When I died they washed me out of the turret with a hose.

Read against the journalistic voices of Shirer and Herr, these poems chime with a new vigor of first-person narrative; they juxtapose aesthetics and anguish; drop us from heights of rhetoric and meter into mud.

Ashes to ashes. Sentences are shortened. The simple declarative takes on a poignancy, as if there remained too little time for oratory. Take Norman Mailer's *Naked and the Dead* (1948).

> Nobody could sleep. When morning came, assault craft would be lowered and a first wave of troops would ride through the surf and charge ashore on the beach at Anopopei. All over the ship, all through the convoy, there was a knowledge that in a few hours some of them were going to be dead.

> (3)

Mailer captures the bluntness of the observation, as if novels now were like dispatches, telegraphed in bits and pieces back to home. When we read them, we are reading like the soldier, looking for the meaning in a scrap of paper or a line of code. And in this world, pictures are everywhere. Shirer's Berlin is a world of maps and photographs. Herr's Vietnam remains a landscape of charts and snapshots. Swofford's Iraq has its cinema. In Mailer, characters engage over a photograph. Here is a dialogue between Sergeant Brown and Private Stanley:

> "Well, now," Brown said, "you're a good kid, and you're smart, but it just don't pay to trust a woman. You take my wife. She's beautiful, I've shown you her picture."
> "She's really a good looking dame," Stanley agreed quickly.
> "No doubt about it, she's beautiful. You think she's gonna sit around and wait for me? No, she ain't. She's out having herself a good time."

"Well, I wouldn't say that," Stanley suggested.

"Why not? You ain't going to hurt any feelings of mine. I know what she's doing, and when I get back I'm going to have a little accounting with her. I'm going to ask her first, 'Been having any dates?' and if she says, 'Yes,' I'll get the rest out of her in two minutes. And if she says, 'No, honey, honest I haven't, you know me,' I'm just going to do a little checking with my friends and if I find she's been lying, well, then I'll have her, and, man, maybe I won't give her some lumps before I kick her out."

(Mailer, *Naked and the Dead*, 15)

Mailer gives us the vernacular of observation. How can we judge the picture? What is the place of beauty in the muck? As if to mime this question in his style, Mailer ensconces in literary prose colloquial pronunciations (*gonna*), grammatical trips (*ain't, just don't pay*), and popular vocabulary (*honey, dame*). So, too, do Herr and Swofford, Thomas, Owen, Reed, and Jarrell. Can we find a place for Japonica in the mud? What happens when a well-coiffed wife reads "Fuck it"?

To my mind, though, the most innovative verbal moment in Mailer, here, is his use of *man*. The *OED* reports its history as a vocative of address or as a parenthetical expletive, and it locates that history as distinctively nonwhite and nonnormative (it defines its realm of usage as "in South Africa, among Blacks, among jazz musicians and enthusiasts"; s.v., *man* def. 2.4.e). The *Dictionary*'s many quotations are in black voice, for example, this quotation from the 1933 issue of *Metronome*: "Trum's greeting was in the Negro dialect he usually employed, 'Man! How is you?'"

Mailer's *man* brings this expression into literature. He renders it accessible for everyone: white, black, soldier, reader. And he reveals what wartime does to language—it brings dialects and idioms together, channels what would have been marginal expressions into the mainstream. Soldiers, whether returning from the South, the Western Front, the Pacific, Indo-China, or the Middle East, bring back many things, and what they bring back is language changed irrevocably by contact with voices they would not have heard at home.

I've argued that war changes language and that such changes inflect the idioms of speech by those who have served and who have not; that there is a new narrative persona that emerges from the journalism and imaginative writing of armed conflict; and that, often, the locutions of the soldier charge martial things with sex. And yet, when I speak to audiences of a certain age, there still come questions about words. What really was the genesis of *jeep*; why do we call soldiers *GI*s; where did *gremlin* come from? No chapter on war and language can ignore them, for their study reveals the mystery of their coinage and the mythologies surrounding them. They distill what many still want that impact to be: the creation of humorous terms for culture-changing gadgets; the making of people into acronyms and abbreviations.

Jeep may have come from the initials "G.P." printed on the sides of "general purpose vehicles" during the 1930s. "Eugene the Jeep" appeared in the Popeye comic strip on March 16, 1936, as a little creature who could do anything. *GI* is usually attributed to the initials for "government issue," words branded on just about everything from soap to shoes. A *gremlin* may have found its name by evocation of the sound of "goblin" and originated with the RAF in World War I to imagine the imps that got into machinery and caused it to malfunction for no clear reason. Some, too, have argued that the word arose, as an article in the *Observer* from 1942 put it, "on account of they were the goblins which came out of Fremlin beer bottles."

Who knows? Scholars love these words. *Jeep* was a particular favorite of Mencken, who devotes two pages in *The American Language* to reviewing, and debunking, possible etymologies, claiming only that it "seems to be authentically American" (759). *GI* similarly gets a full discussion, together with an additional etymological source in "galvanized iron" (and thus, an origin in World War I). Mencken avoids *gremlin* (as it clearly is a word of British origin), but studies published soon after World War II (Partridge's *Dictionary of Forces' Slang* and Taylor's *Language of World War II*) devote extensive space to it.

We love these words because they are safe. They make war into something funny sounding, fill it with cute creatures, turn killing men and machines into toys (GI Joe was the action doll of choice for my childhood, and the American Motors Gremlin puttered through suburban streets during my high school days). They also bring out national identity in war. Mencken looks for something "authentically American," little realizing that the truly authentic American creations—verbal and material—of that war were *napalm* (coined in 1942) and *atom bomb*. British lexicographers use *gremlin* to distill what many might imagine as the quintessence of Englishness: a land filled with mythic creatures, a barely controlled ability with new technologies, a stoic muddle-through-it-ness that makes life simply inexplicable. Gremlins, writes a contributor to the journal *American Speech* in 1944 (in a quotation used by the *OED*), "are mythical creatures who are supposed to cause trouble such as engine failure in aeroplanes, a curious piece of whimsy-whamsy in an activity so severely practical as flying." We are, here, not in Shirer's Berlin or Mailer's Mediterranean (or, for that matter, Herr's Vietnam or Swofford's Iraq), but in the *Wind in the Willows* or the Hundred Acre Wood. War is just another bedtime story.

We'd like to think that such words are the lexicon of war, but they are not. They pacify only those who have not fought. For, in the end, war does not so much change language as challenge it. I have a friend, a veteran of the first Gulf War, who, in moments of despair, thinks back on his time in hundred-degree heat in a hazmat suit, recalls the soul-sickening food, reimagines himself in a military prison after pulling a knife on a compatriot, and says, when I ask him to talk about it, "Words can't describe it."

CHAPTER 19

He Speaks in Your Voice

Everybody's English

EACH YEAR, I GIVE ABOUT A DOZEN LECTURES to community groups, libraries, small colleges, and local public gatherings. I tell them of my teaching
and give outlines of the history of the English language as a way of illustrating how our speech and writing change. I stress that changes in themselves
are neither bad nor good; we cannot rein in alterations in the grammar of
the everyday or stop the flow of new words. I tell them about Samuel Johnson and his *Dictionary*, about Anglo-Saxon scribes, about Chancery and
Chaucer, Shakespeare and the orthoepists. I read passages from literary
dialects, quote Webster, Mencken, Mailer, and Cab Calloway. When it ends,
I take some questions, and the first, inevitably, is: "Why doesn't anyone
speak English anymore?" Such questions come from people stymied in
the bank line, lost on buses in once-known but now unfamiliar neigh-
borhoods, crossing streets while hip-hop shatters their silences, counting
change in grocery stores. New groups of immigrants have filled old social
niches; part-time employees more familiar with text messaging than check
endorsing serve their customers; music and media displace the pace of life
once lived in waltz time. A sea of words breaks over us, and we are lost.

When people ask why nobody speaks English anymore what they are
really asking is: Why doesn't anybody understand *me*? Language now
changes in a lifetime, and the shifts that I have charted toward the close of
this book—war, ethnic diversity, popular culture, and literature—make the
speed of verbal passage seem as fast as technology. In 1999, a story in the
New Yorker magazine called attention to this seeming speediness of language change. That winter, signs started appearing throughout Manhattan
with some familiar words used in odd ways. *Round* seemed to mean "cool."
February connoted "out of style." *Fresno* meant "classic rock." Each poster

had the logo of MTV and the words "Stay Tuned" emblazoned on it. In an interview with the magazine, Allan Broce, an MTV executive, reported: "We made 'em all up. We did it to create buzz. So much that appears on MTV is about buzz, and we wanted to reinforce our position as the place in TV and music where buzz starts." This was, as the *New Yorker* called it, "a commercial substitute for slang." Behind each word was something of a puzzle (I prefer to think of them as modern versions of the Anglo-Saxon riddles or Old English kennings). Round is the opposite of square; February is, by all accounts, an unstylish, forgettable month; Fresno, as the executive explained, "is kind of passé and not the hippest thing in the world." These are, as the *New Yorker* goes on, "plastic etymologies," word histories for a history-free generation.

Beyond the humor of this little story lie some basic questions. Are words commodities, and can we sell them as we sell commercial products? Can we shape a generation's taste in language as in music, art, or hemlines? Can one arbitrate the culture of the word, make something up and make it stick? Years after this account ran in the magazine, I find no evidence that anybody uses any of these words. You cannot sell a language. Verbal arbiters from Samuel Johnson to James A. H. Murray tried, and failed, to keep words in or out. Words are like fashions, and one's personal vocabulary is as much a store of styles as one's garage, houses, cars, tools, or patio furniture. In a commodity culture, language is up for sale.

Still, this may not be new. During the period of British rule in India, for example, language took on the flavor of the exotic. English was something of a stew, and words from other languages became its spices. Like spices, sought-for overseas by travelers and traders, words can be bought and sold to saffron our tongue. Or, like the fetishes and fans from distant lands, words become objects of desire, things to mount on mantelpieces to display our journeys.

One of the most fascinating documents in English literary and linguistic history is *Hobson-Jobson*, a dictionary of colloquial Anglo-Indian words and expressions put together in the 1880s by Colonel Henry Yule and A. C. Burnell. Their "Introductory Remarks" remain as much a classic of lexicographical positioning as Johnson's *Plan* and the preface to his *Dictionary*, Webster's introduction to his *American Dictionary*, or the many comments, introductions, and accounts of Murray and the *OED*. "Words of Indian origin," they begin, "have been insinuating themselves into English ever since the end of the reign of Elizabeth." *Insinuating*: words creep in, by stealth or artifice; they snake their way into the everyday. It is a highly charged word, a Miltonic word ("Close the Serpent sly, Insinuating": *Paradise Lost*, 4.348). Words such as *calico*, *chintz*, and *gingham*, Yule and Burnell note, "had already effected a lodgment in English warehouses and shops, and were lying in wait for entrance into English literature." Are words like some satanic stowaways in English Eden? "Such outlandish guests grew more frequent 120 years ago." *Outlandish*, at its heart, is from another land. These are the interlopers into language. And yet, as with all new immigrants, eventually rights of social use evolve. "Of words that seem to have been admitted to full franchise, we may give examples"; some words have been around so long that they have now been given rights to vote, or citizenship in the lexicon. "There are a good many others, long since fully assimilated, which really originated in the adoption of an Indian word"; *assimilate*, *adopt*: these are the words of national identity and family legitimacy.

Where do the words of *Hobson-Jobson* come from? Many of them are from Indian languages: Urdu, Hindi, Bengali, Tamil, Sinhalese, and others. Many, too, are from the languages of earlier colonial and trade nations: descendants of Dutch, Portuguese, and French terms. Others come from even earlier contacts, from Arabic-speaking slavers and traders, or from China. The words in *Hobson-Jobson* are at times "corruptions," at times "hybrids," as if cross-breeding made them flower into rust or roses.

The editors single out several words in their "Introductory Remarks" that, upon close inspection, reveal the virtuoso juggling and judgments of all lexicographers. Take the word *curry*. Originally, it connoted not the main dish of a meal but the enhancement to the cereal or rice that constituted its center. It was a kind of relish or a condiment, and Yule and Burnell go back to reports from ancient Greece and late Roman antiquity to illustrate the history of Indian culinary habits here. And yet, they go on, curry may have been inspired by the foods of early Europe itself. "The medieval spiced dishes," they announce, "were even coloured like curry," and they quote what they call "the old English poem of King Richard, wherein the Lionheart feasts on the head of a Saracen—"

> sodden full hastily
> With poder and with spysory
> And with saffron of good colour.

(281)

Even the basic spices may have had a European origin. Red pepper, they aver, "was introduced into India by the Portuguese," and, in the end, what we think of as a "curry" may well be an English transformation of these Indian and colonial materials. Indeed, by the time of William Thackeray's novel, *Vanity Fair* (1848), curry has been domesticated in the English household, as they quote: "Now we have seen how Mrs. Sedly had prepared a fine curry for her son" (but just to be precise: *Vanity Fair* is set some thirty years or so before its publication, and that curry meal had been prepared for a son just returned from India—so, in the novel's fictional world, this food may well have been less familiar than in the historical time of its publication).

To read through this entry is to see not simply etymology or literary history but politics at work. *Hobson-Jobson* takes a term, one might well say *the* term, of distinctive Indian identity and makes it European: curry was, in some sense, already there in the Middle Ages (no accident, too, that they quote a passage about Richard the Lionhearted eating a Saracen's head—a little allegory of the English conquest of the East). Its basic elements were imports. Its true form is a hybrid of English, European, and Indian. But to read through this entry, too, is to get a sense of what *Hobson-Jobson* thinks of language itself: that language is a kind of curry, and new words are relishes that spice it up.

Language is also something of a house, and many cultures have among the legacies of conquest and high culture words for architecture that betray a history of contact (witness the Romance-language words in English: *foyer*, *mansard*, *cupola*, *dome*, *rotunda*, *patio*, and so on). *Hobson-Jobson*'s entry for *verandah* is a touchstone for such inquiries. The central question here is whether this is an Indian word at all. One line of argument, they report, is that the word comes from Portuguese and Spanish *baranda*. Another is that it comes from the Sanskrit *veranda*, from the verb *var*, meaning to cover. Wherever it comes from, it was certainly one of the earliest words to emerge from European contact with the Indian subcontinent (*Hobson-Jobson* quotes from the writings of Vasco da Gama from 1498).

But why such an attention to this word? Surely, there are many other household terms of equal philological challenge. In this dictionary *verandah* is another kind of metaphor, a figure for the Anglo-Indian experience. From the range of quotations *Hobson-Jobson* offers, it is obvious that the verandah was a space of interaction, a place in between the closed domestic (and hence, European) rooms of living and the landscape of the local and the other. From 1809, they quote: "In the same verandah are figures of natives of every cast and profession." From 1810: "The viranda keeps off the too great glare of the sun, and affords a dry walk during the rainy season."

And from 1816: "And when Sergeant Browne bethought himself of Mary, and looked to see where she was, she was conversing up and down the verandah, though it was Sunday, with most of the rude boys and girls of the barracks." Such quotations illustrate the social space of the verandah: a place where the English and the Indian can mix, either literally or symbolically; a place that permits the European to experience the landscape, but with covering and shade; a place where a well-born woman can converse with rude boys and girls.

The verandah is the space of language: it enables us to bring together disparate elements from different origins; it keeps us dry and shaded when experiencing the outside. There are many words in *Hobson-Jobson* that give voice to this idea of liminal or bordered spaces: words such as *thug* (originally, an intruding robber who throttled his victims); compounds such as *competition-wallah* (someone who entered the Civil Service through competitive examination—a system developed after the Sepoy Rebellion of 1857); and *hobson-jobson* itself (presented as a corruption of the Islamic cry, "Ya Hasan! Ya Hosain"). These words, and many others, are the verbal equivalents of the verandah or the curry: exemplars of mixing or cross-breeding.

They are, too, from the point of modern historical linguistics, exemplars of how words enter into language and how new locutions form themselves. They all have, to varying degrees, such qualities as onomotopoeia, metonymy, synecdoche, and what the *Cambridge History of the English Language* calls "burlesque metaphor." This idea is a favorite of mine, as it classifies what we often think of as the most creative or colorful of local expressions: *sing*, "to turn informer"; *Arkansas toothpick*, "hunting knife"; *cowboy Cadillac*, "pickup truck"; *oreo*, "a black person aligned with white political interests" (Algeo, *The Cambridge History of the English Language*, 6:225). Indeed, *Hobson-Jobson* itself soon became something of a burlesque metaphor, as H. L. Mencken could note the phenomenon as early as the first edition (1919) of his *American Language*: "Its variations show a familiar effort to bring a new and strange word into harmony with the language—an effort arising from what philologists call the law of Hobson-Jobson." Now, to my knowledge, there is no "law of Hobson-Jobson" in the philological code, and this quotation, which made it into the second edition of the *OED* (s.v., *Hobson-Jobson*), seems as much about scholarly self-reference as it does word history (I'm sure, frankly, Mencken caught on to the term because it simply sounded funny or arcane to him—much as he would coin such locutions as the "booboisie," or much as he would linger over "jeep" and its sonic silliness).

Burlesque metaphor, for all its equally mock-philological impact, seems in the end unable to describe these different kinds of phrases. Like the MTV terms that never caught on, they are something more like riddles or kennings (how are "cowboy Cadillac" or "competition-wallah" any different, really, from "the road of the whale" or "God's candle"?). Our words are often burlesques—a term that came from the Italian *burla*, meaning a theatrical-ized caricature, and that emerged, by the eighteenth century in English, to connote a species of dramatic exaggeration. "Burlesque metaphor" implies, now, something of a theater of word use, a kind of vaudeville of new coin-ages or loan words. Indeed, many of us like to think of such words, and the speakers of their forms of origin, as burlesque actors on the stage of language—as if we were witnessing a parade of stage accents, costumed skits, or semantic stripteases.

But there is far more to world English than burlesque. That of India embraces not just the curiosities of *Hobson-Jobson* but a prose style that, in the hands of writers such as Salman Rushdie, Arundhati Roy, and Vikram Seth, rivals that of Dickens. Australian English offers more than rhyming slang and folk songs and has emerged, in the final decades of the twentieth century, as the vernacular of film and television. Anglophone African litera-ture spans the range of J. M. Coetzee's South Africa to Ben Okri's Nigeria. World English voices more than cola ads or Internet sites. It articulates a vision of imaginative fiction and social change.

A whole book could be written on the subject (and some have been). But what I want to stress, in closing my own book, is how we have become a world of English voices: how imaginative writing makes a speaker present, and often the voice of that speaker has, if not an American accent, then an American audience. English has become the language of commerce, entertainment, computation, and reportage, but it has, as well, become the language of sport. The rhetoricians I grew up with—my Odysseus, my Stentor, my Daniel Webster—were sportscasters. The voices on the radio were voices of the picture makers. Drawing, in part, on the traditions of the war reporter, the sportscaster colored our imaginations of events (the phrase "color commentary" is now used to refer to the interpretations of-fered by professional athletes turned sportscasters). Theirs are the colors of a rhetoric redolent of what Mencken called, nearly a century ago, the "hallmarks of American." The American, recall his phrasing, "from the beginning has been the most ardent of recorded rhetoricians. . . . He exer-cises continually an incomparable capacity for projecting hidden and often fantastic relationships into his speech" (99).

Nowhere in modern fiction is this capacity as incomparable as in the opening of Don DeLillo's *Underworld* (2001).

> He speaks in your voice, American, and there's a shine in his eye that's halfway hopeful.
>
> It's a school day, sure, but he's nowhere near the classroom. He wants to be here instead, standing in the shadow of this old rust-hulk of a structure, and it's hard to blame him—this metropolis of steel and concrete and flaky paint and cropped grass and enormous Chesterfield packs aslant on the scoreboards, a couple of cigarettes jutting from each.
>
> Longing on a large scale is what makes history. This is just a kid with a local yearning but he is part of an assembling crowd, anony-mous thousands off the buses and trains, people in narrow columns tramping over the swing bridge above the river, and even if they are not a migration or a revolution, some vast shaking of the soul, they bring with them the body heat of a great city and their own small reveries and desperations, the unseen something that haunts the day—men in fedoras and sailors on shore leave, the stray tumble of their thoughts, going to a game.
>
> The sky is low and gray, the roily gray of sliding surf.

The "he" of this opening is the African American young man who skips school for the most important baseball game of the age: the Giants-Dodg-ers playoff game of 1951. But to what does the word "American" refer? Is it the apposition of voice, the characterization of the language of the youth? Or is it an apostrophe, an address to the reader—you, the American? The central metaphor for DeLillo's postwar America is not the melting pot but the sports stadium. Notice the words here: *migration, revolution.* Spectators come from all around, anonymous thousands, and the opening of *Under-world* cannot but recall, in my medievalist mind, the General Prologue to Chaucer's *Canterbury Tales* where he describes how pilgrims "from every shires ende" find their way to Beckett's shrine.

Longing on a large scale is what makes history. But it is also what makes the history of a language. Throughout this book, I have attended to tales of desire: the need for Caedmon to give voice to faith, for Frederick Douglass to inscribe himself into his master's copybook; the challenges that sexual desire poses to writers, whether they be Chancery scribes writing up an account of a rape or African American poets and musicians serving up platters of sexual delectables. Sing me something. The angel that comes to Caedmon comes to all of us, as we speak in our, and your, voice to express the beginning of things.

For DeLillo, the ball park is a kind of Eden, and the paradox of *Underworld*'s opening lies precisely in the ways in which that Eden is the site of personal transgression: the young boy playing hooky, or the dignitaries in the stands (J. Edgar Hoover, Jackie Gleason, Frank Sinatra, Toots Shor) whose lives will be entwined in deceit. Have we fallen, too? My public questioners would have me believe so, as their sense of an English in America is now a corrupt thing, its grammar marred by e-mail and the Internet, its spellings shattered by decades of public-school indifference, its accents edged by immigration. What would they make of this e-mail I received from a student in my Chaucer class in 2004?

> *prof. lerer—*
>
> *on my way out to class today i got a piece of glass stuck in my foot.*
> *it was bleeding and hurting a lot so i had to come back and clean it up.*
> *sorry about the absense, but i'll get the notes from someone.*
>
> *apologies*

Sure, there are misspellings, failures of capitalization, run-on colloquialisms—all of them hallmarks of an e-mail style designed not, I believe, to mime precisely speech but to create a kind of faux simplicity. E-mail articulates a studied informality, a carefully framed indifference to the rigors of epistolarity (I still write e-mails as if they were business letters; my students, clearly, do not). But what this e-mail voices, too, is something of a legacy of an American poetics. Modern American poetry is as studied in its informality as such electronic messages. It challenges the conventions of form and rhetoric, gives voice to voice, yet always lets us know that it is a voice captured on the page. On reading this student's message, I could not but be struck by its resemblance to another letter of apology, this one from William Carlos Williams.

This Is Just to Say

I have eaten
the plums
that were in
the icebox

and which
you were probably
saving
for breakfast.

Forgive me
they were delicious
so sweet
and so cold.

Williams's poem from 1919 has the same lilt as my student's message. Both are, in essence, notes tacked on to the kitchen walls of life. They are essays in *ab-sense*—in the ways in which we try to make sense of absence. And they both are letters of apology. I've plucked forbidden fruit. Our fallen status only asks forgiveness. We live in a world of Babel, where our lilt lies only in apology. Witness the rising ending of our spoken sentences. Once reserved for suburban teenagers, this habit now seems everywhere (some linguists have referred to it as "uptalk"). All utterances seem to be questions now. We're always asking for assent, as we speak both unsure of ourselves and somehow guilty as charged.

We should not see our language as debased. The history of English is a history of invention: of finding new words and new selves, of coining phrases that may gather currency in a linguistic marketplace, of singing to the cowherds or to the burlesque theater of self. The mead, the hog meat, the curry, the plums—all are the nourishments of language, the things that have made my foray into history so tempting and so tasty. A nation's language, to recall Mark Twain, is a large matter. And so all I have been able to do here is offer up a sampling. If on the way I've cut my foot, forgive me. I was so anxious to get you these notes on time.

APPENDIX

English Sounds and Their Representation

THROUGHOUT THIS BOOK, I have described the sounds of English and their changes using the terms of articulatory phonetics and a version of the International Phonetic Alphabet. Here, I review the ways of representing those sounds.

Vowels can be held long or short. They can be located in the back of the mouth or the front; they can also be located high or low in the mouth. Vowels can also be single sounds (as in the word "meet"), called monophthongs. Or they can be double sounds (as in the word "boy"—*aw* + *ee*), called diphthongs. We can represent the mouth schematically as a kind of grid, and thus locate vowel sounds on the axes of that grid. Here, for example, are the major vowel sounds of modern spoken English (illustrated by representative words).

	Front		Central		Back	
High	meet		big, bug		loop	
Mid		get			so	
		cat				put, saw
Low			swan			father

The long *a* as in "father" is a low back vowel; the long *ee* sound as in "meet" is a high front vowel; and so on. Some vowels are further back than others (the *a* in "father" is further back than the *o* in "so"). Some are further front (the *ee* in "meet" is further front than the *a* in "swan").

There is also a low mid-vowel sound known as a *schwa* (/ə/, which is the unaccented vowel sound in a word like "the" or at the end of "sofa").

Consonants are described by two features: where they are produced in the mouth, and whether they can be held for any length of time or not. Working backwards from the front of the mouth, we would say that consonants produced with the lips are called labials; those with the teeth are called dentals; those with the hard ridge behind the teeth are called alveolar; those with the hard palate are called palatals; those with the soft palate, or velum, are called velars. Consonants that cannot be held are called stops; those that can be held are called continuants. Those that involve combining two sounds are called affricates. Those that involve moving the mouth from one position to another are called glides. Those that are produced by flipping or rolling the tongue are called liquids. Those that are produced through the nose are called nasals. Consonants can also be voiced or unvoiced. Voiced consonants are those produced by vibrating the vocal chords; unvoiced consonants are produced with the vocal chords silent.

Here are the basic consonants of modern spoken English, illustrated by representative words. When words are paired, the first illustrates the unvoiced, the second the voiced consonant.

	Labial	Dental	Alveolar	Palatal	Velar
Stop	pet, bet		ten, den		cut, gut
Continuant	file, vile	thin, other	sit, zit	plush, pleasure	here
Affricate			cheer, jeer		
Glide	weird		year		
Liquid		love	red		
Nasal	mad		net		sing

Every language, however uses its own spelling conventions to represent sounds. Linguists have therefore developed what is called the International Phonetic Alphabet (or IPA) to transcribe the sounds of any speech. Sometimes these symbols are the same as the letters in modern English spelling; sometimes they are not. Here are the basics of the IPA.

a as in father
æ as in cat
e as in ace
ɛ as in mess
i as in machine

ɪ as in miss
ɔ as in cost
o as in most
ʊ as in put
u as in moose
ə as in the
ai as in lice
au as in mouse
ɔi as in moist
ju as in muse
b as in boy
tʃ as in cheer
d as in dog
f as in fog
g as in gun
dʒ as in jeer
h as in hear
k as in cat
l as in long
m as in man
n as in net
ŋ as in sing
p as in pet
r as in red
s as in sit
ʃ as in sheer
t as in tip
þ as in thin
ð as in there
v as in vet
w as in wet
z as in zero
ʒ as in pleasure

Note, too, that in phonetic transcriptions the colon /:/ is used to represent a long vowel.

ALLITERATION: The repetition of the initial consonant or vowel of words in sequence. Old Germanic poetry was alliterative in structure: the poetic line was shaped not according to the number of syllables but to the number of alliterative words in stressed positions.

ANALOGY: The process by which certain grammatically or morphologically different words or expressions come to share the same form or pronunciation. For example: certain strong verbs, such as *wax* ("to grow") became weak verbs by analogy with other weak verbs; certain nouns that formed their plurals by altering the root vowel of the word (for example, Old English *boc*, "book," *bec*, "books") took on the final -s by analogy with other nouns.

ARGOT: A distinctive way of writing or speaking, often characterized by a unique vocabulary, used by a particular class, profession, or social group.

ARTICULATORY PHONETICS: The study of how sounds are produced in the mouth and the technique of describing those sounds by using special symbols.

CALQUE: A bit-by-bit, or morpheme-by-morpheme, translation of one word in one language into another word in another language, often used to avoid bringing new or loan words into the translating language (e.g., modern German *Fernseher* is a calque on *television*; Afrikaans *apartheid* is a calque on *segregation*).

COGNATE: Two or more words from two or more different, but related, languages that share a common root or original.

COMPARATIVE PHILOLOGY: The study of different, but related, languages in their historical contexts, traditionally with the goal of reconstructing earlier, lost forms of words and sounds in the Indo-European languages.

CREOLE: A new language that develops out of the sustained contact among two or more languages. Often, creoles develop when the language of a colonizing or economically dominant group is imposed upon a subordinate or colonized group. Thus, many creoles have elements of both European and non-European languages. Creoles may emerge over time from pidgins. Creoles are perceived by their speakers as the natural or native language, whereas pidgins are perceived as artificial or ad hoc arrangements for communication (*see* PIDGIN).

DESCRIPTIVISM: The belief that the study of language should describe the linguistic behavior of a group of speakers or writers at a given moment and should not be pressed into the service of prescribing how people should write or speak (*see* PRESCRIPTIVISM).

DIALECT: A variant form of a language, usually defined by region, class, or socioeconomic group, and distinguished by its pronunciation, its vocabulary, and, on occasion, its morphology.

DIALECTOLOGY: The study of different regional variations of a given language, spoken or written at a given time.

DIPHTHONG: A vowel sound made up of two distinct sounds joined together (for example, the sound in the modern English word *house*).

ETYMOLOGY: The study of word origins, roots, and changes. The etymology of a given word is its history, traced back through its various pronunciations and shifts in meaning to its earliest recorded or reconstructed root.

EYE-DIALECT: A way of representing in writing regional or dialect variations by spelling words in nonstandard ways. Spellings such as *sez* (for "says") or *onkores* (for "encores") are eye-dialect forms, as they do not actually record distinctions of speech but rather evoke the flavor of nonstandard language.

GRAMMATICAL GENDER: The organization of nouns in groups or classes depending on how they require special endings or distinctive pronoun, adjective, and article forms. Nouns may be masculine, feminine, or neuter. The grammatical gender of a noun need not be the same as the actual gender of the object it represents.

GREAT VOWEL SHIFT: The systematic shift in the pronunciation of stressed, long vowels in English, which occurred from the middle of the fifteenth century to the middle of the sixteenth century in England and which permanently changed the pronunciation of the English language. It effectively marks the shift from Middle English to Modern English.

INDO-EUROPEAN: The term used to describe the related languages of Europe, India, and Iran, descended from a common tongue spoken roughly in the third millennium B.C. by an agricultural people originating in Southeastern Europe. English is a member of the Germanic branch of the Indo-European languages.

INKHORN TERMS: Words from Latin or Romance languages, often polysyllabic and of arcane, scientific, or aesthetic resonance, coined and introduced into English in the sixteenth and seventeenth centuries.

LEXICOGRAPHY: The practice of making dictionaries.

LEXIS: The vocabulary resources of a given language.

LINGUISTICS: The systematic, professional study of language. Linguists may focus on specific features of language (for example, phonology or syntax), and they may reflect on the theoretical, sociological, cognitive, and/or historical contexts in which a specific language or in which language generally as a form of human behavior develops and may be described.

LOAN WORD: A word that enters one language from another, but that eventually becomes an accepted part of the borrowing language. The Middle English word *prison*, for example, is a loan word from French; the Modern English word *jib* is a loan word from Dutch. The word *Schadenfreude*, however, is not a loan word, as its English users recognize it as a German word and use it, self-consciously, as a technical or untranslatable term from that language.

METATHESIS: The reversing of two sounds in a sequence, occasionally a case of mispronunciation, but also occasionally a historical change in pronunciation. For example, *psghetti* (for "spaghetti") is a case of mispronouncing by metathesis, but Old English and early Middle English *brid* changing into Modern English *bird* is a case of metathesis explaining a permanent, historical change in pronunciation.

MIDDLE ENGLISH: The form of English spoken and written in the British Isles from about the middle of the twelfth century until about the end of the fifteenth century. It is characterized by the loss of inflections and grammatical gender from Old English and an influx of loan words from French and Latin.

MONOPHTHONG: A vowel sound made up of only one continuously produced sound (for example, the sound in the modern English word *feet*).

MORPHEME: A set of one or more sounds in a language which, taken together, make up a unique, meaningful part of a word (e.g., *-ly* is the morpheme indicating manner of action, as in *quickly* or *slowly*; *-s* is a morpheme indicating plurality, as in *dogs*).

MORPHOLOGY: The study of the forms of words that determine relationships of meaning in a sentence in a given language. It includes such issues as case endings in nouns and the formation of tenses in verbs.

OLD ENGLISH: The language spoken and written by the Germanic settlers in the British Isles (known as the Anglo-Saxons) from about the middle of the fifth century until about the middle of the twelfth century. It is characterized by a complex inflectional system of grammar, grammatical gender in the nouns, many classes of strong verbs, and a system of word formation based on compounding.

ORTHOEPISTS: A term used to describe a group of scholars, teachers, and philosophers working from the middle of the sixteenth until the early eighteenth century who were interested in describing forms of speech, developing systems of writing that could represent speech sounds, and reflecting on the philosophical relationships among sound, spelling, and the human vocal apparatus.

ORTHOGRAPHY: From the Greek meaning "right writing," a term referring to the accepted principles of spelling at a particular time.

PARATAXIS: The rhetorical device of stringing words or clauses together in a sentence without indicating one as subordinate to another.

PERIPHRASTIC: A term that refers to a roundabout way of doing something; used in grammar to describe a phrase or idiom that uses new words or more words to express grammatical relationships. The word *do*, for example, has taken on many periphrastic uses: in questions, "Do you know the way?;" in negative statements, "I did not eat the apple"; in the imperative, "Do come to lunch."

PHILOLOGY: From the Greek meaning "love of language," or "love of the word." It refers to the historical study of changes in phonology, morphology, grammar, and lexis (though, in the eighteenth and nineteenth centuries, it referred to the study of language and works of literary artistry generally). Comparative philology is the term used to describe the method of comparing surviving forms of words from related languages to reconstruct older lost forms.

PHONEME: An individual sound that, in contrast with other sounds, contributes to the set of meaningful sounds in a given language. A phoneme is not simply a sound, but rather a sound that is meaningful (e.g., *b* and *p* are phonemes in English because their difference determines two different meaningful words: *bit* and *pit*, for example).

PHONETICS: The study of the pronunciation of sounds of a given language by speakers of that language. Unlike phonology, phonetics is the study of how sounds are actually produced and understood by living speakers of a language.

PHONOLOGY: The study of the system of sounds of a given language. Phonology, as a discipline, is less interested in how living speakers of a language pronounce sounds than in the system of phonemes that make up a language's set of meaningful sounds and sound differences.

PIDGIN: A language that develops to allow two mutually unintelligible groups of speakers to communicate. Pidgins are often ad hoc forms of communication, and they are perceived as artificial by both sets of speakers. Over time, a pidgin may develop into a creole (see CREOLE).

POLYSEMY: The condition in which one word comes to connote several, often very different, meanings. Sometimes, these different meanings come from different historical periods in the language (for example, in early Modern English, the word *silly* could still connote its older sense of "blessed," as well as its newer sense of "foolish").

PRESCRIPTIVISM: The belief that the study of language should lead to certain rules of advice for speaking and writing (see DESCRIPTIVISM).

REGIONALISM: An expression in a language that is unique to a certain geographical area and is not characteristic of the language as a whole. A regionalism may be a matter of vocabulary, pronunciation, or grammar.

STRONG VERB: In the Germanic languages, a verb that signals change in tense through a meaningful change in the root vowel. For example, "Today I run, yesterday I ran"; "Today I think, yesterday I thought." In Old English and other, older forms of the Germanic languages, strong verbs were classified into groups according to the specific sets of vowel changes in their principle parts.

SYNTAX: The way in which a language arranges its words to make well-formed or grammatical utterances.

UPTALK: A way of talking, traditionally associated with young women from Southern California but now characteristic of much American colloquial speech, in which sentences and phrases habitually end with a rising sound, as if the statement were a question.

WEAK VERB: In the Germanic languages, a verb that signals the past tense by adding a suffix. In Modern English, these suffixes have become *-ed* or *-d*. For example, "Today I walk, yesterday I walked." All new verbs that enter the English language (either by coinages or loans) enter as weak verbs.

Introduction

Baugh, Albert C., and Thomas M. Cable. *A History of the English Language.* 5th ed. Englewood Cliffs, N.J.: Prentice-Hall, 2004.

Bryson, Bill. *The Mother Tongue: English and How It Got That Way.* New York: Avon Books, 1990.

Burgess, Anthony. *A Mouthful of Air: Language and Languages.* London: Hutchinson, 1992.

Crystal, David. *The Stories of English.* London: Allen Lane, 2004.

———. *The Cambridge Encyclopedia of the English Language.* 2nd ed. Cambridge: Cambridge University Press, 2003.

Hogg, Richard M., general ed. *The Cambridge History of the English Language.* 6 vols. Cambridge: Cambridge University Press, 1992–2002.

Lerer, Seth. *The History of the English Language.* Videotape. Springfield, Va.: The Teaching Company, 1998.

McCrum, Robert, William Cran, and Robert MacNeil. *The Story of English.* New York: Viking Press, 1986.

Nunberg, Geoffrey. *The Way We Talk Now: Commentaries on Language and Culture from NPR's "Fresh Air."* Boston: Houghton Mifflin, 2001.

Watkins, Calvert. *The American Heritage Dictionary of Indo-European Roots.* Boston: Houghton Mifflin, 1984.

Winchester, Simon. *The Professor and the Madman: A Tale of Murder, Insanity, and the Making of the Oxford English Dictionary.* New York: Harper Collins, 1998.

———. *The Meaning of Everything: The Story of the Oxford English Dictionary.* Oxford: Oxford University Press, 2003.

1. Caedmon Learns to Sing

Baker, Peter S. *Introduction to Old English.* Oxford: Blackwell, 2003.

Barney, Stephen A. *Word-Hoard: An Introduction to Old English Vocabulary.* 2nd ed. New Haven, Conn.: Yale University Press, 1985.

Campbell, Alistair. *Old English Grammar.* Oxford: Oxford University Press, 1959.

Cassidy, F. G., and Richard N. Ringler. *Bright's Old English Grammar and Reader.* 3rd. ed. New York: Holt Reinhart and Winston, 1971.

Klaeber, Friederich. *Beowulf.* 3rd ed. Boston: D. C. Heath, 1950.

Lerer, Seth. *Literacy and Power in Anglo-Saxon Literature.* Lincoln: University of Nebraska Press, 1991.

O'Keefe, Katherine O'Brien. *Visible Song.* Cambridge: Cambridge University Press, 1990.

2. From Beowulf to Wulfstan

Auerbach, Erich. *Mimesis.* Trans. Willard R. Trask. Princeton: Princeton University Press, 1957.

Baker, Peter S. *Introduction to Old English.* Oxford: Blackwell, 2003.

Barney, Stephen A. *Word-Hoard: An Introduction to Old English Vocabulary.* 2nd ed. New Haven, Conn.: Yale University Press, 1985.

Cassidy, F. G., and Richard N. Ringler. *Bright's Old English Grammar and Reader.* 3rd ed. New York: Holt Reinhart and Winston, 1971.

Klaeber, Friederich. *Beowulf.* 3rd ed. Boston: D. C. Heath, 1950.

Krapp, George Philip, and E. V. K. Dobbie, eds. *The Anglo-Saxon Poetic Records.* 6 vols. New York: Columbia University Press, 1931–53.

Godden, Malcolm R. "Literary Language." In *The Cambridge History of the English Language,* vol. 1, *The Beginnings to 1066,* ed. Richard M. Hogg, 490–535. Cambridge: Cambridge University Press, 1992.

Whitelock, Dorothy. *Sweet's Anglo-Saxon Reader.* 15th ed. Oxford: Oxford University Press, 1967.

3. In This Year

Bennett, J. A. W., and G. V. Smithers. *Early Middle-English Verse and Prose.* 2nd ed. Rev. Norman Davis. Oxford: Clarendon Press, 1968.

Brehe, S. K. "Reassembling the *First Worcester Fragment.*" *Speculum* 65 (1990): 521–36.

Burrow, J. A., and Thorlac Turville-Petre. *A Book of Middle English.* 3rd ed. Oxford: Blackwell, 2005.

Clark, Cecily. *The Peterborough Chronicle.* 2nd ed. Oxford: Clarendon Press, 1970.

Lerer, Seth. "Old English and Its Afterlife." In *The Cambridge History of Medieval English Literature,* ed. David Wallace, 7–24. Cambridge: Cambridge University Press, 1999.

——. "The Genre of the Grave and the Origins of the Middle English Lyric." *Modern Language Quarterly* 58 (1997): 127–62.

Orwell, George. "Politics and the English Language." 1946. Reprint, in *The Norton*

Anthology of English Literature, 7th ed., ed. M. H. Abrams et al., 2:2462–71. New York: Norton, 2000.

4. From Kingdom to Realm

Bennett, J. A. W., and G. V. Smithers, rev. Norman Davis. *Early Middle-English Verse and Prose*. 2nd ed. Oxford: Clarendon Press, 1968.

Burrow, J. A., and Thorlac Turville-Petre. *A Book of Middle English*. 3rd ed. Oxford: Blackwell, 2005.

Clanchy, M. T. *From Memory to Written Record: England 1066–1307*. Cambridge, Mass.: Harvard UP, 1979.

Fisher, John Hurt. *The Emergence of Standard English*. Lexington: U of Kentucky P, 1996.

Lerer, Seth. "Medieval English Literature and the Idea of the Anthology." *PMLA* 118 (2003): 1251–67.

Mossé, Fernand. *Handbook of Middle English*. Trans. James A. Walker. Baltimore: Johns Hopkins UP, 1952.

Turville-Petre, Thorlac. *England: The Nation*. Oxford: Clarendon Press, 1996.

Williams, Deanne. *The French Fetish from Chaucer to Shakespeare*. Cambridge: Cambridge UP, 2004.

Wogan-Browne, Jocelyn, et al. *The Idea of the Vernacular*. University Park: Penn State UP, 1999.

5. Lord of This Langage

Benson, Larry D., general editor. *The Riverside Chaucer*. 3rd ed. Boston: Houghton Mifflin, 1987.

Cannon, Christopher. *The Making of Chaucer's English*. Cambridge: Cambridge University Press, 1999.

Justice, Steven V. *Writing and Rebellion: England in 1381*. Berkeley: University of California Press, 1994.

Lerer, Seth. *Chaucer and His Readers*. Princeton, N.J.: Princeton University Press, 1993.

——, ed. *The Yale Companion to Chaucer*. New Haven, Conn.: Yale University Press, 2006.

6. I Is as Ille a Millere as Are Ye

Baugh, Albert C., and Thomas Cable. *A History of the English Language*. 5th ed. Englewood, N.J.: Prentice-Hall, 2004.

Benson, Larry D., general ed. *The Riverside Chaucer*. 3rd ed. Boston: Houghton Mifflin, 1987.

Mossé, Ferdinand. *Handbook of Middle English.* Trans. James Walker. Baltimore, Md.: Johns Hopkins University Press, 1968.

Milroy, James. "Middle English Dialectology." In *The Cambridge History of the English Language,* ed. Norman Blake, vol. 2: *1066–1476,* 156–206. Cambridge: Cambridge University Press, 1992.

Samuels, M. L. *Linguistic Evolution.* Cambridge: Cambridge University Press, 1972.

Strang, B. M. H. *A History of English.* London: Methuen, 1970.

7. The Great Vowel Shift and the Changing Character of English

Baugh, Albert C., and Thomas Cable. *A History of the English Language.* 5th ed. Englewood Cliffs, N.J.: Prentice-Hall, 2004.

Crotch, W. J. B. *The Prologues and Epilogues of William Caxton.* Early English Text Society, Original Series, No. 176. London: Oxford University Press, 1928.

Davis, Norman. *The Paston Letters and Papers of the Fifteenth Century.* 2 vols. Oxford: Clarendon Press, 1971, 1976.

Giancarlo, Matthew. "The Rise and Fall of the Great Vowel Shift? The Changing Ideological Intersections of Philology, Historical Linguistics, and Literary History." *Representations* 76 (2001): 27–60.

Jespersen, Otto. *A Modern English Grammar on Historical Principles.* Vol. 1: *Sounds and Spellings.* Heidelberg: Carl Winter, 1909.

Lass, Roger. "Phonology and Morphology." In Roger Lass, ed. *The Cambridge History of the English Language,* vol. 3: *1476–1776,* 56–186. Cambridge: Cambridge University Press, 1999.

Lerer, Seth. *Courtly Letters in the Age of Henry VIII.* Cambridge: Cambridge University Press, 1997.

8. Chancery, Caxton, and the Making of English Prose

Baugh, Albert C., and Thomas M. Cable. *A History of the English Language.* 5th ed. Englewood Cliffs, N.J.: Prentice Hall, 2002.

Davis, Norman. *The Paston Letters and Papers of the Fifteenth Century.* 2 vols. Oxford: Clarendon Press, 1971, 1976.

——. "The Language of the Pastons." *Proceedings of the British Academy* 40 (1955): 119–44. Reprint, in *Middle English Literature: British Academy Gollancz Lectures,* ed. J. A. Burrow, 45–70. Oxford: Oxford University Press, 1989.

Fisher, John Hurt. "Caxton and Chancery English." In *Fifteenth-Century Studies,* ed. R. F. Yeager, 161–85. New Haven, Conn.: Archon, 1984. Reprint, in Fisher, *The Emergence of Standard English,* 121–44. Lexington: University Press of Kentucky, 1996.

——. "Chancery and the Emergence of Standard Written English." *Speculum* 52 (1977): 870–89. Reprint, in Fisher, *The Emergence of Standard English,* 36–64. Lexington: University Press of Kentucky, 1996.

——. *The Emergence of Standard English*. Lexington: University Press of Kentucky, 1996.

Fisher, John Hurt, Malcolm Richardson, and Jane L. Fisher. *An Anthology of Chancery English*. Knoxville: University of Tennessee Press, 1984.

Hart, John. *An Orthographie*. 1569. Facsimile reprint in *English Linguistics 1500–1800*, ed. R. C. Alston, No. 209. Menston: Scolar Press, 1969.

Lass, Roger. "Phonology and Morphology." In *The Cambridge History of the English Language*, vol. 3: *1476–1776*, ed. Lass, 56–186. Cambridge: Cambridge University Press, 1999.

9. *I Do, I Will*

Alexander, Catherine. *Shakespeare and Language*. Cambridge: Cambridge University Press, 2004.

Bertram, Paul, and Bernice W. Kliman, eds. *The Three-Text Hamlet*. New York: AMS Press, 1996.

Blake, N. F. *A Grammar of Shakespeare's Language*. New York: Palgrave, 2002.

Kermode, Frank. *Shakespeare's Language*. London: Allen Lane, 2000.

Dobson, E. J. *English Pronunciation, 1500–1700*. 2nd edition. Oxford: Oxford University Press, 1968.

Görlach, Manfred. *Early Modern English*. Cambridge: Cambridge University Press, 1992.

Lass, Roger, ed. *The Cambridge History of the English Language*. Vol. 3: *1476–1776*. Cambridge: Cambridge University Press, 1999.

Orgel, Stephen, and A. R. Braunmiller. *The Pelican Shakespeare*. Harmondsworth: Penguin, 2004.

10. *A Universal Hubbub Wild*

Cockeram, Henry. *The English Dictionarie*. London, 1623. Facsimile reprint, English Linguistics 1500–1800, No. 124. Menston: Scolar Press, 1968.

Giamatti, A. Bartlett. *The Earthly Paradise and the English Renaissance Epic*. Princeton, N.J.: Princeton University Press, 1966.

Gil, Alexander. *Logonomia Anglica*. London 1619. Facsimile reprint, English Linguistics 1500–1800, No. 68. Menston: Scolar Press, 1968.

——. *Logonomia Anglica*. Ed. Bror Danielsson and A. Gabrielson. Trans. R. C. Alston. Stockholm: Almqvist and Wiksell, 1972.

Lass, Roger, ed. *The Cambridge History of the English Language*. Vol. 3: *1476–1776*. Cambridge: Cambridge University Press, 1999.

Lerer, Seth. "An Art of the Emetic: Thomas Wilson and the Rhetoric of Parliament." *Studies in Philology* 98 (2001): 158–83.

Mack, Peter. *Elizabethan Rhetoric*. Cambridge: Cambridge University Press, 2002.

Nevalainen, Tertu. "Early Modern English Lexis and Semantics." In *The Cambridge History of the English Language*, vol. 3: *1476–1776*, ed. Lass. Cambridge: Cambridge University Press, 1999.

Puttenham, George. *The Arte of English Poesie*. Facsimile edition. Ed. Baxter Hathaway. Kent, Ohio: Kent State University Press, 1970.

Shawcross, John, ed. *The Complete Poetry of John Milton*. New York: Anchor, 1971.

11. Visible Speech

Cohen, Murray. *Sensible Words: Linguistic Practice in England, 1640–1785*. Baltimore, Md.: Johns Hopkins University Press, 1977.

Dobson, E. J. *English Pronunciation, 1500–1700*. 2nd ed. Oxford: Oxford University Press, 1968.

Gil, Alexander. *Logonomia Anglica*. London 1619. Facsimile reprint, English Linguistics 1500–1800, No. 68. Menston: Scolar Press, 1968.

———. *Logonomia Anglica*. Ed. Bror Danielsson and A. Gabrielson. Trans. R. C. Alston. Stockholm: Almqvist and Wiksell, 1972.

Hart, John. *An Orthographie*. London, 1569. Facsimile reprint, English Linguistics 1500–1800, No. 209. Menston: Scolar Press, 1969.

Lass, Roger, ed. *The Cambridge History of the English Language*. Vol. 3: *1476–1776*. Cambridge: Cambridge University Press, 1999.

———. "Phonology and Morphology." In *The Cambridge History of the English Language*, vol. 3: *1476–1776*, ed. Lass, 56–186. Cambridge: Cambridge University Press, 1999.

Mulcaster, Richard. *The First Part of the Elementarie*. London, 1582. Facsimile reprint, English Linguistics 1500–1800, No. 219. Menston: Scolar Press, 1970.

Price, Owen. *The Vocal Organ*. London, 1665. Facsimile reprint, English Linguistics 1500–1800, No. 227. Menston: Scolar Press, 1970.

Wallis, John. *Grammar of the English Language, with an Introductory Grammatico-physical Treatise on Speech*. Translated with a commentary by J. A. Kemp. London: Longman, 1972.

Wilkins, John. *An Essay Towards a Real Character, and a Philosophical Language*. London, 1668. Facsimile reprint, English Linguistics 1500–1800, No. 119. Menston: Scolar Press, 1968.

12. A Harmless Drudge

Fix, Stephen. "Johnson and the 'Duty' of Reading *Paradise Lost*." *ELH: A Journal of English Literary History* 52 (1985): 649–71.

Hedrick, Elizabeth. "Locke's Theory of Language and Johnson's *Dictionary*." *Eighteenth-Century Studies* 20 (1987): 422–44.

Johnson, Samuel. *A Dictionary of the English Language*. 2 vols. London, 1755.

——. *The Plan of a Dictionary*. London, 1747. Facsimile reprint, English Linguistics 1500–1800. No. 223. Menston: Scolar Press, 1970.

Lass, Roger, ed. *The Cambridge History of the English Language*. Vol. 3: *1476–1776*. Cambridge: Cambridge University Press, 1999.

Lowth, Robert. *A Short Introduction to English Grammar*. London: J. Hughs, 1762.

Mack, Ruth. "The Historicity of Johnson's Lexicographer." *Representations* 76 (2001): 61–87.

Priestley, Joseph. *The Rudiments of English Grammar*. London, 1761. Facsimile reprint, English Linguistics 1500–1800. No. 210. Menston: Scolar Press, 1969.

Reddick, Allen. *The Making of Johnson's Dictionary, 1746–1773*. Rev. ed. Cambridge: Cambridge University Press, 1996.

Wimsatt, W. K. *Philosophic Words: A Study of Style and Meaning in the* Rambler *and the* Dictionary *of Samuel Johnson*. New Haven, Conn.: Yale University Press, 1948.

13. Horrid, Hooting Stanzas

Algeo, John. *The Cambridge History of the English Language*. Vol. 6: *English in North America*. Cambridge. Cambridge University Press, 2001.

Deppman, Jed. " 'I could not have defined the change': Rereading Dickinson's Definition Poetry." *The Emily Dickinson Journal* 11 (2002): 49–80.

The Emily Dickinson Lexicon. http://linguistics.byu.edu/faculty/hallenc/EDLexicon/nehgrant.html.

Hedrick, Elizabeth. "Locke's Theory of Language and Johnson's *Dictionary*." *Eighteenth-Century Studies* 20 (1987): 422–44.

Johnson, Thomas H., ed. *The Complete Poems of Emily Dickinson*. Boston: Little, Brown, 1958.

Johnson, Samuel. *A Dictionary of the English Language*. 2 vols. London, 1755.

Jones, Gavin. *Strange Talk: The Politics of Dialect Literature in Gilded Age America*. Berkeley: University of California Press, 1999.

Mencken, H. L. *The American Language*. 4th ed., with supplements, revised and abridged by Raven I. McDavid Jr. New York: Knopf, 1977.

Simpson, David. *The Politics of American English, 1776–1865*. Oxford: Oxford University Press, 1986.

Webster, Noah. *An American Dictionary of the English Language*. New York, 1828. Facsimile reprint, Foundation for American Christian Education: Anaheim, 1967.

——. *The American Spelling-Book: Containing an Easy Standard of Pronunciation*. Part 1 of *A Grammatical Institute of the English Language*. 14th ed. New York: Samuel Campbell, 1792.

——. *A Grammatical Institute of the English Language*. Hartford: Hudson and Goodwin, 1783.

14. Antses in the Sugar

Algeo, John. *The Cambridge History of the English Language*. Vol. 6: *English in North America*. Cambridge. Cambridge University Press, 2001.

——. *Problems in the Origin and Development of the English Language*. 2nd ed. New York: Harcourt, Brace, Jovanovich, 1972.

Carver, Craig. *American Regional Dialects: A Word Geography*. Ann Arbor: University of Michigan Press, 1987.

Cassidy, Frederic G., ed. *Dictionary of American Regional English*. Cambridge, Mass.: Harvard University Press, 1985–.

Jones, Gavin. *Strange Talk: The Politics of Dialect Literature in Gilded Age America*. Berkeley: University of California Press, 1999.

Lerer, Seth. *Error and the Academic Self: The Scholarly Imagination, Medieval to Modern*. New York: Columbia University Press, 2002.

Labov, William. *The Social Stratification of English in New York City*. Washington, D.C.: Center for Applied Linguistics, 1965.

——. "The Dialects of North American English." In *The Atlas of North American English*, ed. Labov et al. http://www.ling.upenn.edu/phonoatlas/Atlas_chapters/Ch11/Ch11.pdf.

Mencken, H. L. *The American Language*. 4th ed., with supplements, revised and abridged by Raven I. McDavid Jr. New York: Knopf, 1977.

15. Hello, Dude

Jones, Gavin. *Strange Talk: The Politics of Dialect Literature in Gilded Age America*. Berkeley: University of California Press, 1999.

Lerer, Seth. "Hello, Dude: Philology, Performance, and Technology in Mark Twain's *Connecticut Yankee*." *American Literary History* 15 (2003): 471–503.

Lovell, Charles J. "The Background of Mark Twain's Vocabulary." *American Speech* 22 (1940): 88–98.

Marvin, Carolyn. *When Old Technologies Were New: Thinking About Electric Communication in the Late Nineteenth Century*. Oxford: Oxford University Press, 1988.

Miller, Francis Trevelyan. *Thomas A. Edison, Benefactor of Mankind*. London: Stanley and Paul, 1932.

Murray, K. M. Elizabeth. *Caught in the Web of Words: James A. H. Murray and the Oxford English Dictionary*. New Haven, Conn.: Yale University Press, 1977.

Murray, James A. H., ed. *A New English Dictionary on Historical Principles*. Vol. 3: *D and E*. Oxford: Clarendon Press, 1897.

Twain, Mark. *A Connecticut Yankee in King Arthur's Court*. Ed. Bernard L. Stein. Berkeley: University of California Press, 1984.

Whitney, William Dwight, ed. *The Century Dictionary*. New York: The Century Company, 1889–91.

———. *Life and Growth of Language*. New York: D. Appleton, 1875.

16. Ready for the Funk

Campbell, Kermit E. *"Gettin' our Groove On": Rhetoric, Language, and Literacy for the Hip-Hop Generation*. Detroit: Wayne State University Press, 2005.

Dillard, J. L. *Black English*. New York: Random House, 1972.

Douglass, Frederick. *The Life and Times of Frederick Douglass*. 1892. New York: Bonanza Books, 1962.

Ellison, Ralph. *Invisible Man*. New York: Random House, 1952.

Gates, Henry Louis, Jr. *The Signifying Monkey*. New York: Oxford University Press, 1988.

Johnson, James Weldon. *The Book of American Negro Poetry*. New York: Harcourt Brace, 1922.

Labov, William. "Objectivity and Commitment in Linguistic Science: The Case of the Black English Trial in Ann Arbor." *Language in Society* 11 (1982): 165–201.

McRae, Rick. " 'What is hip?' and Other Inquiries in Jazz Slang Lexicography." *Notes: Quarterly Journal of the Music Library Association* 57 (2001): 574–84.

Mufwene, Salikoko S. "African-American English." In *The Cambridge History of the English Language*, vol. 6: *English in North America*, ed. John Algeo, 291–324. Cambridge: Cambridge University Press, 2001.

Rickford, John Russell, and Russell John Rickford. *Spoken Soul: The Story of Black English*. New York: John Wiley, 2000.

Sidnell, Jack. "African American Vernacular English (Ebonics)." *Language Varieties*. http://www.une.edu.au/langnet/aave.htm.

17. Pioneers Through an Untrodden Forest

Aarsleff, Hans. *The Study of Language in England, 1780–1860*. 2nd ed. Minneapolis: University of Minnesota Press, 1983.

Lerer, Seth. *Error and the Academic Self: The Scholarly Imagination, Medieval to Modern*. New York. Columbia University Press, 2002.

Mugglestone, Linda, ed. *Lexicography and the OED*. Oxford: Oxford University Press, 2002.

———. *Lost for Words: The Hidden History of the Oxford English Dictionary*. New Haven, Conn.: Yale University Press, 2005.

Murray, James A. H., et al. *A New English Dictionary on Historical Principles* [*NED*]. Oxford: Oxford University Press, 1889–1928; Supplement, 1933; Second edition, 1989.

Murray, K.M. Elisabeth. *Caught in the Web of Words: James A. H. Murray and the Oxford English Dictionary*. New Haven, Conn.: Yale University Press, 1977.

The Oxford English Dictionary. 3rd ed., with supplements. http://dictionary.oed.com.

Willinsky, John. *Empire of Words: The Reign of the OED*. Princeton, N.J.: Princeton University Press, 1994.

Winchester, Simon. *The Meaning of Everything*. Oxford: Oxford University Press, 2003.

18. Listening to Private Ryan

Dickson, Paul. *War Slang: American Fighting Words and Phrases Since the Civil War*. Washington, D.C.: Brassey's, 2004.

Herr, Michael. *Dispatches*. New York: Knopf, 1978.

Jones, Terry. "Why Grammar Is the First Casualty of War." *London Daily Telegraph*, January 12, 2002.

Mailer, Norman. *The Naked and the Dead*. New York: Rinehart, 1948.

McAlpine, R.W. "A Word About Slang." *The United States Service Magazine* (June 1865): 535–40.

Mencken, H.L. *The American Language*. 4th ed., with supplements, revised and abridged by Raven I. McDavid Jr. New York: Knopf, 1977.

Orwell, George. "Politics and the English Language." 1948. Reprint, in *The Norton Anthology of English Literature*, ed. M.H. Abrams and Stephen Greenblatt, 7th ed, 2462–71. New York: Norton, 2000.

Partridge, Eric. *A Dictionary of Forces' Slang, 1939–1945*. London: Secker and Warburg, 1948.

Reinberg, Linda. *In the Field: The Language of the Vietnam War*. New York: Facts on File, 1991.

Shirer, William L. *Berlin Diary: The Journal of a Foreign Correspondent, 1934–1941*. New York: Knopf, 1941.

Swofford, Anthony. *Jarhead*. New York: Scribner, 2003.

Taylor, A. Marjorie. *The Language of World War II*. New York: H.W. Wilson, 1948.

"Voices from World War I" [poetry of Edward Thomas, Wilfred Owen, and David Jones, et al.]. In *The Norton Anthology of English Literature*, ed. M.H. Abrams and Stephen Greenblatt, 7th ed., 2048–84. New York: Norton, 2000.

19. He Speaks in Your Voice

Algeo, John. *The Cambridge History of the English Language*. Vol. 6: *English in North America*. Cambridge: Cambridge University Press, 2001.

DeLillo, Don. *Underworld*. New York: Scribner, 1997.

Savan, Leslie. "Decoding the New MTV-Speak." *The New Yorker*, March 29, 1999, 45–46.

Yule, Colonel Henry, and A. C. Burnell. *Hobson-Jobson*. 2nd ed., ed. William Crooke, with a new foreword by Anthony Burgess. London: Routledge and Kegan Paul, 1985.

Appendix

Bolton, W. F. *A Living Language: The History and Structure of English*. New York: Random House, 1982.

Pullum, Geoffrey K., and William A. Ladusaw. *Phonetic Symbol Guide*. Chicago: University of Chicago Press, 1986.

ACKNOWLEDGMENTS

I am most grateful to my students, who have taught me how to make what fascinates me fascinating to a larger audience. I am particularly grateful to the fall quarter 2005 History of the English Language class at Stanford, many of whose participants commented critically on chapters of this book and added to its scope. The Stanford Humanities Fellows Program provided the opportunity to have a complete draft of this book read by a remarkably perceptive group of postdoctoral teaching and research fellows. Their comments have improved its structure, tone, and exposition immeasurably. Anna North, my former student and the current administrator of the Fellows Program, read through the entire book and offered a level of detailed and deft response that made it better.

In the mid-1990s, Tom Rollins of the Teaching Company invited me to prepare a series of video and audiotape lectures on the history of the English language, and this series has enabled me to reach an audience much wider and much more diverse than any I could find at school. This book does not reproduce those lectures, but for those who know me through the Teaching Company it may provide a different, complementary insight into the subject and into my personal engagement with it.

This book is filled not just with facts or interpretations but also with personal experience, and I could not have written it without the store of memorable teachers, colleagues, friends, and family who have contributed to my understanding. The teachers I recall best include, from Oxford, Ursula Dronke, Anne Hudson, Patricia Ingham, and the late E. J. Dobson; and from Chicago, Jay Schleusener, Michael Murrin, and David Bevington. Colleagues who have contributed to my thinking on this subject include, Jay Fliegelman, Nicholas Jenkins, Gavin Jones, Stephen Orgel, and Jennifer Summit, and, from Princeton, the incomparable Hans Aarsleff. My friends with whom I have shared this work and from whom I have learned to improve it include Lisa Cooper, Joseph Dane, John Ganim, Brian Stock, Kathryn Temple, and Deanne Williams. My mother, brother, wife, and son remain my toughest audience.

Jennifer Crewe of Columbia University Press welcomed this book and was instrumental in securing supportive and valuable critiques from the Press's readers.

I wish to thank those anonymous readers for their careful attentions to my errors and infelicities, but also for their sustaining agreement with the scope and plan of this book.

Research and writing for this book in its present form took place at Stanford University and the Huntington Library, and I am grateful to the staffs, librarians, and administrations of these institutions for providing support and materials.

I am happy to acknowledge those libraries, publishers, and editors who have granted permissions to reproduce pictures, extracts, and some texts.

The Bodleian Library, Oxford, for permission to reproduce MS Tanner 10, folio 100r, containing the Old English text of *Caedmon's Hymn*.

The Huntington Library, San Marino, California, for permission to reproduce MS Ellesemere 26 C9 folio 1r, the opening of Chaucer's *Canterbury Tales*.

Cambridge University Press, for permission to reproduce Middle English dialect maps from M. L. Samuels, *Linguistic Evolution* (Cambridge: Cambridge University Press, 1972), 70.

Thomson Learning Global Rights Group, for permission to reprint selections from the literary representation of American dialects, from John Algeo, *Problems in the Origin and Development of the English Language*, 2nd ed. (New York: Harcourt, Brace, Jovanovich, 1972), 238–41.

Harvard University Press, for permission to reproduce figure 14.2, illustrating the regional distribution of the terms *mosquito hawk* and *skeeter hawk*, from Frederic G. Cassidy, ed., *The Dictionary of American Regional English*, vol. 1: *A–C* (Cambridge, Mass.: The Belknap Press of Harvard University Press, 1985), xxvii.

Oxford University Press and the editors of *American Literary History*, for permission to incorporate material from my article, "Hello, Dude: Philology, Performance, and Technology in Mark Twain's *Connecticut Yankee*," *American Literary History* 15 (2003): 471–503, in chapter 15.

Page locators in italics indicate figures

Cable, Thomas M., 3, 103

Cadmus (Thornton), 182

Caedmon's Hymn, 12–13, 15–16, *18*, 51, 222, 264, 265; calques in, 29; miraculous quality of, 21, 24; setting of, 23–24; translations of, 17–18

Calloway, Cab, 229, 233, 234

calques, 29, 32

Cambridge History of the English Language, 3, 99, 103, 163–64, 262

"can," as idiom for knowing, 30–31, 80–81

canebrake (word), 202–3

Cannon, Christopher, 71

canon of writers, 7, 168, 178

Canterbury Tales (Chaucer): Caxton's 1483 edition, 119–20; "Clerk's Tale," 76, 125–26; Ellesemere Manuscript, 73, 120; General Prologue, 71–76, 264; "Knight's Tale," 109; "Pardoner's Tale," 76; as performed, 74, 79; Prologue to the "Clerk's Tale," 77; pronouns in, 76; "Reeve's Tale," 79, 87, 93–94, 194, 218; social relationships in, 76; "Tale of Sir Thopas," 78–79. *See also* Chaucer, Geoffrey

Carver, Craig, 205

case endings, 6, 27, 31, 67; weakening of, 39–40, 45

castles, 41, 43–44, 52

Caxton, William, 99, 172; Chancery Standard and, 116, 119–22; Chaucer, view of, 70; *Eneydos*, translation of, 112–13, 118, 121, 126; literary history in writings of, 121–22

Cecilia (Burney), 180

Celtic languages, 9–10

censorship, cultural, 244

Central French (Parisian) dialect, 61, 69

Century Dictionary, 216–17

Chambers, Ephraim, 169

Chancery, 115–16

Chancery Standard, 115–16, 202; French legal prose as model for, 117; northern dialect and, 119–20; spelling, 118–19, 127; translations of Middle English literature, 112–13, 118–21, 126; William Pulle petition, 122–27; word order, 118, 119

character, 104–6, 111, 113

Chaucer, Geoffrey, 1, 2; context of achievement, 65, 70; French used by, 63–64, 72–74, 78–79; Gil's critique of, 148; high style in, 78, 84; language, concern with, 71, 81–82; as linguistic innovator, 71–73; loan words in works of, 72–74, 77–79; persona of writer, 71; pronunciation in, 79, 93–94; range of, 76–77; social context in, 70–71, 82; sound of speech in, 79; sources, concern with, 74, 77, 82; translations and adaptations, 77–81; *Treatise on the Astrolabe*, 80–84, 117, 142–43; trilingualism in, 70, 82–84; *Troilus and Criseyde*, 78, 99; "Truth," 109; "usurp" used by, 142–43; viewed as inventor of new language, 70, 75, 84. *See also Beowulf; Canterbury Tales*

Chesterfield, Lord, 171, 172

Christianity: Passion imagery, 59–60; translation of pagan concepts to, 15–16, 28–29

Christ (Wulfstan), 36

City of God (Augustine), 87

Clemens, Samuel L. *See* Twain, Mark

clerics, 62–63

Cockeram, Henry, 146–47, 169

cognates, 8–10, 15–16, 48

Cohen, Murray, 164

coinage: Chancery Standard and, 125; Civil War era, 248–49; by Eliot, 241; by Shakespeare, 71, 129, 135–37

Coleridge, Herbert, 237

Coles, Elisha, 169

Colloquy (Ælfric of Eynsham), 30–32, 38, 53

commerce, Renaissance England, 146, 157

compound words, 13–14, 16, 45; in *Beowulf*, 26–27, 29–30; calques, 29, 32

Connecticut Yankee in New York (Twain), 208–14, *213*, *214*

Consolation of Philosophy (Boethius), 27, 79–81

consonant clusters, 15, 39, 51, 90–93

consonants, 268, *268*; Middle English, 65–66; Old English, 15, 39

Continental verse, 42

copia, 143–47

copula, 137

couplets, 42–44, 52

Cranmer, Thomas, 131

creation, Anglo-Saxon interest in, 21–24

creole languages, 223, 224–25

Crystal, David, 3

cultivated standard, 87

curry (word), 260–61

Cursor Mundi, 58–59, 87

cycle plays, Northern English, 95

Cyclopaedia (Chambers), 169

Danes, 35

Daniel, 25, 26

DARE. See *Dictionary of American Regional English*

dative case, 40

Davis, Daniel Webster, 222, 226–27

Davis, Norman, 110

death, lexicography of, 29–30, 47–48

"Death of the Ball Turret Gunner" (Jarrell), 254

decasyllabic line, 65, 74

declensions, 13

De conscribendis epistolis (*On Writing Letters*) (Erasmus), 105–6

definite article, 27

DeLillo, Don, 264–65

descriptivism, 4, 178–79

Desert of Religion, 126

diachronic change, 99, 102

dialect literature, American, 196–99

dialectology, 85–86, 99; American, 194–96, 203; as form of social history, 86; lexical variation, focus on, 203–5, *204*; main points of, 89. *See also* philology

dialects: eye dialect, 96, 196, 218–19, 226; French, 39, 42–44, 61, 69; geographical boundaries, 87, 89–90, *91*, *92*, 102, *193*, 194; Middle English, 75–76, 86–93, *92*, 98, 99, 194. *See also* African American English; American regional dialects

dialects, English, 5, 45, 85–86; Chancery Standard and, 119; content with other languages, 19; East Midlands, 75, 89, 99; Kentish, 89, 96–97; London Middle English, 75–76, 99; metathesis, 5, 66–67; Middle English, 75, 86–87, 99, 194; Northumbrian, 16–19, 88–90; Old English, 16–19; parody of, 94–96; prestige, 111; sounds of, 90–93, *92*; Southern, 89, 94–96; verb forms, 94–96; West Midlands, 89

Dickens, Charles, 7

Dickinson, Emily, 187–88, 232

Dictionairre (Cockeram), 146–47, 169

dictionaries, 142–43; as arbiters of language, 168, 171–72; early Modern English, 146–47; of war language, 247. *See also* vocabulary

Dictionary (Bailey), 146, 176

Dictionary (Johnson), 167, 236; American words in, 181; canon and, 168,

extension in lexis, 143
eye dialect, 96, 196, 218–19, 226

Faerie Queene (Spenser), 150
felonousely (word), 125
Fighting Indians, 212–13
Filostrato, Il (Boccaccio), 78
First Worcester Fragment, The, 50
Fisher, John Hurt, 116, 122
Florio, John, 151
food metaphors, 229
formulaic phrasing, 20, 25–26, 57
Fowler, William Chauncey, 208
Francis of Assisi, 35
French, 5; as language of government
    and culture, 61, 63–64
French dialects: Norman, 39, 42–44,
    61, 69; Parisian, 61, 69
French idioms, 54, 57–58
French legal prose, 117
French literature, medieval, 61
French words: in Chaucer, 63–64,
    72–74, 78–79; in Johnson's *Diction-
    ary*, 174; in personal letters, 109–11;
    political and administrative, 46–47,
    54–55, 57–58, 68; polysyllabic, 55,
    68, 78–79; pronunciation and spell-
    ings, 68–69
frumsceaft (creation), 24
fultum (aid), 56–57

Gates, Henry Louis, Jr., 232
gender: nineteenth-century social
    idioms, 212, 215–16. *See also* gram-
    matical gender
Genesis, 25, 36
German comparative philology, 236,
    237, 242–43
Germanic languages, 8–9, 39, 130;
    Early Modern English spelling and,
    159; Latin words in, 10; meter, 20;
    monosyllabic words, 8, 68; shared

mythology, 15–16, 28–29, 37. *See
    also* Old English
Germanic poetry, 35
"Gettysburg Address" (Lincoln), 230–31
Giancarlo, Matthew, 111
Gil, Alexander, 147–49, 154, 159–61,
    165, 166; on American English, 181
Gildersleeve, Basil Lanneau, 196
ginne (ingenuity), 51–53
GI (word), 256
Gothic language, 13
Gower, John, 63–64, 99
grammar, 6, 13–14; American usage,
    182; Early Modern English, 154
grammarians, eighteenth-century,
    178–79
Grammatica (Wallis), 161, 162
grammatical gender, 39–40, 45, 62
*Grammatical Institute of the English
    Language, A* (Webster), 185
Grant, Ulysses S., 212–14
Grave, The, 50, 51
Great Expectations (Dickens), 7
Great Vowel Shift, 5–6, 101–2, 106;
    rhymes, changes in, 103, 114; in
    Shakespeare, 114, 133–34; spelling
    and, 106–8, 113–14; visual repre-
    sentations of, 102–4, 104, 105, 163;
    worldly reasons for, 111–12. *See also*
    pronunciation
Gregory the Great, 33
gremlin (word), 256–57
Grendel (*Beowulf*), 1, 28–29, 32–34
Gullah dialect, 224–25
"Gullible's Travels" (Lardner), 198, 202

Hamlet (Shakespeare), 138–40, 151
*Handbuch der mittelenglischen Gramma-
    tik* (Jordan), 85
Handwörterbuch der griechischen Sprache
    (Passow), 237
handwriting, 105–6, 121

hard-word books, 169–70

Harley 2253 Manuscript, 59, 64

Harris, Joel Chandler, 196, 199, 202–3, 222

Hart, John, 115, 127, 153, 154–57, 165

Heaney, Seamus, 2

heinouse (word), 126

hello (word), 208–10

hello-girls, 209, 210–12

Henry III, Proclamation of 1258, 55–58, 61, 62, 82

Henry IV, 83

Henry IV (Shakespeare), 130–32

Henry V (Shakespeare), 140, 150, 218

Henry VIII, 131

heroic vocabulary, 23, 25, 46

Herr, Michael, 247, 251–52, 254

Higden, Ranulf, 87

Hill, Adams Sherman, 195–96

History of English (Strang), 86–87

History of the English Church and People (Bede), 13, 16, 17, 18, 23

History of the English Language (Baugh and Cable), 3

History of the English Language, The (Teaching Company), 3

Hitler, Adolf, 250–51

hobson-jobson (word), 262

Hobson-Jobson (Yule and Burnell), 259–62

Hoccleve, Thomas, 70

"Hog Meat" (Davis), 226–28, 229

Hoosier poetry, 227–28

horrible (word), 125, 149

horrid (word), 189–90

household list, 122

hubbub (word), 149–50

Huckleberry Finn (Twain), 196, 198–99, 202; attention to dialect in, 218–19; preface, 207, 208

Hudson, Anne, 85

Hughes, Ted, 2

Hume, David, 179

Humphries, Jennet, 238, 239, 240

idioms: can, as idiom for knowing, 30–31, 80–81; French, 54, 57–58; Old English, 54, 97; war language and, 255–57

Idler essays (Johnson), 178, 184

"I have a dream" (King), 230–32

imagination, 19, 64, 137–38, 143; American English and, 182, 185–86, 188, 216; Johnson's *Dictionary* and, 176–78

Indian words, 259–62

Indo-European Languages, 8–10, 236

inflected language, 6–7, 13

"In Parenthesis" (Jones), 246

International Phonetic Alphabet (IPA), 104, 267–69

invent (word), 2

invention of language, self and, 2–3

Invisible Man (Ellison), 228–30

inwit (conscience), 97

Irving, Washington, 2, 182–83

italics, 185, 186–87

Ivanhoe (Scott), 161

Jarhead (Swofford), 252

Jarrell, Randell, 254

jeep (word), 256

Jespersen, Otto, 101–3, 105, 156

Jeu d'Adam, 61

Jewett, Sarah Orne, 196, 197, 200–201

"Jive Talk Dictionary," 229

John, King, 55

Johnson, James Weldon, 226

Johnson, Samuel: on Americans, 181; as canon maker, 168, 178; *Idler* essays, 178, 184; on lexicographer, 167–68; pathologized, 167–68; patronage and, 171–73. *See also Dictionary*

Swofford, Anthony, 252, 254
syllables, 66; monosyllabic words, 8, 55, 68, 125, 147, 161; polysyllabic words, 55, 68, 78–79, 110, 125, 145, 186, 251; stressed, 40, 102, 191
synchronic variation, 99, 102
syncretism, 59
synonymy, 26, 35
syntax, 34; African American English, 223–25; war and, 247–48

Taps for Private Tussie (Stuart), 199, 202
Teaching Company, 3
technological innovation, 208–9
telephone, 209–12
Telephony, 211–12
tense, 6, 14, 130, 225
textbooks, Latin, 14–15
Thackeray, William, 261
theatricality, 143–44, 150, 151
theology, language of, 64–65
"This Is Just to Say" (Williams), 265–66
Thomas, Edward, 252–53
Thomas A. Edison: Benefactor of Mankind, 210
thorn, 15, 45, 134–35
Thornton, William, 182
Tolkien, J. R. R., 2, 16, 28
tongue, 24
Tonson, Jacob, 170
Tout, T. F., 115
Traité sur la lange française (Walter of Bibbesworth), 61–63
Transactions of Philological Society, 240
translations: of *Caedmon's Hymn*, 17–18; by Chaucer, 77–81; in Middle English, 56, 112–13, 118–21, 126; into Old English, 27
Treatise on Education (Locke), 186
Treatise on the Astrolabe (Chaucer), 80–84, 117, 142–43

tresor (treasure), 45, 46, 58
Trevisa, John of, 87–89, 96
Troilus and Criseyde (Chaucer), 78, 99
"Truth" (Chaucer), 109
Turville-Petre, Thorlac, 55
Twain, Mark (Samuel L. Clemens), 246; *Connecticut Yankee in King Arthur's Court*, 208–14, 213, 214; cultural debate on dialect and, 207–8; *Huckleberry Finn*, 196, 198–99, 202, 207–8, 218–19; as linguistic innovator, 217–18
typefaces, 121

Underworld (DeLillo), 264–65
unforsceawodlice (unforeseen), 31–32
universal language, 153, 154
uptalk, 266
usurp (word), 82–84, 142–43

Vanity Fair (Thackeray), 261
verandah (word), 261–62
verba, 74–75
verbs: dialect forms, 94–96; disappearance of classes, 67; Old English, 13–14, 16, 45; periphrastic, 130; strong and weak, 14, 39, 67; tense, 6, 14, 130, 225; third-person endings, 47, 67–68, 75, 92, 94, 96, 99, 108, 119–20, 200
vernacular authority, 82–83, 107
vernacular literacy, 21, 94, 104, 111, 156
vertu, 72
Victorian literary practices, 235–36, 239–40, 242–43
Vietnam war, 251–52
Vikings, 19
visual representation of sound, 102–4, 104, 105, 161–64
vocabulary: administrative, 46–47, 54–55, 57–58, 68; calques, 29, 32; core,

8, 68; heroic, 23, 25, 46; Middle English, 68–69. *See also* dictionaries
Vocal Organ, The (Price), 161, *163*, 164
voice, in Old English literature, 27–28
vowels, 267; chain of, 102–3, *105*; changes from Old English to Middle English, 66; diphthongs, 19, 103, 163–64, 224, 267; monophthongs, 101–2, 267; in plural forms, 75; West-Saxon, 19. *See also* Great Vowel Shift
vowel-shift, as phrase, 101

Wakefield Cycle, 87, 94–96
Wallis, John, 161, 162, 164
Walter of Bibbesworth, 61–63
Walysby, William, petition of, 116–17, 118
war, language of, 246; coinage, Civil War era, 248–49; dictionaries, 247; idioms, 255–57; journalism, 250–51; obscenity, 250; poetry, 253–54; as sexualized, 248–49, 253; syntax and, 247–48
Watkins, Calvert, 9
Watreman, W., 150
Way We Talk Now, The (Nunberg), 3
weapons, words as, 36, 38
Webster, Noah, 168, 182, 184–87, 193, 220, 259
West Midlands dialect, 89
West-Saxon dialect, 17–19
When Old Technologies Were New (Marvin), 210
when/then clauses, 27, 33–34, 46
Whitman, Walt, 1
Whitney, William Dwight, 195, 207, 216–17

Wilkins, John, 154, 161, 164
to will (verb), 130
Williams, William Carlos, 265–66
William the Conqueror, 39, 41–44, 52
Wilson, Thomas, 143, 145
Witherspoon, John, 183
women, as contributors to *New English Dictionary*, 239–40, 243
"Word About Slang, A" (McAlpine), 248–49
word endings, 10, 16, 39–40, 67–68; adverbs, 119, 200; American, 185; verbs, 75, 119, 120. *See also* case endings
word order, 6, 27, 39, 169; Chancery Standard, 118, 119; to form questions, 130; Middle English, 54, 75–76; multiple negation, 75–76
words, sources for, 7–9
wordum wrixlan, 20, 36
world English, 263
World War I, 246
World War II, 246
writing, speech sounds distinguished from, 61–62, 115
Writing and Rebellion: England in 1381 (Justice), 83
wrought (word), 21–22
Wulfstan, Archbishop, 26, 28, 35–37, 35–38, 202
Wulfstan of Worcester, 44
Wycliff, John, 82

Yiddish, 1
Yule, Henry, 259–62